Portland Hill Walks

Portland HILL WALKS

TWENTY EXPLORATIONS IN
PARKS AND NEIGHBORHOODS

LAURA O. FOSTER

TIMBER PRESS
PORTLAND • LONDON

REGIONAL
ARTS & CULTURE
COUNCIL
This book is funded in part by the Regional Arts and Culture Council.

Published in 2005 by
Timber Press, Inc.

The Haseltine Building
133 S.W. Second Avenue, Suite 450
Portland, Oregon 97204-3527
www.timberpress.com

2 The Quadrant
135 Salusbury Road
London NW6 6RJ
www.timberpress.co.uk

Fifth printing 2011

Printed in the United States of America

Library of Congress Cataloging-in-Publication Data

Foster, Laura O.
  Portland hill walks : twenty explorations in parks and neighborhoods /
Laura O. Foster.
     p. cm.
  Includes bibliographical references and index.
  ISBN-13: 978-0-88192-692-7 (pbk.)
  1. Walking—Oregon—Portland—Guidebooks. 2. Portland
(Or.)—Guidebooks. I. Title.
  GV199.42.O72P6737 2005
  917.95'490444—dc22
                                        2004017631

To my parents, Mike and Dorothy O'Brien, who showed me that it's fun to get lost, and to my husband, Kevin Foster, for always being interested in what I discover

CONTENTS

Northeast Portland

North Portland

FOREWORD by Earl Blumenauer

One of the great pleasures of growing up in Portland was the opportunity to explore its many neighborhoods on foot and by bike. My friends and I spent countless hours discovering the shortest ways between home and friends' houses, the best routes to parks, the quickest shortcuts to the local store. It was an ideal way to learn about my neighborhood and my city.

Little did I know that these early explorations would be the beginning of my passion for community issues. Since I was first elected to political office in 1972, my priority has been to strengthen communities and support citizens' efforts to make them better. After more than thirty years of public service, I remain convinced that issues that affect our communities lie at the heart of good public policy. And there is no better way to get to know a community and the people who live there than by walking or biking through it.

A livable community is one that you can safely and enjoyably navigate on foot or by bike. The slow pace enables you to notice the details, greet the residents, and better understand how people and place interact to create a sense of belonging and stewardship. It's what gives each community its unique character and feel.

Portland's numerous parks and vibrant green neighborhoods continue to inspire my work on livable communities. Not a week goes by when I'm in Portland that I'm not out running or biking, following familiar routes, noticing the changes, and meeting people along the way. Nothing restores my spirit and health like a walk, run, or bicycle ride through the neighborhoods and parks that I call home.

Laura Foster has written a wonderful walking guide to many of Portland's fine neighborhoods, adding a wealth of information and historical context along the way. It's apparent she's not only familiar with these routes, she's fond of them. With her book as your guide, I invite you to take your own walk through Portland's wonderful neighborhoods and parks. It's the best way to get to know one of America's most livable cities.

Earl Blumenauer represents Oregon's Third Congressional District, which includes Portland, in the U.S. House of Representatives.

PREFACE

"The city is most fortunate, in comparison with the majority of American cities, in possessing such varied and wonderfully strong and interesting landscape features." So wrote the Olmsted Brothers, landscape architects of Central Park fame, in the City of Portland's 1903 *Report of the Park Board*. More than a hundred years later, most Portlanders and visitors agree with the assessment. Portland is a walking mecca, in large part because walkers are rewarded for their efforts with stunning views of volcanoes, rivers, and cityscapes at just about any elevation.

In this city, where the largest river and lava floods on the face of the earth once took place, the land reveals its fascinating past in the varied landforms left behind by the cataclysms. The twenty walks detailed in this book take you through every aspect of Portland's landscapes and through every section of the city. Twelve walks explore the long, steep ridge of hills on Portland's west side, with its fabulous views of the city and distant Cascade mountains. Some walks lead you along the broad valley floor with its spring-carved ravines and gentle inclines. Some lead you up the slopes of volcanoes. One walk lets you dip your feet in the Willamette River, while another carries you up and down a 4-mile ridge of gravel and sand laid down by floods.

Every walk in this book celebrates Portland's successful weaving together of natural areas and neighborhoods, as walks thread their way in and out of the city's numerous parks and cemeteries. I have a fondness for city staircases and unmapped pedestrian access paths, and many of these have been included.

Portland is not only a walking mecca but an eating mecca too, where local foods are celebrated and a person can walk for miles without seeing a chain restaurant. Most hill walks pass by, or near, interesting restaurants or coffee shops. I have included those that are locally owned, many of which have been in business for decades.

Like the city, the book is laid out in five sections: Northwest, Southwest, Southeast, Northeast, and North. In all, thirty-seven neighborhoods are covered. In Portland, the neighborhoods and their personalities have formed independently of the automobile. Many started out as separate towns, and most have thriving business districts with shops, libraries, restaurants, and community centers just steps away from residents' front doors.

Each hill walk focuses on the city's history, geology, and built environment, with anecdotes sprinkled throughout about colorful past residents like Oswald West, Maurine Neuberger, or Lilla Leach. Each route also provides offbeat horticultural information, even delving into the uses American Indians made of native Northwest plants. Some walks reveal the secrets held within the city's public art; others reveal the secrets of our much-altered landscape: which mountainside was terraced in stairsteps, which lake was buried under tons of muck, and which prominent rock shuddered in the onslaught of the earth's most catastrophic floods.

Each chapter begins with an overview of the walk, including how to get to the starting point and what to bring along. Mileage, elevation, safety issues, and the location of restrooms and drinking fountains are also included. A map of each walk follows the route through a series of numbered route junctions that correspond to the text. Route junctions appear as **1**, **2**, **3**, and so on. TriMet information is given from downtown Portland for bus or MAX light rail routes and stops. Call TriMet at 503-238-RIDE or visit www.trimet.org for specific bus schedules and routes.

All but three of the walks in this book are loops. Some can only charitably be called hill walks, specifically the Albina Riverfront to Hilltop Loop and the Willamette Cove to Saint Johns Bridge Loop; the hills on these walks are gentle inclines rising away from the Willamette River, but they are included because of the rich history of these areas, both of which are often neglected by walking books. Some of the walks are steep enough to challenge a marathon walker. Some, such as the Multnomah Village to Vermont Hills Loop, are short and not too steep, while others, such as the Hillsdale to Healy Heights Loop, are long and calf-building. In every case, walks can be shortened by a detour of your own design back to the starting point. For that purpose, each map shows streets that are contiguous to the walk route. The difficulty of each walk can be gauged by the elevation gain and distance of the walk, provided at the beginning of each chapter.

I researched this book by walking alone, but solitude has its risks. Use good judgment when walking in areas that are remote or seldom visited, but also keep in mind that the rare assault gets more media coverage than the thousands of unremarkable walks people take in parks and woodlands.

Dogs are a big part of walking for many people. To some, leashing a dog in a natural area seems cruel. I had a dog once, and I believed it was her canine birthright to run wherever her four paws could take her. I have since been educated. Dogs are seemingly everywhere in the city, and in an urban environment their impact is high—not just their byproducts but their presence itself, storming through underbrush, kicking up gravel in streambeds, and knocking elderly people off their feet. In a city well populated with dogs, less adaptable species can easily be overwhelmed. Please keep your dog on a leash during the hill walks.

I hope you enjoy reading this book and walking around Portland. The American Podiatric Association says that Portland is among the country's most walkable cities. Come see why.

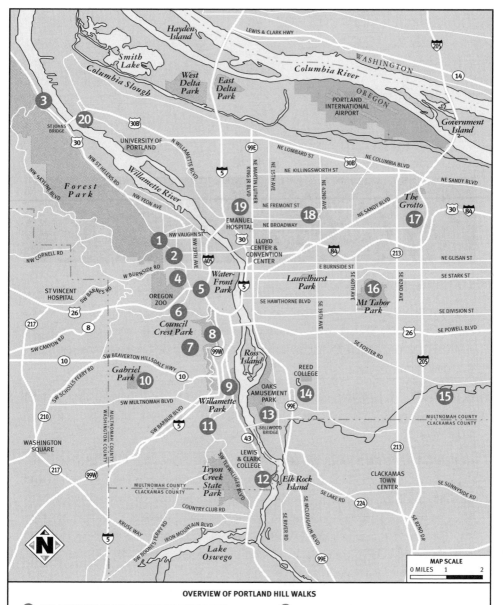

OVERVIEW OF PORTLAND HILL WALKS

1. WILLAMETTE HEIGHTS TO BALCH CREEK CANYON LOOP
2. NOB HILL TO KINGS HEIGHTS AND PITTOCK MANSION LOOP
3. LINNTON TO FOREST PARK
4. WASHINGTON PARK TO ARLINGTON HEIGHTS LOOP
5. PORTLAND HEIGHTS TO PARK BLOCKS AND GOOSE HOLLOW LOOP
6. PORTLAND HEIGHTS TO COUNCIL CREST LOOP
7. HILLSDALE TO HEALY HEIGHTS LOOP
8. LAIR HILL TO OHSU LOOP
9. WILLAMETTE PARK TO TERWILLIGER LOOP
10. MULTNOMAH VILLAGE TO VERMONT HILLS LOOP
11. MARSHALL PARK CANYON TO CEMETERIES LOOP
12. DUNTHORPE GARDENS
13. SELLWOOD RIVERFRONT TO JOHNSON CREEK LOOP
14. REED CANYON TO EASTMORELAND LOOP
15. LEACH BOTANICAL GARDEN TO MOUNT SCOTT LOOP
16. MOUNT TABOR NEIGHBORHOODS AND PARK LOOP
17. ROCKY BUTTE BASE TO PEAK
18. ALAMEDA RIDGE LOOP
19. ALBINA RIVERFRONT TO HILLTOP LOOP
20. WILLAMETTE COVE TO SAINT JOHNS BRIDGE LOOP

WILLAMETTE HEIGHTS TO BALCH CREEK CANYON LOOP

STARTING POINT NW 29th Avenue and Wilson Street

DISTANCE 4.5 miles or less (eliminating the Thurman-to-Leif Erikson-to-Aspen section by taking the Thurman-to-Aspen stairs shortens the walk to 2.75 miles; eliminating the Balch Creek portion by taking the Thurman-to-Aspen stairs shortens it to 3 miles)

ELEVATION 50 feet at the starting point; 350 feet at Leif Erikson Drive, with ups and downs; 350 feet at the intersection of Lower Macleay Trail and Wildwood Trail

GETTING THERE AND PARKING From W Burnside Street and NW 23rd Avenue, drive north on 23rd. This is the Alphabet District: streets running north of and parallel to Burnside are in alphabetical order. Follow the alphabet to NW Vaughn Street. Turn left on Vaughn and left again at the stoplight at NW 27th Avenue. Drive one block and turn right on NW Upshur Street. Turn right on NW 29th and drive two blocks to the intersection with NW Wilson Street. There is ample street parking at this intersection.

TriMet: From downtown, take bus 17 (NW 21st Avenue/Saint Helens Road) to the stop at NW Nicolai and Wardway (just past the nine-story Montgomery Park building). Walk 0.3 mile south (uphill) on 29th to its intersection with Wilson.

RESTROOMS AND DRINKING FOUNTAINS You'll find a drinking fountain at the NW Thurman Street entrance into Forest Park, a drinking fountain and restrooms at Macleay Park, and a portable toilet on Leif Erikson Drive.

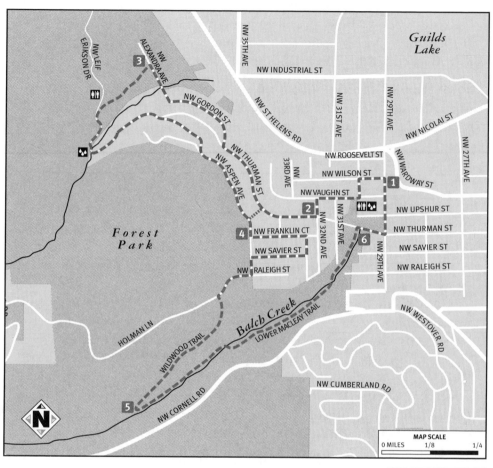

WALK 1. *Willamette Heights to Balch Creek Canyon Loop*

FOOD AND DRINK A couple of restaurants are located close to the starting point. Besaw's Café at 2301 NW Savier Street is open Monday through Saturday for breakfast, lunch, and dinner, and Sunday for breakfast and lunch; 503-228-2619. Portland Brewing Company's Taproom Restaurant, located at 2730 NW 31st Avenue, is open daily for lunch and dinner; 503-228-5269.

NOTE The areas of Forest Park covered in this hill walk are among the most popular in the park. Heavy use by people and dogs can overwhelm native plants and wildlife; please keep dogs leashed and out of the fragile ecosystem of Balch Creek.

B ORDERED ON ONE SIDE BY THE STEEP CANYON of Balch Creek and on another side by Forest Park, the Willamette Heights neighborhood delights explorers with its steep streets, densely wooded properties, wonderful Arts and Crafts homes, and proximity to Balch Creek, arguably the city's loveliest wild area.

Although sparsely settled when Portland's world's fair, the Lewis and Clark Exposition, opened on June 1, 1905, in the lowlands next door, Willamette Heights was already on its way to becoming a neighborhood of distinguished houses. Its developers, the Scottish American Investment Company, had asked Emil Schacht to design the early spec houses that were built here, and to provide a selection of plans for buyers. The resulting homes were among the first in Portland built in the Arts and Crafts style, with prices designed to appeal to the middle class. Houses that were originally $5500, however, now sell for $500,000 or more, and today this neighborhood, like many in Portland's inner city, is home to both middle-class folks who bought when the houses were affordable (before the real estate boom of the 1990s) and to newcomers who possess a large bank account or an ability to stomach a large mortgage.

1 The hill walk starts at NW 29th Avenue and Wilson Street, a location on the former shore of Guilds Lake, the site of the 1905 Lewis and Clark Exposition. In addition to commemorating the centennial of the Lewis and Clark expedition, the fair was intended to showcase Oregon's investment potential. It was deemed a huge success—more than 1.6 million people attended, and the organizers made a profit.

The fair's main entrance was at 26th and Upshur, now the site of a 1920s-era building. (The amazingly unchanged Fairmount apartment building at this intersection was built to house workers for the fair and then became a hotel for fairgoers.) The carriage entrance was at 28th and Thurman. Oregon's exhibits at the fair were housed in the Forestry Building, the world's largest log cabin, which was designed to show the world the immense bounties of Oregon's forests. The Forestry Building sat between Upshur and Vaughn at 28th, where the Old Forestry Condominiums now sit. The landmark Montgomery Park building at 28th and Vaughn (a former Montgomery Ward distribution center and now an exhibit space and meeting hall) sits where the fair's sunken gardens used to be.

The fair lasted only four and a half months, so most of the buildings, despite their grand appearances, were cheaply built, just plaster skins over wooden frames. There were exceptions, such as the timbered Forestry Building and a few conventionally built structures that still survive. One of these, the Masonic Building, is at NW 26th and Northrup. In Saint Johns, what was originally the National Cash Register Building now houses the McMenamins-owned Saint Johns Theater and Pub. (See Walk 20 for more information.) The Massachusetts Building was moved to Mount Tabor to become a sanatorium but was torn down in 1940.

The Forestry Building, a uniquely Northwest landmark of old growth and unpeeled timbers, went into a period of neglect after the fair, interspersed with periodic spasms of civic concern. Despite not being adequately maintained, it continued to be a tourist attraction, and its parklike grounds remained popular until the building burned to the ground in 1964.

GUILDS LAKE

A century after the world's fair took place, its location, Guilds Lake, is a bit of a mystery to many Portlanders. This is understandable, since the lake that the fair was built around no longer exists.

At the time of the fair, Guilds Lake was a large, shallow (less than 3-foot-deep) bottomland adjacent to the Willamette River, just downslope of Willamette Heights. It was originally a meander of the Willamette River and became a swampy wetland when the river changed its course to the east. The swamp became a bona fide lake in 1888 when a rail line went in, impounding the water. It was named for Peter and Eliza Guild, who settled there in 1847.

When New York City's Olmsted Brothers came to town in 1903 to help develop a system of parks, they recommended that Guilds Lake, with its backdrop of scenic mountains, be the site of the upcoming world's fair. One distinct advantage of the site over others was that the fair could be served by existing streetcar lines.

Once the fair was over, the Olmsted Brothers proposed that the site be converted to a public open space, with a park linking Macleay Park to the riverfront; but the fate of the fair site was sealed, literally, beginning around 1905, when Lafe Pence, a peripatetic lawyer, miner, and entrepreneur, breezed into town.

Pence, who was in Portland for the world's fair, allegedly hiked up into the hills above the fair site. Sitting on Scot's Nubbin, he envisioned the money he could make filling the swampy fair site with silt from the hillside and developing the land for industry. No matter that he owned neither the hillside nor the bottomland: after the fair was over, he commenced work on his scheme.

High up in the Balch Creek drainage, he cut trees to construct miles of wooden flumes to carry rocks and soil downhill. He milled logs at a mill that he built in the woods, and obtained water from Balch Creek and streams in the Tualatin River watershed (on the western side of these hills). Once all elements were in place, Pence began to sluice the ground down the hill into Guilds Lake.

Incensed at Pence's temerity, city fathers brought their axes up into the hills in 1906 and personally demolished the flume. In 1960 Thornton Munger noted in his *History of Portland's Forest Park* that part of the flume, which ran along the western side of Balch Creek, was still visible under the Thurman Street Bridge. Today it is no longer visible there, but a revised edition (1998) of Munger's book notes that remains can be seen in the form of a ditch alongside the Wildwood Trail, between the Birch and Wild Cherry trails.

Pence's idea, if not his ethics, had merit, because in 1910 the neighborhood to the south, Westover Terraces (also called Westover Heights, now Kings Heights), was developed into a series of terraces by sluicing the hillside away into Guilds Lake. The mudflats created by the tons of debris that came down off Westover later became the industrial park they are today.

Walk west on NW Wilson one block. What was once a sparkling showcase of the world's bounties is now a very unlovely sight: barbed wire, weedy vacant lots, and prefabricated buildings are scattered along the northern side of the street. At Wilson and 30th sits the oldest home in Willamette Heights. The home was built in 1874 and served as a stagecoach inn along Linnton Road (now Saint Helens Highway). In 2003 the house was moved from its original location at 2149 NW 32nd (north of the intersection of 32nd and Wilson) and settled here, with a new daylight basement below it.

Just steps from the end of NW Upshur Street is Balch Creek, one of only two year-round creeks in Forest Park and home to native cutthroat trout.

Turn left on 30th, a gravel road. At sewers on this road, stop and listen a moment for the buried sounds of Balch Creek. Walk uphill to a dead end of NW Vaughn Street, turn right, and climb the concrete stairs leading up. From midway up the stairs, look to your left to see the 1903 Thurman Street Bridge and Balch Creek Canyon. Although you're downstream, you are actually at a higher elevation due to the pile of fill dumped here. In 1903 John Olmsted praised the extreme natural beauty of Balch Creek within Macleay Park, recommending that the park remain little developed and be extended to Saint Helens Road. Instead, the creek plunges underground at Thurman. If ever a buried creek should be "daylighted," it should be Balch Creek: uncovering its lower portions would reap big rewards for a relatively small amount of work.

At the top of the steps, take the short path on the right that leads uphill to an upper section of Vaughn. Here Vaughn shucks the commercial skin it wears at lower elevations and becomes a quiet, steep, charming street of bungalows. There are views here down into Guilds Lake Industrial Area and across the Willamette to North Portland. The red-roofed building tucked amongst the warehouses is the Portland Brewing Company, an excellent place for lunch. It was established in 1986 by Portland's MacTarnahan family and sold in 2004 to Pyramid Breweries of Seattle.

Turn left on NW 32nd Avenue. Before you do, you may want to explore the end of Vaughn or the few streets on the slope below it. Both are very satisfying for the urban explorer, offering peeks into a little-driven and very quaint corner of the city.

2 Walk one block on 32nd and turn right onto NW Thurman Street. The house on the northwestern corner was built in 1904 for Charles Swigert, who came here in 1880 to construct the first bridge over the Willamette. The anachronistic dwelling at 3245 used to be a row of garages. The homes at 3309 and 3321 are 100 percent behind Portland's tradition of planting roses in the parking strip. An unusual placement of wisteria adorns the narrow parking strip at 3407. This plant, a rapidly growing vine, is usually trellised against a large structure, and even then its unmannerly growth and insidious tendrils can quickly overwhelm a timid gardener. The street starts to curve into the forest just past here, and Forest Park looms ahead.

Thurman Street was named for G. William Thurman, an assistant manager at the Pacific Postal Telegraph Cable Company. How does such a lowly minion get his name on a street? As is often the case, it's whom you know. Thurman was buddies with Portland's superintendent of streets, who renamed many of the city's streets in 1891.

In Thurman's 3400 block are wonderful views to the north. A public staircase at 3418 leads up to NW Aspen Avenue, if you want to take a shorter walk.

Turn right at leafy NW Gordon Street, which runs northwest at the 200-foot elevation toward a creek valley. Many of the homes on this street are newer and share a neo–Arts and Crafts style, with wood shingles and muted yet unconventional trim colors.

Gordon ends at the very high Alexandra Street Bridge, built in 1922, which serves just one property plus a city water tank. The bridge is distinctive in that it is one of the few old bridges in town in which the decorative ironwork has not been obscured by much safer but quite ugly concrete barriers. Peer over the side for a bird's-eye view of the tree canopy. The creek below is a good size; it drains an area of Forest Park just north of the Balch Creek watershed.

At the bridge's midway point, look to the northeast to the blue and white cranes. These are located at the Port of Portland's Terminal 2. According to the Port, this 55-acre facility on the western side of the river handles virtually all types of cargo, including lumber, forest products, steel, machinery, and packaged goods. It also has a low-level dock for "ro-ro" (cargo that can be rolled on or off a ship, such as autos, trucks, or construction equipment, or that can be driven on or off by a truck). Terminal 2 is among the most modern multipurpose marine facilities on the West Coast.

The bridge ends at the only occupant of NW Alexandra Avenue, the Salvation Army's White Shield Center, which provides residential treatment for pregnant teens. This 1914 Colonial Revival house was built as the Home for Unwed Mothers by E. Henry Wemme, who struck it rich in the late 1890s selling canvas tents to Klondike gold rushers. Once, in the 1920s, some of the younger girls here tried to attend nearby Chapman Elementary School, but the mothers of Chapman students objected to their presence, so a small school was set up inside the White Shield Center. From the 1940s through the 1960s, babies were born at the Wemme Memorial Hospital at the rear of the building. To this day, residents of the White Shield Center may reside there until their child reaches the age of three. The center also offers short-term emergency shelter for girls who have left abusive situations. Though one might not guess so from its name, the Salvation Army is an evangelical Christian church. Its mission is to make a difference, one human being at a time.

3 Pass the entrance to the White Shield Center. Next to a locked gate that leads to a City of Portland water tank is a pedestrian path that leads into Forest Park. Take this path uphill, on the left side of the tank. The trail steepens as you climb the creek valley.

Stinging nettles line the trail here. In this plant, hollow hairs cover the stalks, leaf stems, and undersides of leaves. When you brush against the plant, the tips of the hairs break and the hair functions like a tiny hypodermic needle, injecting a stinging, though harmless, venom into your skin. The plant's name, in fact, comes from the Anglo-Saxon word for "needle." Nettles have fascinated people for centuries. The ancient Roman Petronius wrote that a man could be thrashed about the kidneys and below the navel with nettles in order to improve his virility. Science is finding that many folk remedies using nettles have merit (but perhaps not that one!). As a food, nettles are a rich source of vitamin C. Young shoots are edible raw; later, after they are mature and sting-laden, the leaves can be steamed like spinach. Once cooked, they lose their sting.

Further up the trail you can see the grown-over evidence that this trail was once an old road: steeply cut banks above a wide, level bed.

The top of the trail intersects with Leif Erikson Drive, a premier hiking and biking trail. Originally called Hillside Drive, it was built in 1914 and 1915 to provide access to several subdivisions planned along its route, with names like Glen Harbor Heights, Maybrook, Ridgewood, Marine View, and Regents Heights. The route was first proposed in 1903 by the Olmsted Brothers, who called it the "Northwest Hillside Parkway" and said it "could be continued . . . as many miles as can be afforded along the northern flank of the hill . . . on a level in the mist of the woods, bending into the ravines and out around the spurs, with pretty glimpses between trees of the distant landscape and of the snow-capped peaks." Unfortunately, although the road could be continued, it could not be maintained. The route of Leif Erikson, from its start at Thurman to its terminus 11 miles north at NW Germantown Road, crosses numerous steep drainages, and seasonal torrents caused repeated washouts. The first washout came one year after the road was built. It soon became apparent the road would be too expensive to maintain, and the plans for subdivisions were abandoned. Many lots had already been sold, but none were ever built upon. Most were later forfeited to the city for unpaid taxes, thereby building up the acreage that would later become the park. In the 1930s the road became a Depression-related work relief project. In an effort to provide the maximum hand labor for the unemployed, it was graded and graveled, but slides soon made it again impassable. Its name was changed from Hillside to Leif Erikson in 1933 upon a petition by the Sons of Norway fraternal organization. (For more information, see Walk 3, which covers the last 1.5 miles of Leif Erikson.)

Turn left onto Leif Erikson (a portable toilet sits to the right a few hundred feet), and you will immediately cross one of the very steep valleys that doomed the road.

As the road hairpins around the valley, it has a very pleasant downhill grade, just enough to let gravity help you stretch your stride. You're at about 350 feet elevation here. Watch out for cyclists who can come bombing down this last stretch of Leif Erikson after working out further back in the woods.

Exit Leif Erikson and Forest Park at Thurman Street, the busiest street in Willamette Heights. Thurman's terminus is one of Forest Park's most popular entrances. The Friends of Forest Park are working to create another entrance on Saint Helens Highway to take the heat off this street.

Where Thurman splits, go right, uphill, onto NW Aspen Avenue. Stay left on Aspen where NW Belgrave Street comes in on your right. There's great house watching on Aspen. A set of fraternal twins sits at 2112 and 2102. It's also fun to look at the site-specific designs of private staircases that allow people to inhabit these very steep lots. Just past 1846 is the top of the staircase that leads to Thurman.

4 For a slight detour onto some of the quieter streets in Willamette Heights, turn left onto NW Franklin Court, a great sledding street that drops smoothly in the first block and then levels out a bit so you can bail out before sailing on down the hill into Balch Creek. Many Arts and Crafts homes are situated here; the homes at 3449 and 3437 were built during the first decade of the twentieth century. A very self-possessed American Basic is at 3339, its third story addition gracefully blending with the existing lines.

Turn right on NW 33rd Avenue and right again after one block, onto NW Savier Street. Savier is steep, with correspondingly good views. After the first block, however, the road levels out, probably from Lafe Pence's sluicing. The high ground to the left is Scot's Nubbin, a 400-foot-tall ridge that is now an isolated bump, having had its western side sluiced away, leaving flat ground that you'll soon cover as you reenter Forest Park.

The geology of this neighborhood enabled Pence to wash the hillside away. The rock under most of Willamette Heights is the Troutdale Formation, not the Columbia River Basalts more typical of the West Hills. The Troutdale Formation was laid down as flood deposits two to ten million years ago over the Columbia River Basalts. It is exposed in Willamette Heights and in other places along the eastern side of the West Hills by faulting or folding. The Troutdale Formation is fun to find, a welcome change from the usual dark basaltic rock more typical of western Oregon. It consists of conglomerates of well-rounded cobbles and pebbles. Some rocks in the formation consist of sandstone, quartzite, schists, and granites from the ancestral Columbia River and source regions to the east; others are basaltic, eroded from the ancient Cascade Mountains. Water pressure was able to erode the conglomerates and wash them downhill.

Go left on Aspen to NW Raleigh Street. Turn right into a more peaceful, less frequently used entrance into Forest Park. The trail is called Holman Lane, named for the family that once ran a small dairy here. It was also called Mountain View Park Road after a subdivision was platted here in 1882. Running uphill to NW 53rd Avenue, the road-turned-trail once had several summer cabins situated along it.

Walk up the trail. A grassy area on the left is a good place to romp with your dog before leashing him for the park trails. This flat meadow was the site of the Holman dairy in the 1920s and later, a Girl Scout day camp. In 1939 the owners of the dairy donated this land, still called Holman Park, to the city, which incorporated it into Forest Park.

Just past the meadow, turn left at the intersection with the Wildwood Trail. As you begin walking on the Wildwood, stop for a moment to look at the tree trunks. Many lean—some uphill, some downhill. Others, like a large fir on the uphill side of the trail, have smooth curves on their lower trunks. These are signs that this hillside is on the move: the soil is creeping downhill beneath the trees. In the case of the wildly skewed trees, the ground has moved rapidly, knocking the trees awry; the trees with the gentle curves have adapted to a slow creep by realigning themselves so that they can continue to grow vertically.

Within minutes of walking on the Wildwood Trail, you're in the Balch Creek Canyon, hiking on a level trail that runs along the hillside a few hundred feet upslope from the creek. The Wildwood is the longest trail in Forest Park, at 30 miles. It was started in 1909 to connect the upper reaches of Macleay Park with the Forestry Building. In this stretch are some of the largest Douglas firs in Forest Park, and the walk has the same hushed feel you get in a cathedral. The traffic noise audible here emanates from NW Cornell Road, which climbs along the opposite canyon wall. Far down the slope, Balch Creek runs year-round.

As the trail descends toward the creek, the air grows cooler and there are increasing numbers of big firs. This section of Forest Park was originally called Macleay Park. Donald Macleay owned this land in the late nineteenth century. In 1897, while paying his property taxes, he grumbled to the property assessor that he'd rather give the land away than pay such high taxes. "Well then, why don't you?" replied the assessor, and Macleay did.

5 The Wildwood Trail meets Balch Creek at the intersection with the Lower Macleay Trail. The stone shelter at the intersection was built in the 1930s by the Works Progress Administration, or WPA. (For more information on the WPA, see Walk 14.) It was a bathroom until the Columbus Day storm of 1962 destroyed its water supply. The wooden roof disappeared sometime later. The comfort station wasn't renovated, and today the abandoned shell, with its romantic fringe of ferns and moss, is a beloved landmark.

Turn left on the Lower Macleay and follow it as it runs downhill along the creek. Watch for the enormous Douglas fir on the creek bank. This is a Portland Heritage Tree and the biggest tree in Forest Park.

Balch Creek was named for Danford Balch. With his wife and nine children, he emigrated to Oregon in 1847, and in 1850 filed a donation land claim for the area bounded by Vaughn Street and Saint Helens Road to the north, 22nd Avenue to the east, Cornell Road to the south, and Aspen Avenue to the west. He built a home along the creek that bears his name. In 1859 Balch was hanged for shooting the man who ran off and married his fifteen-year-old daughter. His daughter witnessed the execution along with five hundred other Portlanders.

Balch Creek is a fabulous gem at any time of year. Just 2 miles from downtown Portland and blocks from neighborhood yards, this stream has it all: huge, downed trees lying across the water right where nature left them, lacy vine maples dripping with moss and arching across the streambed, and best of all, the wild, rushing sound of untamed water running to the sea. In winter the water roars as one foaming, rushing torrent; in late summer, at its lowest level, the creek pools and drops as it quietly stairsteps downhill. On the upper reaches, ivy has been removed to reveal the native vegetation. The delicacy of these plants contrasts with the green shag-carpet effect of the ivy along the lower reaches of the creek.

Near the bottom of the canyon, the trail is paved. When Macleay donated this land he stipulated that any trails developed along the creek be wide and flat enough to accommodate wheelchairs so that patients at nearby Good Samaritan and Saint Vincent Hospitals could receive the healthful benefits of mountain air. In 1994 one of Macleay's descendants, Judy Weinsoft, died. It was her wish, too, that a wheelchair-accessible trail be installed in the park. Family and friends worked to make this come to fruition.

When you emerge from the canyon into a meadow, you can see two wire-mesh structures designed to catch debris, and an older wooden weir at the place where the water runs into a culvert. As you enter the meadow underneath the Thurman Street Bridge, the change in topography is striking: the ground becomes unnaturally flat and suddenly streamless. The creek valley has been filled, either when homes were constructed on the hillside above or as a result of Lafe Pence's sluicing. The stream doesn't see daylight until it hits the Willamette River about a mile from here.

Balch Creek in 1934, just south of the Thurman Street Bridge. WPA workers installed a "trash trap," which still exists, and lined the bank with rock. The creek valley had been filled in by this date. Photo courtesy of the City of Portland Archives.

This place has a rich history. Under this artificial meadow is the site of the home Danford Balch built in 1850. Later, from the 1860s until water from the Bull Run watershed came on line in 1895, Balch Creek was used to supply water to Portland. The concrete intake pipe was located here, and Peter Guild was paid $200 to give up rights to the water that had previously flowed into his lake.

Gypsies camped under the Thurman Street Bridge in the early 1900s, giving the canyon an air of mystery and danger to local children.

Today the land under this vintage 1903 bridge is the busiest portal to the 5000-acre Forest Park. Here you'll find restrooms, a water fountain, a picnic shelter, grassy fields, and the Forest Park Field House, home to the No Ivy League, which works to eradicate the noxious invasive plant from urban forests. The field house was built in 1951 as the original headquarters for the newly formed Forest Park.

6 Take the stairs on the eastern end of the bridge, up to Thurman. Turn left at the top and walk downhill on Thurman one block to NW 29th Avenue. Turn left on a paved pedestrian walkway. The pavement peters out into a well-worn but rutted dirt path. In the exposed dirt in this path are rounded, hand-sized

From the Thurman Street Bridge, looking down into Balch Creek Canyon, site of Danford Balch's home and much human engineering in the years since then. Upstream from here, beyond the water-control structures, the canyon is wild and the creek runs freely.

cobbles, evidence of the Troutdale Formation. In one block the path deposits you at Upshur, where 29th turns back into a street. From here, walk two blocks to your starting point at 29th and Wilson.

Two nearby restaurants are always good. Besaw's Café was established in 1903 by two French Canadian loggers, George Besaw and Medric Liberty, with seed money from brewer Henry Weinhard. Today it offers period furnishings and fresh Northwest ingredients. Portland Brewing Company's Taproom is a brewery and restaurant located in the historic Guilds Lake Industrial Area, a few blocks from the hill walk's end.

NOB HILL TO KINGS HEIGHTS AND PITTOCK MANSION LOOP

STARTING POINT Wallace Park: NW 25th Avenue and Raleigh Street

DISTANCE 4.75 miles

ELEVATION 110 feet at the starting point; 930 feet at the Pittock Mansion

GETTING THERE AND PARKING From downtown Portland, drive west on Burnside Street. Turn right on NW 23rd Avenue into the Alphabet District. Turn left on NW Raleigh Street and drive two blocks to the intersection with NW 25th Avenue. Park along the street.

TriMet: From downtown, take bus 15 (NW 23rd Avenue) to the stop at NW 23rd Avenue and Raleigh Street. Walk west on Raleigh two blocks to 25th.

RESTROOMS AND DRINKING FOUNTAINS You'll find restrooms and drinking fountains at Pittock Mansion, Wallace Park, and the Hillside Community Center, located near the route of the walk and open daylight hours, Monday through Friday.

FOOD AND DRINK Tara Thai Northwest, located at 1310 NW 23rd Avenue, is open daily for lunch and dinner; 503-222-7840. A smorgasbord of other dining options can be found on NW 23rd between Burnside and Vaughn.

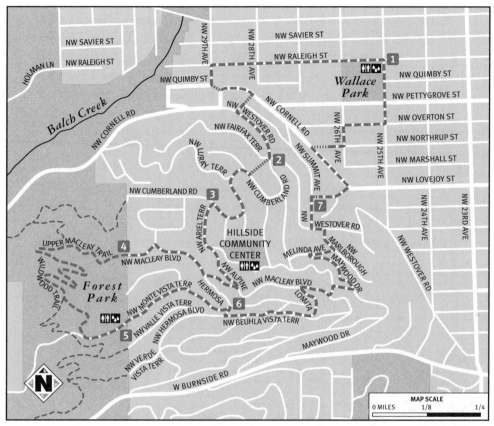

NW SAVIER ST
NW RALEIGH ST
HOLMAN LN
NW QUIMBY ST
Balch Creek
NW CORNELL RD
NW 29TH AVE
NW 28TH AVE
NW SAVIER ST
NW RALEIGH ST
1
NW QUIMBY ST
Wallace Park
NW PETTYGROVE ST
NW OVERTON ST
NW NORTHRUP ST
NW MARSHALL ST
NW LOVEJOY ST
NW 26TH AVE
NW 25TH AVE
NW 24TH AVE
NW 23RD AVE
NW WESTOVER RD
NW CORNELL RD
NW FAIRFAX TERR
NW LURAY TERR
NW WESTOVER RD
NW CUMBERLAND RD
2
NW CUMBERLAND RD
NW SUMMIT AVE
NW CUMBERLAND RD
3
NW ARIEL TERR
HILLSIDE COMMUNITY CENTER
7
NW WESTOVER RD
UPPER MACLEAY TRAIL
4
NW MACLEAY BLVD
NW ALPINE
MELINDA AVE
NW MARLBOROUGH
NW MAYWOOD DR
WILDWOOD TRAIL
Forest Park
NW MONTE VISTA TERR
HERMOSA
NW MACLEAY BLVD
LOMITA
NW VALLE VISTA TERR
NW HERMOSA BLVD
6
NW BEUHLA VISTA TERR
5
NW VERDE VISTA TERR
MAYWOOD DR
W BURNSIDE RD
N
MAP SCALE
0 MILES   1/8   1/4

WALK 2. *Nob Hill to Kings Heights and Pittock Mansion Loop*

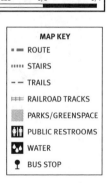

MAP KEY
▪ ▬ ROUTE
▪▪▪▪▪ STAIRS
– – TRAILS
┼┼┼ RAILROAD TRACKS
░░ PARKS/GREENSPACE
🚻 PUBLIC RESTROOMS
💧 WATER
🚏 BUS STOP

THIS HILL WALK TRAVERSES TWO NEIGHBORHOODS: Nob Hill and Kings Heights. Nob Hill is home to large homes and many small restaurants and shops. Along NW 21st and 23rd Avenues is a stroller's paradise. This walk bypasses the neighborhood's mercantile core and heads up to Nob Hill's higher reaches before climbing into Kings Heights, a neighborhood literally blasted out of the face of the Tualatin Mountains. The people who live in Kings Heights pay a lot of money for the privilege of owning a home that looks out at four Cascade peaks: Rainier, Adams, Saint Helens, and Hood. Save this walk for a crystal-clear day when the mountains appear in their glorious white majesty.

1 Begin the hill walk at Wallace Park, located in Nob Hill. This park is bounded by NW Pettygrove and Raleigh Streets and NW 25th and 26th Avenues, and is adjacent to Chapman Elementary School. Before Chapman was built, in the 1920s, this area was an open space where the circus set up its big tents when it came to town. In the early 1900s, American Indians also came here to sell baskets.

Walk west on Raleigh past modest duplexes and garden apartments. The hills you see above Chapman are in Kings Heights, which you'll pass through on your way to even higher ground at the Pittock Mansion. At NW 28th Avenue,

Layers of homes in Kings Heights.

Raleigh begins to climb the lower flanks of the Tualatin Mountains in earnest. The gently sloping land you're leaving consists of deposits laid down across the Portland area and the Willamette Valley thirteen to twenty thousand years ago by the Missoula Floods. (See Walks 14 and 17 for more on the floods.) As the hill steepens, you're walking atop the much older Troutdale Formation, gravels and cobbles laid down millions of years ago and uplifted as the Tualatin Mountains were born.

Turn left on NW 29th Avenue, one block before Raleigh dead-ends into the canyon of Balch Creek. NW 29th dead-ends in one block as well, but the sidewalk doesn't. Keep walking and you'll emerge onto an especially charming section of NW Quimby Street that ends at a shady, paved path leading to twenty-four stairs. Take the stairs out of this quiet neighborhood and up to busy NW Cornell Road. At the top of the stairs and across the road at 2870 Cornell are two umbrella pines. Related to the redwood and native to a small area in Japan, this tree is named for the way its needles are arrayed, like the ribs of an umbrella.

Cornell was formerly Balch Creek Road, named for Danford Balch. (See Walk 1 for more on Balch.)

Turn left onto Cornell. You'll pass a large Camperdown elm at 2855, its Medusa-like mass of twisting, coiling branches perched atop a single trunk. In 1640 the Earl of Camperdown in Dundee, Scotland, noticed a branch creeping along the floor of his elm forest. He grafted it to a Scotch elm tree, and voilà!— the world's first Camperdown elm. The Camperdown is a mutant and cannot reproduce without human intervention; each one is a part of the original that has been grafted to an elm rootstock. The droopy, pendulous branches and mushroom-like growth habit of the Camperdown elm are an exotic, though acquired, taste.

Across from the home at 2840 is an unobstructed view of Montgomery Park above Nob Hill rooftops. Built in 1922, this was the first West Coast warehouse for retail giant Montgomery Ward. After its first useful life ended, the warehouse was reincarnated in 1986 as office space and a convention and event center. From this spot on a clear day you can also see Mount Rainier peaking over the left shoulder of Mount Saint Helens, which blew its top 1300 feet off in 1980. Mount Adams sits off to the east of Saint Helens. All three of these Cascade peaks are in Washington. To the left of Montgomery Park is a sea of warehouses in Guilds Lake, a swampy river meander that was filled for industrial use in the early 1900s. Beyond it to the north you can see the Burlington Northern Railroad Bridge, and 1 mile north of that, the elegant spires of the Saint Johns Bridge. This is an industrial scene today but was once a beautiful bottomland. In 1903 the Olmsted Brothers proposed a "Northwestern River

Parkway" along Saint Helens Road, which "in the low land at the base of the steep hills . . . is nearly level, and commands at present exceedingly beautiful scenery." At that point in time, its beautiful days were numbered.

Two houses past this swell view is 2815 Cornell. Here, carefully cross the road, which is used by commuters, and take the flight of seventy-three steps that lead steeply uphill alongside a quaint, moss-lined concrete gutter. At the top of the steps you're on NW Summit Avenue. Turn right, and in a few steps you're at the intersection of Summit and NW Westover Road.

The house on the corner, at 2877 Westover, is the oldest home in this fascinating neighborhood. It was built in 1911 as a model home to entice homebuyers up the newly leveled hillside to look at the lots.

Westover Terraces (Kings Heights) during or shortly after the sluicing of the hillside, circa 1911. The house at far right, 2877 NW Westover Road, was the first in the neighborhood. Guilds Lake, still a body of water at that time, is visible in the background, as are the homes of Willamette Heights. Photo courtesy of the Multnomah County Library.

The history of Kings Heights could never be repeated today, in this more ecologically sensitive era. The neighborhood began to be developed in 1910 when the Lewis-Wiley Hydraulic Company installed pumps to bring water up from Guilds Lake as ammunition for a water cannon called "the giant," which was used to attack the hillside to create workable road grades and level lots. The rock and gravel brought down by the hydraulic mining flowed through steel-lined flumes to its final resting place in the soon-to-disappear Guilds Lake. Like the hydraulic giants used to mine for gold in California, where "hydraulicking" was invented, this water cannon knocked down trees, rolled boulders, and flushed everything down hill.

Most street names in the neighborhood include the word *terrace*, because that was the salient selling point of the Westover Terraces, as the area was called. Advertisements noted that "each home sits on a plateau of its own: distinct, separate and complete."

The sluicing of the hillside would not have been practicable if the Columbia River Basalts, present under most West Hills neighborhoods, had existed here. But as with Willamette Heights, the underlying rock in the lower flanks of Kings Heights is the Troutdale Formation. (For more information on the Troutdale Formation, see Walk 1.)

If you look at a detailed topographic map of this neighborhood, you'll see contour lines consisting of a series of flat planes and right angles; these indicate places where vertical cuts were made on the steep hillside and land was scraped away, or where fill was placed on a slope to make flat, buildable spots. (In contrast, the hillside just west of the Pittock Mansion remains in a more natural state, with smoothly curving contour lines.) Developers crowed about the lots never needing retaining walls because "only superfluous earth, or earth that has a tendency to slide, ever require [sic] walls to retain it. And it is this earth that is now being removed—once and for all—from Westover Terraces." For each lot, the developers estimated that an average of 10,000 cubic yards of "superfluous earth" was removed. Evidently they didn't get it all, because the land is still prone to sliding.

Some of the newer homes were built on unterraced ground using more sophisticated building techniques. Instead of sitting on a flat building site, they sit on stilts and foundations sunk into stable soil and rock.

Today, making cuts and placing fills on what are now known to be the very unstable slopes of Portland's West Hills are two surefire ways to invite intense attention from your neighbors and their lawyers.

On Westover Road, turn left and begin walking uphill past a lineup of grand homes. The house at 2808 Westover, where Westover intersects with NW

Fairfax Terrace and Cumberland Road, once belonged to Richard and Maurine Neuberger. Richard won a seat in the Oregon Senate in 1948, and Maurine won a seat in the Oregon House in 1950. After Richard ran successfully for U.S. Senate in 1954, Maurine caused a minor scandal when at a Democratic fundraiser in Washington she joined other Senate wives in modeling clothes from her home state. Instead of wearing a decorous wool suit from Pendleton Woolen Mills, she showed off her still-great figure in a black one-piece swimming suit from Jantzen! Some people said that she had besmirched the dignity of the Senate, but she professed to not understand what the fuss was about. After Richard died suddenly in 1960, Maurine ran for his seat and won. As a senator, she championed consumer's rights, saying, "No industry I know of has ever been able to regulate itself to the interest of the consumer public." After taking on the meat, tobacco, and cosmetics industries, she left the Senate after one term and returned to teaching. She died in Portland in 2000 at age ninety-three.

2 At the intersection of Westover, Fairfax, and Cumberland, turn right onto Fairfax. Next to the corner is a staircase leading uphill. The steepness of this staircase, built on an unterraced slope, indicates the challenges of developing this mountainside. One hundred forty-one steps bring you to Cumberland. This staircase and the one below it, running from Summit to Westover, have a total of 280 steps. Firefighters use the two flights of steps to practice running stairs at top speed.

Turn right and walk uphill on Cumberland past four streets: Shenandoah, Luray, Rapidan, and Winchester Terraces. At Winchester is the grand mansion called Ariel Terraces. Built in 1926, this was the home of Clarissa McKeyes Inman, inventor of the electric curling iron. When she sold her rights to the iron after twelve years, she invested the proceeds into this house. Just past the intersection with NW Ariel Terrace is a fine view over a driveway and down into the industrial district. Across the river is Swan Island. Now industrial land, this was the site of the first Portland airport. The main river channel used to run along the eastern side of Swan Island before that area was filled and the channel diverted to the western side.

3 Turn left on NW Ariel Terrace, which traverses the inner core of Kings Heights. Just off the hill walk route, further downhill on Ariel, is the hard-to-believe-it's-not-a-country-club Hillside Community Center. While now part of Portland Parks and Recreation, this site indeed had its origins in the private sector. From 1916 to 1958 it was home to the Catlin Hillside School. After Catlin's merger with the Gabel Country Day School, the combined school, Catlin Gabel, moved to the current campus on SW Barnes Road. After Catlin Gabel School left, neighbors went to work raising money to buy the property in order to keep it out of a developer's hands. When donations weren't enough, twelve neighbors borrowed money, using their own homes as collateral, with the expectation that the City of Portland would buy them out. They were called the "trembling twelve," but their faith was well placed. The community center's jewel is a gymnasium designed by world-famous architect Pietro Belluschi in 1947 in the Northwest Regional style. After leaving Portland in 1950, Belluschi returned to the city to retire in 1972, moving into a home that he had originally designed for a client, located up the hill from the gymnasium. The gymnasium is a beautiful building with clear vertical-grain fir walls, a high barrel-vault ceiling, and large windows that open to the tree-covered hills behind. Since a fire in 2003, the building has been beautifully restored. Restrooms and water are available inside. The center is closed on weekends.

Turn right off Ariel onto NW Alpine Terrace, and climb this narrow street. Turn right onto NW Macleay Boulevard, which follows the hillside about 70 feet above Alpine, giving you wonderful views to the northwest.

On Macleay, just past NW Hermosa Boulevard, is a newer home towering high above. To build this house, which sits on an unterraced lot, contractors had to create level ground out of thin air, which is what the building has whistling through its vast superstructure of steel and laminated beams. Although some of the older homes on Macleay are surprisingly plain-Jane, their views are anything but. Stay on Macleay (left) at an intersection with NW Warrenton Terrace.

4 Macleay ends one block from here, in the woods, at one of the unadvertised backdoor entrances to Forest Park. The trail to the right is the Macleay Trail, which in a short distance becomes one with the Wildwood Trail. Take the trail to the left, the Upper Macleay Trail. It also intersects with the Wildwood Trail.

On the Upper Macleay Trail, begin traversing the side of a hill, at the 650-foot elevation line. Water flowing on the slopes here runs into Balch Creek, one of the few year-round streams in Portland. A bit further on, the trail is really lovely, with deep shade, large trees, and abundant sword ferns. American Indians found the sword fern to be a versatile plant. They used its leaves as bedding, floor coverings, ceremonial headgear, placemats for feasts, and as an early-day wax paper, lining their food storage boxes and berry baskets with its fronds.

When you come to the intersection with the Wildwood Trail, take the left-most trail, which is the Wildwood. The woods here are cathedral-like, sun shafts streaming through the trees on a cloudless late-summer noon. The trail steepens and begins to switchback up to the elevation of Pittock Mansion, one of

Portland's most beloved landmarks and the former home of Henry and Georgiana Pittock.

Emerging from the woods, you'll see a parking lot. Walk through the lot until you see the western face of the mansion. It was built between 1909 and 1914, near the end of Henry Pittock's life. Henry came to Oregon from England at age nineteen in 1853. Penniless, he took a job with the *Weekly Oregonian*. When his employer couldn't pay him, he gave Henry the paper. Henry changed the paper to a daily, the *Morning Oregonian*, and published it from 1860 until his death in 1919 at age eighty-five. He was an avid hiker, and in 1857 was in the first climbing party to gain the top of Mount Hood. He helped found the Mazamas hiking club in 1894 and laid out and built many of the trails around the mansion. He was also a bike rider and into his seventies would ride from Portland to one of his daughter's homes in Camas, east of Vancouver. Even today, with smooth roads and multigeared bikes, that ride is a challenge.

Georgiana, his wife, came to Oregon as a child in a wagon train in 1854. She was reportedly kidnapped along the way by Sioux Indians, who were so charmed by her that they returned to ask for permission to keep her. Georgiana's parents refused (politely, I assume), and their daughter was returned. She has been described as a warm-hearted and generous woman; in her later years she was dedicated to improving the welfare of women and children. She started, with others, the Martha Washington Home "for wage-earning girls and women strangers" and was active in the Ladies Relief Society, the Parry Center, and the Fruit and Flower Mission.

Two of the Pittocks' seven children moved into the mansion after being married; the outdoorsy Pittocks thus had the fun of raising three grandchildren on the property. One grandchild, Robert "Peter" Gantenbein, was born in the house and lived in it until 1958.

The home was vacant, with Gantenbein looking for a buyer, when the infamous Columbus Day storm of 1962 hit the city. The mansion was badly damaged by winds up to 100 miles per hour. Because of the damage, demolition was on everyone's mind, but once again citizen activists saved the day. Through fundraising and help from the federal government, Portlanders raised the $225,000 needed to purchase the property. Today the mansion is maintained by the Pittock Mansion Society.

You'll come first to the garage and caretaker's quarters, now a gift shop, with restrooms, water, and a pay phone. You can buy a history of the mansion or get a free walking-tour map of the grounds. Tours of the interior are given daily, with different hours from June through August and September through May. The mansion is closed in January, though the grounds are open. The tour is worth its price ($5.50 for adults, less for children and seniors), both for the trip it offers back in time and up the social stratum, and for the help it provides to the folks who have restored and now maintain the home.

You actually approach the back of the home; the front faces the view east, over Kings Heights. After looking at the back of the house, most folks walk around the house and head straight out to the grassy promontory overlooking the city. It's true that the views from the promontory are not to be missed, but I also like to hang out on Mr. and Mrs. Pittock's front porch, which many people ignore. Tiled in red, the porch swoops around the home, giving access to every angle of the city views. The view of Mount Hood from here is classic, captured by photographers of every level, from professionals to the little girl visiting from Indiana with her disposable camera. Exterior stone window seats are a perfect place to curl up, soak in the sun, and spin a little fantasy of wealth. From the porch, gigantic windows afford a good peek into the various rooms of the house; the nice people who run the museum have thoughtfully placed outward-facing cards in the windows that explain interior features for outdoor gawkers.

No matter how many times I see the Pittocks' home, I am still delighted by its beauty and the accord it has achieved with its surroundings. While more imposing than most architecture of the Northwest, it still seems to embody a Northwest spirit of quiet satisfaction without braggadocio. The home, in the French Renaissance Revival style, is grand but not vulgar, elegant but not stuffy. And as big as it is, it sits atop its promontory not like a "look at me" tiara but more like part of the mountain itself—a more highly evolved bit of stone, but still a part of the rock on which it sits. The home is fireproof, constructed of reinforced concrete covered with Tenino stone, a fine-grained sandstone from Tenino, Washington. Inside are steel-reinforced concrete floors topped with wood and marble, and interior walls of hollow tile block.

From the front porch, walk out into the lawn and then along the paved road that curves downhill around the southern side of the house toward the Gate Lodge, the home for thirty-nine years of the Skene family. James Skene served the family as gardener, chauffeur, and custodian until 1953. Follow the road past the gate lodge and turn left, toward downtown.

5 Walk downhill on a paved road toward a gate that marks the boundary of Forest Park. Pedestrians can pass through it to NW Monte Vista Terrace. Sunny Monte Vista runs along the top of a ridgeline here, the same ridge on which the Pittock Mansion sits. Homes on the right look south across a steep canyon into Washington Park; homes on the left look north toward the industrial area of

Northwest Portland and the Willamette River. Walkers can look over the rooftops on both sides.

At the intersection with NW Rio Vista Terrace is a view of the Fremont Bridge framed between two pines. The classical lines of this interstate highway bridge were designed to soothe Portlanders who were miffed at the ugliness of the Marquam Bridge. (For more on the Fremont Bridge, see Walk 19.)

On the right, the road downslope of Monte Vista is NW Valle Vista Terrace. This street, now a dead end, once had a rail line along its route that ran from Kings Heights to the corner of W Burnside Street and NW Skyline Boulevard, to the Mount Calvary Cemetery. This was during the early 1900s, when cemeteries were recreational destinations for families.

On the spot where NW Hermosa Boulevard comes in is the Otho Poole home, a large, picturesque building in the Spanish Mission style, built in 1928, that curves gracefully around a swimming pool in the backyard. It is on the National Register of Historic Places.

6 Turn right onto Hermosa and take an immediate left to NW Beuhla Vista Terrace, which parallels Monte Vista on the southern side of the ridge and offers views of downtown Portland and the forests of Washington Park.

Pass NW Verde Vista Terrace on the right and Rainier Terrace on the left. At this intersection are four generations of retaining walls—each with a story, I'm certain, of angst and hope. Judging from the relatively new landscaping and young age of the plants above the new mortared stone wall, a landslide probably occurred here since the 1990s. Nevertheless, hope springs eternal where the views are stunning.

Pass NW Calumet Terrace on the right and turn left on NW Lomita Terrace, a beautiful street that runs along the prow of the ridge, giving a view to the east. Turn right onto Macleay and check out the enormous (5-foot or taller) carved basalt blocks that were somehow muscled into an interlocking perfection to retain the slope. Macleay is dark and canyonlike here. In places you can see old streetcar tracks. One neighbor told me that meter readers would take the streetcar to the top of Macleay and walk their route, downhill.

Turn left at NW Albemarle Terrace, right at NW Roanoke Street, and left at NW Maywood Drive. You're at 450 feet elevation here, about halfway down from the top at Pittock Mansion. From near the bottom of Maywood you can see about thirteen levels of homes layered like frosting on the mountain.

Turn right on NW Melinda Avenue and walk practically under the elevated roadbed of Maywood. A heritage ginkgo tree sits by the home at 662. Individual ginkgoes are either male or female, and the females are usually avoided by homeowners because they produce stinky, naked seeds. However, there is a silver lining for those who end up with a female ginkgo tree: once the smelly covering of the seed is stripped off, the hard inner seed can be cracked open and eaten. In fact, this is a delicacy in China, where the trees are grown, plantation-style, for their seeds.

Turn left onto NW Marlborough and left again onto Westover. Walk half a block on Westover and turn right on NW Summit Avenue.

7 Walk past four homes on Summit. Across the street from 850, an entire slope has been extravagantly tiled in large basalt blocks, with a stone staircase cutting through it toward the house above.

Across from this masterpiece is a staircase leading downhill. Take these stairs to the end of NW Lovejoy Street. At the bottom of the steps is a giant sequoia. The first home on the right, at 2670 Lovejoy, is a 1901 Colonial Revival that Stewart Holbrook once lived in. Holbrook came to Oregon in 1923 as an unemployed ex-logger. Over the next forty years he made a national name for himself as "the Lumberjack Boswell," telling the stories of loggers, cooks, and other humble figures seldom discussed in history books.

At 2642 Lovejoy is a red-brick 1909 Colonial Revival designed by A. E. Doyle. This house, once home to psychiatrist Anna Neils, is on the National

A quiet dead end where NW Northrup Street meets the steep hillside at Cornell Road. Ernest Hemingway once visited the home on the right.

Register of Historic Places. Where Lovejoy intersects with the start of Cornell Road, turn left onto Cornell and walk two blocks. Take the stairs on the right, which mark the intersection with NW Northrup Street. Note the grand old home on the left. This house, at 2665 Cornell, was built in 1916 for Simeon Winch, the editor of the *Oregon Journal*. Ernest Hemingway once visited there. Halfway down the stairs on the right is Gedney Gardens, a large 1908 home turned bed-and-breakfast. The last flight of stairs puts you on Northrup, and you're off the hillside, back in the land of linear streets.

Walk one block to NW 26th Avenue. Turn left. On the corner at 1209 NW 26th is a 1905 Colonial Revival home that was built as the Masonic Building for the Lewis and Clark Exposition in nearby Guilds Lake and moved here afterwards. (See Walk 1 for more on the exposition.)

At the corner of NW Overton Street, turn right. The home at 2559 was built in 1923 for Oswald West, governor of Oregon from 1910 to 1914. A progressive and a reformer, Governor West saw women's suffrage come to pass under his watch. He also reined in banks and corporations and took steps to protect workers' rights. He formed the Fish and Game Commission and the State Forester's office, but West earned his high place in the pantheon of great Oregonians when he signed a law that protected Oregon beaches for public use. He did so by designating the entire Oregon shoreline a state highway, thereby putting it in the public domain. While you can no longer drive on Oregon's beaches, they remain unfenced and open, unlike those of our neighbor state to the south. After accomplishing all he set out to do in his first term, West declined to run again. He moved to Portland at age forty-one to practice law. Oswald West State Park, located south of Cannon Beach on the Oregon Coast, features groves of old-growth Sitka spruce and Short Sands Beach, among the state's most beautiful beaches.

Turn left on NW 25th, across from an enormous deodar cedar, and walk three blocks to the starting point at NW 25th and Raleigh. Tara Thai Northwest at NW 23rd and Overton is one of the restaurants closest to the end of the walk. Its outdoor deck under an enormous Oregon white oak is a great place to enjoy Nob Hill's ambience.

A magnificent staircase and rock wall on Summit Avenue.

WALK 3

LINNTON TO FOREST PARK

STARTING POINT NW Springville Road and Ogden Street

DISTANCE 3–4 miles one way, plus a 1.2-mile bus ride along Highway 30 back to the starting point

ELEVATION 400 feet at the starting point; 700 feet at NW Leif Erikson Drive; 50 feet at Highway 30 and NW 107th Avenue

GETTING THERE AND PARKING From Northwest Portland, drive northwest on Highway 30 (also called Saint Helens Road). From the stoplight at NW Kittridge Avenue, drive 2.9 miles to the first stoplight after the road goes under the span of the Saint Johns Bridge. Turn left, climb the hill, and pass NW Germantown Road. In less than 0.1 mile, turn right onto the inconspicuous NW Springville Road. Drive 0.3 mile uphill on Springville to its intersection with NW Ogden Street. Park along the shoulder.

TriMet: From downtown, take bus 17 (NW 21st Avenue/Saint Helens Road) to the stop at NW Bridge Avenue and Springville Road. Walk on Springville 0.3 mile (uphill) to the starting point of the hill walk.

RESTROOMS AND DRINKING FOUNTAINS At the walk's end is a drinking fountain at NW 107th Avenue and Saint Helens Road.

FOOD AND DRINK The Decoy Saloon is located at 10710 NW Saint Helens Road; 503-286-3208.

NOTE This is a long, fairly strenuous walk with a twist: after walking through three of Linnton's separate neighborhoods, you return to your starting point via

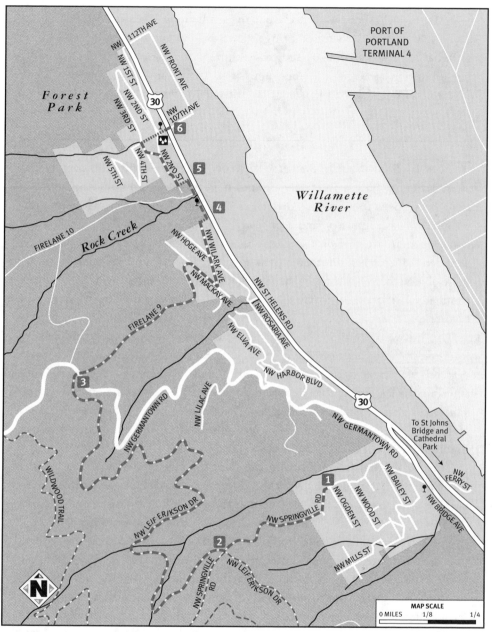

WALK 3. *Linnton to Forest Park*

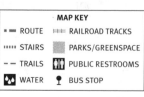

MAP KEY

- ▪▬ ROUTE
- ⁞⁞⁞⁞⁞ STAIRS
- – – TRAILS
- 🌊 WATER
- ▦ RAILROAD TRACKS
- ▨ PARKS/GREENSPACE
- 🚻 PUBLIC RESTROOMS
- 🚏 BUS STOP

PORT OF
PORTLAND
TERMINAL 4

*Willamette
River*

*Forest
Park*

NW 112TH AVE
NW FRONT AVE
NW 1ST ST
NW 2ND ST
NW 3RD ST
30
NW 107TH AVE
6
NW 4TH ST
NW 5TH ST
NW 2ND ST
5
4

FIRELANE 10
Rock Creek
NW HOGE AVE
NW WILARK AVE
NW MACKAY AVE
3
FIRELANE 9
NW ELVA AVE
NW ST HELENS RD
NW ROSARIA AVE
NW HARBOR BLVD
NW GERMANTOWN RD
NW LILAC AVE
30
To St Johns
Bridge and
Cathedral
Park
NW GERMANTOWN RD
NW BAILEY ST
NW WOOD ST
NW OGDEN ST
NW FERRY ST
NW BRIDGE AVE
WILDWOOD TRAIL
NW LEIF ER/KSON DR
1
NW SPRINGVILLE RD
NW MILLS ST
2
NW SPRINGVILLE RD
NW LEIF ER/KSON DR

MAP SCALE
0 MILES   1/8   1/4

N

a TriMet bus. (You can walk back, but the stroll along Highway 30, though on a sidewalk with nice river and bridge views, is loud and not too pleasant.) The walk has some steep portions and passes through quiet stretches of Forest Park. Use discretion about hiking alone on park trails. You might want to take a bus schedule with you so that you can time the end of your walk with the arrival of the bus.

Linnton, an early Portland rival and once a thriving commercial district, is now a relatively unknown Portland neighborhood. Linnton's front door opens to a working stretch of the Willamette River, with shipping terminals, heavy industry, and a grittiness that is easy to dismiss. But its back doors open to the nation's largest city park, and its streets have a quirky, secluded feel that is more than a little inviting. Portlanders on their way to the more obvious scenic charms of Sauvie Island often zoom through Linnton's small commercial strip on Highway 30, never looking up the hill into its steep and picturesque streets.

This hill walk starts in the Whitwood Court area in Linnton, then loops up into Forest Park via the historic Springville Road and Leif Erikson Drive and descends via a steep firelane into Linnton's Waldemere neighborhood. The route continues on a staircase that leads you down to the highway and around a creek valley. For those who are strong of leg, there is an optional tour via a steep set of stairs past Linnton School (now condominiums) to the most central hill in Linnton: Linnton Hill.

This walk beautifully embodies the Olmsted Brothers' vision of accessible urban forests. In Linnton you enter the forest not at official portals complete with parking lots, restrooms, and well-marked trailheads but at quiet neighborhood dead ends, where you can step from road to path casually and inconspicuously.

Linnton is actually a collection of seven small neighborhoods spread over 5 miles and separated from each other by steep creek drainages. It ranges from the Willbridge area along Highway 30, across from the Burlington Northern Railroad Bridge, to the lower flanks of Newberry Road, across from Sauvie Island. Had it become the big city of its early dreams, its hills and valleys probably would have been filled, terraced, and built upon to create one seamless city along Highway 30. As it is now, Linnton is a quiet community and a great entry point for exploring Forest Park's northern reaches.

1 Start in Linnton's Whitwood Court neighborhood, uphill from the site of one of the earliest communities on the Willamette, Springville, established around 1843 (prior to Portland). Springville was originally called Cazeno, for the Multnomah Indian chief who lived in the area.

This community was described in Harvey and Leslie Scott's *History of the Oregon Country*: "At [Springville] C.B. Comstock and Lafayette Scoggin established a warehouse, which served as a shipping point for farmers of Tualatin Valley, and which, about 1860, was regarded with jealousy by Portland and Saint Helens." The road the farmers used, originally called the Cazeno-Hillsboro Road but soon changed to Springville Road, is the first leg of this walk. It was among the earliest Portland roads leading to the breadbasket of the Tualatin Plains, having been surveyed in 1852. Because Portland's Canyon Road was more centrally located relative to the farms of the valley, it became the preferred route to bring products to market, and Springville was less used. After the warehouse burned in 1872, the Springville post office closed.

Downhill of the neighborhood on the river was the Whitwood Court landing for the Saint Johns ferry. In the early 1900s cattle were driven down to the river via Springville or Germantown Roads and loaded aboard the ferry for the trip to Saint Johns. Once off the boat they were herded through North Portland to the stockyards in Kenton.

After parking near the intersection of Ogden and Springville, begin walking uphill on Springville, which soon turns to gravel. Walk past the Springville

A view of the Saint Johns Bridge from Whitwood Court.

Pump Station and then a gate, where the road runs steep and wide along the southern flank of a steep creek ravine. Earlier historians noted that the old trees along Springville still bore the rope marks from produce-laden wagons being let down the steep hillside. I couldn't find any, but they may still be there.

Pass the Whitwood Tank, a water tank for the city. Where the road forks at a private home, stay to the right. Come to an intersection with a broad, unmarked road. This is Leif Erikson Drive, the ill-fated road that was punched through the forest in 1914 and 1915. (See Walk 1 for its history.) Because of the highly unstable Portland Hills Silt mantling the basalt along much of its route, frequent washouts of the roadbed in ravines put an end to its future as a parkway. The silt consists of soils lifted by winds from the Columbia River Valley in eastern Washington 34,000 to 700,000 years ago. This windborne soil, called loess, has been the cause of many a homeowner's heartache, as it is prone to sliding when saturated by rain.

A loss for vehicles became a gain for hikers and bicyclists. Leif Erikson runs 11 car-free miles from NW Thurman Street to NW Germantown Road.

2   Turn right onto Leif Erikson. Before you do, however, you may want to investigate the remains of a farmhouse that sits on Leif Erikson just to the south (left) of this intersection. The Springville intersection, at mile 9.4, is near the end of the road.

At about 9.5 miles, just downhill of Leif Erikson, is a 90-foot-tall Douglas fir snag. Before it lost its top, this was the tallest tree in the park. How this tree escaped the saws of early loggers is a mystery. With its proximity to settlements and the river, the forest here was logged early, its wood used for firewood, steamboat fuel, and construction.

Walk along the road for 1.8 miles. This part of the walk is nearly level, at an elevation of about 700 feet. As noted in Walk 1, many residential building lots were sold along Leif Erikson. Not one was ever built upon. Most of the lots were forfeited to the city and later incorporated into the park.

Cross the Willalatin Trail. Platted out in 1910 as a road, this is now just a trail that starts on Skyline Road. Its name comes from combining "Willamette" and "Tualatin."

Salal is a common understory plant here. Northwest Indians would mash and dry its edible blue-black berries, form them into cakes, and dip them in whale or seal oil. A more appetizing recipe involves layering branches of salal, with the leaves attached, between fillets of fish as they are cooked. The Hesquiat Indians of coastal British Columbia spiced their fish in this way.

Leif Erikson ends at NW Germantown Road. This, along with Springville Road, was among the first market roads to the Tualatin Plains, and it followed an old Indian trail between the river and the valley. It was named Germantown because it ended in North Plains, a Tualatin Valley town settled predominantly by Germans. The trail was widened for wagons in 1845 and predates Canyon Road, which ultimately became the preferred route. Other early roads used to bring produce to market were Cornelius Pass, Newberry, and Cornell.

3 At the end of Leif Erikson is a parking lot on Germantown Road. Walk through the parking lot. Carefully cross Germantown, which has become a busy commuter road on weekdays between North Portland and Hillsboro. Just across from the parking lot's uphill exit is a gated firelane, inconspicuously marked Firelane 9.

Begin the steep descent down Firelane 9. It loses 500 feet in elevation in a quick 0.64 mile, doing so by avoiding such niceties as switchbacks as it runs right down the front of a spur. Watch your step when the ground is wet. Even when it's dry, Douglas fir cones can get under your shoe and roll you off of your feet.

Firelane 9 heads for Linnton's Waldemere neighborhood. Here, Forest Park is called Clark and Wilson Park, after Clark Wilson Lumber Mill, the timber company that donated this tract of land. It was the company's desire to preserve a bit of the ancient forest from which their profits had sprung; at some point, however, the land was logged.

Toward the bottom, the trail crosses a seasonal creek. If the creek bed is dry, you can see the exposed bedrock, which consists of Columbia River Basalt. (See Walk 5 for more information on Columbia River Basalt, the most commonly seen rock in western Oregon.)

Walk to a T intersection. In July, the large cottonwood on the left carpets this intersection with thick clumps of cotton. Seeds are attached to the strands of cotton, which then get picked up and dispersed by the wind. Cottonwoods are the tallest broadleaf trees in the western United States. They are distributed over a wide range, from Alaska to Baja California and east to the Dakotas, but grow only along rivers and streams. To early pioneers trekking west, a stand of cottonwoods was a welcome sight, signaling water and shade. Native peoples in British Columbia used the seed fluff (the "cotton") to stuff mattresses and pillows.

Turn right at the cottonwood intersection; you'll see the concrete remains of an old reservoir, and you'll pass over the creek as it dives below the road on its way to the Willamette River. More cottonwoods create a beautiful mess on the now-paved trail, just before it ends at a gate at the intersection of NW Mackay and Wilark.

As a city, Linnton predates Portland by two years. It was founded in 1843 by two entrepreneurs, Peter Burnett and Morton McCarver, who named it to honor Senator Lewis Linn of Missouri, a strong advocate of free land for settlers in the new Oregon Country. The men hoped that, with its river frontage and a road they had built over the mountains to the farms of the Tualatin Plains, Linnton would become the preeminent port on the Willamette.

Just one year later they realized that the hills fronting the river were too steep to support a large population and that the road they had built was too arduous for farmers to bring their produce to Linnton docks. They turned their attention elsewhere. Burnett became the first governor of California in 1849, one year before the state was admitted to the Union. McCarver speculated again on land in the new town of Sacramento and later bought and helped develop Tacoma, Washington. Despite its founders' lack of faith, Linnton didn't die. It continued to exist, though it didn't exactly flourish until 1891, when a smelter set up shop along the river and a horse cannery, which canned horses for pet food and for the European market, came to town. After that, sawmills and other industry came, and Linnton prospered.

By the time it was incorporated into Portland in 1915, Linnton had two newspapers, seven saloons, a cannery, large lumber mills, rail service to Portland with seventeen passenger trains each day, and its own jail and police force. The population was mostly working-class, as the mills attracted immigrants, many of whom were Italian and whose descendants still live in Linnton.

When Prohibition reigned, Linnton's hills were the perfect place for producing fine, homemade spirits. As one resident said, "There was nothing but bootlegging from here to Saint Helens. People had to try and keep from selling it to each other."

With the Depression, however, Linnton began a slow decline. Fires destroyed the two largest mills in 1945 and 1950, and neither was rebuilt. The final insult came in the early 1960s when Highway 30 was widened to four lanes. More than half of Linnton's businesses, including a butcher shop, barber shop, pharmacy, department store, and grocery, were wiped out. Redevelopment plans never got off the drawing board. When the Linnton School closed in 1971, the neighborhood lost another piece of its identity.

Today the fact that Linnton seemed to fall off city planners' radar for several decades has become part of its allure. The community is no longer exclusively working-class; it is also home to artists (most notably Chuck Palahniuk) and high-tech types who enjoy its mountain views, its combination of remoteness and accessibility to the city, and its proximity to Forest Park.

Turn left onto NW Wilark Avenue, which was named by combining "Wilson" and "Clark" of the Clark Wilson Lumber Mill. On the right is a wide-open view of Mount Rainier, Mount Saint Helens, and the immense parking lot leased by Toyota Motor Sales USA at the Port of Portland's Terminal 4. This terminal is the largest auto-handling port on the West Coast, and the third largest in the United States. Cars unloaded from ships here are destined for car dealerships as far away as the Midwest.

Walk down Wilark to Hoge Avenue. Turn around for a view of Mount Hood and the elegant Saint Johns Bridge (whose history is discussed in Walk 20). A side trip up the short end of Hoge reveals some of Linnton's hidden charms. The homes nestled next to the forest here have found that harmonious balance between the wild and the cultivated.

4 To exit the neighborhood, follow Wilark to the set of steel stairs at its dead end. These forty-one stairs take you to a walkway elevated above the highway. This walkway dates to the highway-widening project that gutted Linnton's main street and turned the town into an insignificant blip on the highway to Astoria.

The half-wild charms of a Linnton front yard.

For forty years after the road was widened, the neighborhood was ruled by the automobiles zipping through it, effectively cutting off Linnton residents from what was left of their commercial district. In 2000, however, a group of activists decided to take back their street. They found funding to construct traffic-calming brick medians planted with trees and convinced the Oregon Department of Transportation to slow (and enforce) the speed limit to 35 miles per hour.

In case any motorists fail to recognize that their commuter route is someone else's main street, these Linnton boosters occasionally march along the highway at rush hour, forcing the cars to heel. At the bus stops and along the road are decorative galvanized-steel "Linnton" signs, fish-backed benches, and quirky bus shelter icons, all made by nationally known artist and Linnton resident Ivan McLean.

The elevated walkway descends to street level at a bus stop on the highway. Here at the base of the Tualatin Mountains runs the Portland Hills Fault, a 30-mile-long fault line. It starts north of here, near the northern boundary of Forest Park, and runs south along the foot of the hills to about Burnside Street. From there the fault runs beneath downtown Portland, crosses the Willamette River between the Marquam and Ross Island bridges, and continues along the eastern side of the river before ending in Clackamas County. The last large quake along this fault line is believed to have occurred about ten thousand years ago. Geologists estimate it to have been about magnitude 6.5, far greater than any recent quake in the Portland area.

Nestled in a steep creek valley, the bus stop here is among the most scenic in the city, complete with a trail into the forest behind it. Most of the year, the creek rushes down in an undammed hurry, so you can cool your toes in it while waiting to catch bus 17 back to the stop at NW Bridge Avenue and Springville. To see a bit more of Linnton's attractions, keep walking on the sidewalk another 0.1 mile to a concrete staircase, which leads up into the oldest and largest section of Linnton's homes, on the hills above the old downtown.

5 Take the stairs up to a sidewalk that runs along the fenced, former Linnton School, the alma mater of Portland's reigning drag queen, Darcelle. The school operated until 1971, when Linnton kids began attending Skyline Elementary School. The building sat vacant for years until it was developed into twelve upscale condominiums known as Linnton School Place. Although the inside of the building has been completely gutted and renovated, the outside still has all the charms of a grade school: the baseball backstop now curves around mounds of rhododendrons, and the playing field is a grassy lawn accented by rose gardens. The garages under the school are an addition; the existing grade had to be lowered 3 feet to accommodate them. For unknown reasons, the school was built facing up the hill. The portion you can see from the sidewalk is actually the back of the school; children entered at the front, on the other side. Behind the school, a trail leads into the woods from NW 3rd Street. Records indicate that a road built around 1844 went up to Skyline Boulevard from there; this was probably the road built by Burnett and McCarver.

Turn right onto NW 2nd Street. The first two homes on the right were owned by the Clarks and the Wilsons of Clark Wilson Lumber Mill. Many of the small homes in this area were built in the early twentieth century by the sawmills, as company-owned housing for employees.

So many Italians settled in Linnton in the early 1900s that NW 1st and 2nd Streets became known as Italian Way. Most of them came to work in the sawmills or at the Portland Gas and Coke Company (Gasco) oil gasification plant in Linnton. (See Walk 20 for information on the Gasco plant.) New immigrants, including people from Yugoslavia, Greece, Japan, and the Philippines, initially settled in separate camps of makeshift shacks along the Willamette.

Among the Italian immigrants was Joseph Lemma. Apprenticed at age nine as a shoemaker in Altamura, a small village in southern Italy, he came here as a young man in 1906. In a shack next to the river in Linnton, he began repairing shoes for the men who were then building the Columbia River Highway and a railroad line to Astoria. As his son John tells it, Joseph made plans to expand his business. Soon after arriving, he paid the five cents to ride the sternwheeler into Portland. On a handshake only, with no credit history and just a little shaky English, he managed to secure a load of dry goods—shoes, coats, boots, clothes—to sell to the construction crews.

Lemma prospered as Linnton grew. The building he constructed in 1918 to house his family of ten children and his many businesses—a grocery, a silent movie theater, a drugstore, a department store, and a de facto bank—is still on Highway 30. Its façade, at 10818 Saint Helens Road, is covered with a patchwork of stone, concrete, and glass block.

In 1933, at the end of Prohibition, Joseph Lemma saw another opportunity and incorporated a new business, the Lemma Department Store and Winery, processing California-grown grapes in the basement of his multitasking building. By then his sons were old enough to drive a truck into town to fetch the grapes, which were delivered via rail car at the produce row under the Morrison Bridge in Southeast Portland.

John Lemma, who was born in 1920, remembers taking half a day off from Lincoln High School during grape season. He and his brothers would load grapes in their wagon and proceed down Linnton's Italian Way. At each Italian-owned home (the northern Europeans in the neighborhood didn't drink wine from grapes, he says, preferring to make wine from local berries), they would unload forty to fifty boxes of grapes into their portable crusher. Each box yielded 2 gallons of juice, and the 80–100 gallons would be the family's wine supply for the coming year. At each stop, John says, he and his brothers were offered samples of last year's wine, making for a very pleasant day off from school.

At 2nd Street's intersection with NW 3rd Court, turn left, walking uphill. Stay right at the next intersection, which is NW 3rd Street, and then left where 3rd splits into an upper and lower section. Walk a few steps to the intersection of NW 3rd and 107th Avenue (a road that is just a set of stairs at this point). NW 3rd is a fine street for taking in some of Portland's lesser known sight lines. Just beyond the stairs, you're instantly rewarded with views of Mount Adams, Mount Rainier, and Mount Saint Helens. In the foreground are the Willamette River and the Port of Portland's Terminal 4. Built in 1919 on the Ogden slough, Terminal 4 is the Port's oldest operating marine terminal. Soda ash mined in Wyoming is unloaded here and is the second biggest export product, by tonnage, for the Port. The terminal also handles automobiles, as previously mentioned, as well as grains, minerals, and "breakbulk" cargo (cargo not in containers, such as large single pieces like yachts, machines, lumber, or steel). During World War II, this terminal was occupied by the U.S. Army and served as the port of embarkation for soldiers and materiel. Just adjacent downstream of Terminal 4 was a Kaiser shipyard that built Liberty Ships for the war.

Terminal 4 is part of the 6-mile-long Portland Harbor, a designated Superfund site. (See Walk 20 for more on the Portland Harbor and the Superfund program.) Starting in 2007, the terminal is slated to be the first of many harbor properties to be cleaned of its toxic past. Sixty-nine businesses and government entities within the harbor reach have been named by the Environmental Protection Agency as potential responsible parties for the cleanup. The Port of Portland is part of the ten-member Lower Willamette Group that has agreed to undertake cleanup efforts at its site.

The immense wood frame building on the river to your right is the old Linnton Plywood Mill, a worker-owned cooperative. The last mill in Linnton, it closed in 2001.

If you have time and energy, follow the streets up and up until they end, surprisingly, at a small private farm. In the late 1800s, Linnton was farmed all the way up the slope to Skyline Boulevard, an area called Linnton Park. The 287 acres of Linnton Park were donated to the city by the estate of Aaron Meier (cofounder of the Meier and Frank department store) in 1938 and are now part of Forest Park. Meier had hung onto the old-growth acreage for years. Before giving it to the city, his estate sold the timber rights and the land was logged off by a fuel dealer. This was not unlike the way in which much of Forest Park was acquired. Property owners took the only thing of value—the timber—and then abandoned the land, which the city acquired in forfeit for the unpaid taxes.

6 From 3rd Street, take the 107th Avenue steps all the way down to Highway 30. It is 1.2 miles back to the bottom of Springville Road. You can either walk the sidewalk along Highway 30 or take the bus.

At the bus stop here you'll find a water fountain and a sign that lists the names of the many Linnton businesses that were displaced by the widening of the highway. The sign sits on flat ground blasted out of the hillside.

If you're hungry, check out the Decoy Saloon, located across the highway. Established in 1978, the Decoy is popular with hunters and fishermen, especially during duck season when doors open at 5:00 a.m.

Today 107th ends one block east of the highway, near the river, at Front Avenue. Now just a jumble of industrial artifacts that sprawl across its roadway, Front used to include homes and a fire station. A few interesting remnants testify to the riverside's once-residential past. Plans are on the drawing board to create a greenway trail in this stretch of Linnton.

WPA workers build a retaining wall on Italian Way (now NW 1st Street), circa 1935. Photo courtesy of the City of Portland Archives.

WALK 4

WASHINGTON PARK TO ARLINGTON HEIGHTS LOOP

STARTING POINT Northern entrance of Washington Park: NW 24th Place and W Burnside Street

DISTANCE 3.5 miles, or 4.5 miles with Rutland Terrace loop

ELEVATION 200 feet at the starting point; 460 feet at the highest point on the main walk; 640 feet at the highest point on the optional loop

GETTING THERE AND PARKING From downtown Portland, drive west on Burnside Street to NW 23rd Avenue. Turn right (north) on 23rd, and park on a neighborhood street north of Burnside (there is no parking at Washington Park's Burnside entrance). Be careful: some streets, especially those close to the shopping district on NW 23rd Avenue, have a two-hour parking maximum.

TriMet: From downtown, take bus 20 (Burnside/Stark) to the stop at W Burnside and NW 23rd Place. Walk west on Burnside to 24th.

RESTROOMS AND DRINKING FOUNTAINS Bathrooms and a drinking fountain are located at the Rose Garden and inside the Elephant House, and there are numerous other facilities along the route in Washington Park.

FOOD AND DRINK Midway through the walk is a food kiosk, located in the Rose Garden and open daylight hours, spring through fall.

NOTE This walk starts low, deep within a forested valley inside 332-acre Washington Park, and climbs high through twisty urban streets to a vertiginous

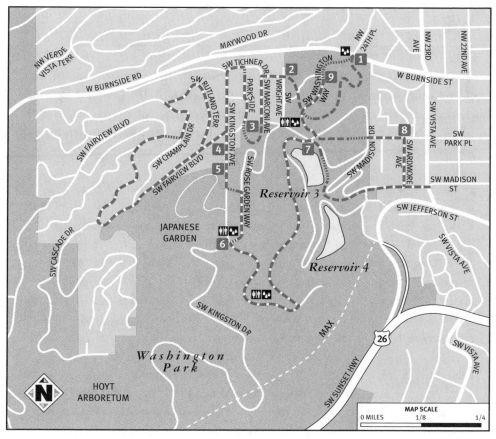

WALK 4. *Washington Park to Arlington Heights Loop*

MAP KEY

- ▪ ▬ ROUTE
- ⋯⋯ STAIRS
- – – TRAILS
- ▦▦ RAILROAD TRACKS
- PARKS/GREENSPACE
- 🚻 PUBLIC RESTROOMS
- 💧 WATER
- ⚲ BUS STOP

viewpoint at the top of one of Portland's longest public stairways. Along the way you'll hear about landslides, lawsuits, Communists, roses, goiter, and plank roads.

IN 1849, WHEN THE OREGON TERRITORY was being divvied up, the federal government deeded to Amos Nahum King (1822–1921) a donation land claim adjacent to the new town site called Portland. Over the course of his long life, King's 513 acres of wilderness were logged off and divided into posh neighborhoods, making him one of Portland's earliest real estate speculators and millionaires.

In 1871, when only eight thousand people lived in Portland, King resided at what is now NW 20th and Burnside and ran a leather tannery at the site of PGE Park, SW 19th and Salmon. With surprising prescience, given that Portland at the time was surrounded by seemingly unending wilderness, the city purchased from King 40 acres for a city park. The price was $800 per acre, with King reserving the right to pipe water from a spring in the park to his home. For about fifteen years the park, then called City Park, was undeveloped. In the mid 1880s a seaman from Germany, the park's first keeper, began laying out trails and gardens based on his memories of European parks.

1 At NW 24th Place and W Burnside Street, you stand at what was in the late 1800s the main entrance to City Park. When the Olmsted Brothers came to Portland in 1903 to create a citywide park plan, they recommended a grander approach to City Park and a more distinguished name. City fathers listened to the wisdom of the great men from the East. Soon after, this northern entrance became a backwater, and a grand entrance was constructed at SW Park Place. A more illustrious moniker, Washington Park, was also bestowed upon the land.

There are three ways to ascend the forested hillside in front of you. The maze of stairs and trails is confusing, but when in doubt, climb: they all end up in essentially the same place. To your far left, tucked next to apartment buildings, is Osage Street. From it, 178 stairs lead efficiently up into the park, but these steps are charmless and are often inhabited. To your right is a set of old stone stairs marked "Stearns Road Trail to Rose Garden." You'll descend these at the end of the walk. For now, take the middle path, a gated asphalt road that leads upward into the forest. Turn right at the intersection with a paved path. Come to another intersection and stay straight (walking away from Burnside).

Now you're on a neglected concrete driveway that was the main road into the park until 1903. In the 1960s, proto-skateboarders on homemade boards loved

The Washington Street (now Burnside Street) entrance to City Park (now Washington Park) as it appeared around 1905. The walls were built of cement salvaged from the park's reservoirs, the liners of which cracked and required extensive repairs after a landslide. Parts of these walls are still visible. The trees in this photograph are about fifty years old. Photo courtesy of Don Nelson.

its undulating surface, but today it's too cracked for that kind of fun. Accented by old street lamps, this wide, wavy drive gently climbs the bottom of the U-shaped valley. Look up: the trees in this valley are some of the largest in the park. While most of the trees had been logged when Amos King sold his land to the city in 1871, after many years of unmolested growth, this forest again seems primeval. The poetically decrepit steps that climb into the trees here and there used to lead to picnic tables. In the park's earliest days, this area housed its collection of zoo animals, scattered around the hillside.

You are strolling through the childhood haunts of John Reed, the only American buried in the Kremlin in Moscow. Reed was born in 1887 just east of the park boundary at his grandparents' 5-acre estate. As a World War I correspondent he witnessed the October Revolution in Saint Petersburg, Russia, which toppled the Romanoff monarchy and brought the Communists to power. In 1917, infused with the idealism of the early Communists, Reed wrote, "I suddenly realized that the devout Russian people no longer needed priests to pray them into heaven. On earth they were building a kingdom more bright than any heaven had to offer, and for which it was a glory to die." Reed chronicled the revolution in the book *Ten Days That Shook the World* and founded the American

Communist Labor Party. When he was indicted for sedition in 1919, he fled to Russia, where he died of typhus in 1920 at age thirty-two. He is not, incidentally, the Reed of Reed College, Portland's highly rated liberal arts and sciences college; this was named for early Oregon pioneers Simeon and Amanda Reed. (See Walk 14 for more on the Reeds and Reed College.)

The concrete road ends at an elegant flight of thirty-nine steps that lead up to SW Washington Way. Turn around at the top for a lovely view of a graceful vine maple arching over the steps and of the road as it curves back into the woods waiting to ferry its next passenger up the hill. Indians called the native vine maple the basket tree and used its long, straight shoots to make baskets. In front of you, across the road, sits what looks like Snow White's home, or at least her bathroom. This brick English Tudor restroom is backed, somewhat incongruously, by a vibrant swath of giant bamboo. The restroom is closed in winter, but the water fountain outside is available year-round. Behind the restroom is the Oregon Holocaust Memorial, built in 2004.

Go right on Washington Way, and pass a white iron gate in the road. On your left are thirteen steps nestled into English ivy under the swooping limbs of a horsechestnut tree. The lustrous brown seeds of this tree species, native to mountainous Greece and Albania, are not related to edible chestnuts. Climb the thirteen stairs and continue up a steep concrete path to three more steps leading into a grassy field.

Walk past the picnic table under a towering Douglas fir to a bronze statue of two American Indians called "The Coming of the White Man." This sculpture was created in 1904 by Hermon Atkins MacNeil, who later designed the "Standing Liberty" quarter, minted from 1916 to 1930. In "The Coming of the White Man," the two figures are looking eastward at their fate. One is a chief, reportedly Chief Multnomah. His mouth is turned emphatically downward and his arms are crossed imperiously, but his excitement and worry are betrayed if you walk behind the statue where you can see that he is on tiptoe, reaching for the best view. The young man next to him excitedly points; you can practically hear his shouts of alarm. The stone for the statue's base (and for the Sacajawea statue later in the walk) came from a basalt quarry at Fisher's Landing, on the Columbia River east of Vancouver. Behind "The Coming of the White Man" lies a large chunk of the base that broke off when the statue was installed.

MULTNOMAH

The first written record of the Indian word *Multnomah*, for which Multnomah County is named, came from Lewis and Clark. In 1805 they wrote of the river "Mult-no-mâh" (now the Willamette River), attributing the name to the Indians who lived along the lower part of the river near its confluence with the Columbia. Some linguists believe the word is a corruption of the Chinookan *nematlnomaq*, meaning "the people living downriver," in reference to those who inhabited the land downriver of the falls of the Willamette, near today's Oregon City.

Indians never settled at the site of present-day Portland, although they used it for a resting place as they traveled between the Columbia River and the falls of the Willamette. To them, Portland was known simply as "the clearing."

The Indians who greeted Lewis and Clark had once been among the continent's most fortunate. Living in a garden of earthly delights, where salmon, berries, nuts, roots, and eels were bountiful, they built large, permanent villages. Their luck ran out, however, even before Lewis and Clark visited: diseases introduced by white fur traders decimated their population, and by the time white settlement occurred in the 1840s, virtually none were left.

From behind the statue, take three basalt steps that lead down into a small parking area. Cross it and continue straight across another quiet grassy lawn.

2 A faint dirt pathway between a Douglas fir and bigleaf maple takes you to the intersection of SW Tichner Drive and Wright Avenue. You are now out of the park and in the Arlington Heights neighborhood, which was subdivided in 1909 from Amos King's original donation land claim.

Go straight onto Tichner for one block, and turn left on Marconi Avenue, named in 1909 for the Italian inventor of wireless communication, Guglielmo Marconi, after he won the Nobel Prize in physics. Walk past a panoply of architectural styles. At 122 is a house with elements of the Italianate and Prairie styles. This was once the home of John Bennes, architect of many homes in this neighborhood and of the Hollywood Theatre in Northeast Portland. Next comes a 1950 tract home; a 1974 modern, minimalist, contemporary home with bonsai-like trees; a tidy Colonial; an English Tudor; and another version of a Colonial.

Midway through the block, on the western, uphill side of Marconi, is a fabulously decrepit stucco and basalt staircase leading up the steep hillside. Complete with grotto, decaying lamps, inlaid benches, and a crumbling stone arch, these stairs hint of long-ago evening trysts and private musings. They're not public, unfortunately. A large beech leans outward over the stairs, menacing trespassers. These stairs are part of the property of the home above, at 226 SW

Parkside Drive. The grotto and stairs were built in 1913 for Edwin Jorgenson, the home's first owner, as a family picnic spot. Jorgenson owned the Lenox Hotel, which may have impressed his neighbors, but I'm more impressed by stories of how he enjoyed trapping moles, tanning the hides, and sewing them into moleskin coats. He was also reputedly the first person to ski on Mount Hood.

Next door is the site of a recent landslide. A former home at the site was undermined and later destroyed. The new home presumably has deeper foundations. The cause for much of the sliding in this area is the unstable Portland Hills Silt, a wind-deposited soil that can't hold itself together when it gets saturated. (See Walk 3 for more on this soil.)

The last house on the western side of Marconi, just before you reenter the park, is the Villa Marconi. Contrast the grace of this Mediterranean residence with today's grand homes, where size often seems to trump style.

Marconi Avenue ends at four flagstone stairs that lead you back into an especially lovely corner of Washington Park. At the top of these steps begins a cobblestone path, where banks of yellow, pink, purple, white, and orange azalea are the ooh-aah highlight of spring bus tours. In an island of pruned lawn on your left resides a trio of elegant trees. The first, a deodar cedar, is native to the Himalayas. *Deodara* derives from the Sanskrit *devadara*, meaning "tree of the gods." Its wood was used to build temples in India, and it is still an important timber species there. The second tree is a ginkgo. This tree species has survived 150 million years and may be the world's oldest living seed plant; fossils of ginkgoes have been found in North America, although today it is native to China. The third tree is an Oregon white oak. Native to the valleys of Western Oregon, this tree's pedigree is humbler. It is best known as an ornamental tree and as a good source of firewood, as it burns hot and splits well.

The steep cobblestone path ends at four flagstone steps. While you're catching your breath, turn around for a "stop and smell the roses" moment. Views like this are an antidote for many of life's ills.

Now onward into the "peanut bowl," an isolated, grassy field tucked into the base of a hill. Note the shape of the field: 100 percent goober. This is a great place to take five, an oasis enclosed by just about every conceivable arboreal texture: lacy maples, spiky sweet gums, misty smoke trees, sentinel-like cedars, spiny barberries, stiff pines, floating dogwoods, and languid willows. The tranquility of this spot followed a violent episode: a home occupied this site until 1933, when a retaining wall on the hillside above it, at 288 SW Parkside Drive, gave way and destroyed it.

Take the gravel path that leads out onto the main park road as it twists up the hillside toward the tennis courts. Don't take the road, but stay on the path as it switchbacks up the hill, and you'll arrive at a forty-four-step staircase that ascends through a murky thicket of Portuguese laurel.

3 At the top of the stairs, you're on SW Parkside Drive, back in Arlington Heights. Turn right. Where Parkside Drive curves left, stay straight and enter a tiny lane marked "dead end." This is Parkside Lane, and it's not a dead end if you're walking. On this narrow alley, large, elegant homes fit together neatly, like puzzle pieces, creating a pleasant, neighborly atmosphere. An exuberant orange-flowered trumpet creeper vine climbs high up a utility pole on the left. This is a rambunctious grower; according to plant expert Michael Dirr, you should "keep your feet moving when in the vicinity of this plant." In counterpoint to its rowdy neighbor, an incredibly refined yew hedge flanks a driveway on the right. Yews have been cultivated for thousands of years, and every part of them is extremely toxic, except, surprisingly, the plant's most ominous-looking part, the blood-red pulp surrounding the fruit. Parkside Lane ends at a staircase. Take the stairs down to SW Tichner Drive.

The wall to your left, which begins at the stairs and curves around the corner, was built around 1915, probably from basalt blasted from the now-retired quarry at today's SW Tichner and W Burnside (just north and downhill from where you stand). Unlike many basalt walls, which use raw and sharp-edged rock pieces freshly dynamited out of a quarry, each block in this wall, including the capstones, was hand-sculpted, for an effect that is both naturalistic and sophisticated. It was built by Italian stonemasons who came to Oregon in 1913 to build the bridges and retaining walls of the Columbia River Highway (now a National Historic Landmark), east of Portland. After the highway was complete, many of these craftsmen remained in the Northwest. Some were also responsible for the magnificent stonework at Rocky Butte and at Timberline Lodge, built by the WPA in 1937 on Mount Hood.

At the bottom of the steps, turn left. Follow the wall up Tichner Drive and left onto SW Kingston Avenue (named for Amos King), around a large home. This home was built in 1918 by Abe Tichner, an early real estate broker, and designed by John Bennes, whose home you walked by on Marconi Avenue.

Much of the parking strip on Kingston is devoted to old and gnarly roses. Each June, Portland celebrates its beloved roses with parades, the coronation of a Rose Queen, and even, incongruously, ear-splitting jet air shows. The city has come a long way from the festival's "happy hands at home" origins in 1904. Back then, residents were encouraged to plant hybrid roses along their parking strips and, if they were lucky enough to have a utility pole, to plant climbing roses at its base. A few days before the rose parade, firefighters would politely

The elegant and secluded Parkside Lane, adjacent to Washington Park.

knock on neighborhood doors and ask to cut roses for the parade. Back at the firehouse, the roses were affixed to the trucks, and on the big day the trucks were paraded down the street to the cheers of the residents. Contrast that homegrown event with today's Rose Festival parade, where corporations sponsor enormous, computerized floats that are built in secret, using big-bloom roses imported from South America.

A fine example sits at 226, complete with old roses climbing up the telephone pole.

Walking south on Kingston, you'll pass several homes listed on the Historic Register. At 226, a stone mansion with elements of Italianate and Prairie styles, sits a contestant for loveliest garage in the city. Wisteria old enough to bear fruit covers a wooden arbor that elevates the humble garage to the level of fine art. This home was also designed by John Bennes. Stay straight on Kingston until you come to the intersection with SW Fairview Boulevard. From this intersection you can take the optional loop up to the Champlain stairs. If you want to skip it, jump to route junction 5.

4 The Fairview-Rutland-Champlain 1-mile loop is a heart-thumping climb through a neighborhood of homes on hillside lots that must have challenged their architects. City and mountain views get better and better with each step. At the pinnacle of the loop lies one of Portland's best view stairs.

At the intersection of SW Kingston Avenue and Fairview Boulevard, begin the loop by walking up Fairview. This road switchbacks up the mountain to an ultimate elevation of 960 feet along the ridgeline of the Tualatin Mountains; however, you'll travel up Fairview just a short way before turning right onto SW Rutland Terrace. Near the corner of Rutland and Fairview, high in the trees above you, sits a green-and-black-striped home. Note the unusual use of roofing as siding, as designed by the owners, both architects.

The home at 2870 Rutland once belonged to Terrible Ted Thye, who traveled the world to promote wrestling.

After 0.15 mile, turn left onto Champlain Drive and walk about two blocks to a concrete staircase on the western side of the road, just past a large home at 2864. There are eighty steps, but several terraces along the way allow you to catch your breath and savor the views. The landscaping at the adjoining home would impress any style guru. Each impeccably groomed terrace has its own personality, with individual terraces accommodating a rose garden, a solitary park bench, a children's play yard, a tiny glass greenhouse, and, at the top terrace, a vineyard and apiary. Don't forget to turn around at the top of the steps for the view from the summit.

You're now back on Fairview Boulevard. Turn left at the top of the stairs. As you walk, you'll pass the all-stone Canterbury Castle at 2910, built in 1930 by a real estate speculator. An early sales brochure brags of its indoor swimming pool and drawbridge! During the record-setting wet winter of 1996 this road was popular with television crews, who filmed the effects of one landslide after another. A streetcar line ran up Fairview from 1913 to 1941. It ended at 2990.

The stroll down Fairview is a twisty downhill walk on a cool, shady road. After you pass Cascade Drive, you'll be walking down a forest canyon. The homes on the right sit atop an ancient streambed that ran along the base of the southern canyon wall (under the backyards of the current occupants). During the wet season you can hear the stream running under the sewer cap at the corner of Fairview and Kingston.

Just past the intersection with Champlain is a gabion wall (a retaining wall constructed of wire cages filled with rock), an increasingly common sight in Portland's West Hills since the floods and mudslides of 1996. Across from 2766, a mortared stone retaining wall bulges out, providing evidence of the soil's uneasy perch on the slope. Look up the slope above the retaining wall: the trees lean crazily, another sign of a creeping slope.

At the intersection of Fairview and Kingston, turn right to rejoin the main walk route.

5 Walk south down Kingston to where it enters Washington Park. The road here had an unusual work crew when it was first cut into the hillside. Contractors borrowed elephants from the nearby zoo to drag the grader along the road bed, flattening it before it was paved.

Here you'll encounter some of the world's most beautifully sited tennis courts. Climbing roses weaving up the courts' fence and a view of Mount Hood through black columns of towering Douglas fir help assuage the pain of even a love-40 loss.

These courts sit on the northern edge of an ancient landslide that has been reactivated several times since the 1890s, to the dismay of real estate developers and the Portland Water Bureau. The slide has left its calling card on the top rail of the chain-link fence along the first pair of tennis courts. The rail swoons and dips at the point where the land is moving. The first court sits on stable ground; the side scarp of the slide begins at the wall between the first and second courts. Walk into the second court and you can see the drop in the concrete surface as the land sags eastward down the slope; the asphalt's cracks give it the appearance of a moist cake slowly oozing off a plate. The gap in height between the two courts has been patched and filled repeatedly.

A view from the top terrace of the Rose Garden, with downtown Portland in the background.

Turn left onto an asphalt path between the first and second pairs of tennis courts. You'll see a sign: "Rose Garden Amphitheatre: .25 miles." At the top of a thirty-two-step staircase, you can see several terraces. In the 1890s these terraces were cut into the hillside and graded flat in order to make the land suitable for homesites. At about that time, further downslope, laborers were hand-digging the Washington Park reservoirs, near the toe of the landslide that you're standing on. After enough land had been excavated, the hillside started to move. The homesites were abandoned as unsalable, and the developer sued the city. Not only did the city win the lawsuit, it ultimately got hold of the land, which was added to the park. In 1917 the first rose slips (cuttings from older bushes) were planted here, in the city's new International Rose Test Garden.

A trip through the Rose Garden is an outing of its own, and much has been written about this Portland landmark, the oldest official and continuously operated public rose test garden in the United States. It owes its existence to World War I. European rose gardeners, concerned about the loss of historic roses to bombs and trench warfare, had been searching for an American repository for old rose varieties. After considering many cities in the United States, they selected Portland. Since then the garden has bloomed into one of the city's signature attractions. Roses bloom from May to November. It's a wonderful sight in any weather, but I recommend visiting on a misty day, when the roses glow in the gray and luminous light.

Descend the thirty-two concrete stairs to a small parking lot for the Rose Garden. To your right is a tiny, storybook-quaint brick building from 1926, the offices of the chief rose gardener. A magnificent swath of the king of vines, the climbing hydrangea, blankets the roof of the building, and cuttings from roses brought west by Oregon Trail pioneers grow along its back wall.

Walk through the parking lot to two flights of flagstone steps that lead into the garden. At the top of these thirty steps, Mount Hood is visible off to the right. The first rounded butte just past the towers of downtown is Mount Tabor, an extinct volcano.

Halfway down the steps is a spot at which you can rest, tucked into a bench nestled into the stone wall, and catch conversational snippets as people pass by. A few more steps down and you're in the Rose Garden. Turn right and stroll along the promenade toward the garden's information kiosk, which is staffed with knowledgeable volunteers on summer Saturdays, and the stainless steel Beech Memorial Fountain.

Just beyond the fountain is a flight of six basalt stairs. Take them, turn right, and follow a red-brick walkway through the rose beds to a flight of stone stairs. A bench located partway up these stairs soaks up late morning sun and invites contemplation. A few more steps and you're in the busy, beating heart of Washington Park, where the tour buses disgorge visitors. Here you'll find the Rose Garden store (open year-round), benches nestled under a rose-covered trellis, restrooms (open year-round), a food kiosk (open during pleasant weather), and picnic tables. Look east for a postcard view of Mount Hood, with the quintessential tree of the Northwest, the Douglas fir, in the foreground.

The Douglas fir is among the country's most important timber species and defines the silhouette of Portland's hillsides. Although first scientifically described by Archibald Menzies on Vancouver Island, the tree was named for David Douglas, a Scottish botanist. In 1823 Douglas was sent to find and collect the unknown plants of the Oregon Territory for the Royal Horticultural Society. He spent the rest of his life as a plant explorer and introduced more than fifty tree species to the gardening world. Unfortunately, Douglas met his end in an especially gruesome way for someone who followed such gentle pursuits. In 1834, at age thirty-six, he was walking the 100 miles from the Kohala Coast to Hilo on the Big Island of Hawaii, collecting plant specimens. At that time, wild bulls—descendants of cattle given to King Kamehameha I by Captain George Vancouver in 1791—had become a dangerous pest. The prevailing method of capturing the wild cattle was to dig and camouflage a deep pit along the trails. Despite warnings about the pits, Douglas, whose eyesight was poor, stepped into one, either before or after it had received its intended occupant. He was gored to death.

OTHER PARK ATTRACTIONS

Washington Park has expanded far beyond its original 40 acres. The following are among the highlights:

Japanese Garden: Five traditional Japanese gardens with a Northwest signature. Emphasis is on form and texture rather than flowers. Located just uphill from the Rose Garden; park on SW Kingston Avenue. Fee charged.

Hoyt Arboretum: Ten miles of trails surrounded by eight hundred species of trees from around the world. Located on the site of the old Multnomah County Poor Farm in the western reaches of Washington Park.

Pittock Mansion: Early-twentieth-century mansion with views of five mountains. Located on NW Pittock Drive and accessible by car or the Wildwood Trail. Fee charged for a home tour; the grounds, with their magnificent views, are free.

Oregon Zoo: Nine major exhibits representing distinct ecosystems from around the globe. Located on the former site of the Multnomah County Poor Farm. Fee charged.

Washington Park and Zoo Railway: Four-mile trip on narrow-gauge track through the forest from the Rose Garden to the zoo. This is the last operating U.S. railroad with its own official Railway Postal Cancellation, making it popular with stamp collectors. Three different historic trains operate during spring and summer, and on December evenings during Zoolights festival. Fee charged.

Children's Museum: Hands-on exhibits and programs for kids six months to ten years of age. Located near the zoo. Fee charged.

World Forestry Center: Exhibits provide an even-handed look at forestry, conservation, and products from Oregon forests. Located near the zoo. Fee charged.

Rose Garden Children's Park: State-of-the-art, accessible destination with a playground and picnic area for families.

6 From the Rose Garden restroom, walk along the road down a steep hillside. This was home to the Washington Park Zoo from 1887 to 1959, when the zoo moved up the hill to its present location. As you walk downhill, you'll hear and then see the Rose Garden Children's Park. Flanked by giant sequoias and comfortable benches, this is a lovely spot to watch children cavort on the playground beneath a living ceiling of sycamores.

Just past the playground is the Elephant House. This former elephant cage was renovated in 1995. All that remains of the pachyderms are the holes in the ceiling left by the cage bars; inside is a brick bas-relief of a mommy elephant and her baby. The few bars that remain give you the feel of just how small a space the elephants were allotted. Inside the Elephant House are picnic tables, bathrooms, and a drinking fountain. Outside around the doorways are cheerful ceramic wildlife murals made by a local artist and schoolchildren.

Across from the Elephant House, a trail leads into the forest. This trail connects with the 30-mile-long Wildwood Trail. The Wildwood passes by many of Washington Park's other attractions and runs the entire length of the 5000-acre Forest Park, the largest wilderness park in the United States contained within a city's limits.

Stay on the road and pass a soccer field, maintenance shed, and some parking pullouts. On the right you'll soon see a 6-foot-tall chain-link fence designed to keep people away from the park's reservoirs. Through the links you can peer at the graceful Vista Bridge in the distance. The cars snaking along under the bridge are on historic Canyon Road, which travels through a pass in the mountains before joining the roaring six lanes of Highway 26 that pass through the Tualatin River Valley on their way to the Pacific Ocean.

The canyon was formerly known as Tanner Gulch, named for Amos King's tannery. At the tannery, creek water, hemlock bark, and animal hides were combined in wooden vats. The tannins that leached from the bark tanned the hides. Much of King's acre-wide field of wooden vats is still intact, deep under the foundations of the PGE Park stadium.

In the mid to late nineteenth century, this gulch made for the lowest, quickest route through the Tualatin Mountains. Unfortunately, the narrow path along the creek floor turned into a muddy quagmire during winter. Conditions improved in 1851 when investors paid to lay planks along the path. (A commemorative sign marking the first plank in the old Plank Road sits at the corner of SW Jefferson and Park, downtown.)

This slippery, mossy road was a slight but crucial improvement over the mud trail, and the road's development was well timed. In 1849 gold was discovered in the Sierras. Decades of growth followed in California, and demand for timber, food, and other products was voracious. Because the Plank Road was the fastest route for Tualatin Valley farmers to get their goods to a river port, it was instrumental in helping Portland gain preeminence over the other river towns of Linnton, Milwaukie, Oregon City, and Saint Helens, each of which was trying to bill themselves as the best deepwater port in the region.

Where is Tanner Creek today? Like nearly 400 miles of streams in the Portland area, it has been piped, culverted, or filled. The narrow canyon floor where it flowed has been widened and filled innumerable times since 1851 and now carries traffic from autos and light rail.

Walk on the park road as it descends and curves around the higher of Washington Park's two reservoirs, which store treated water on its way to Portlanders' taps. A small tributary of Tanner Creek drained this valley until the reservoirs were constructed in the 1890s.

By the 1880s, Portland and other towns along the Willamette River had been dumping household and industrial sewage into the river for forty years, and the Willamette's waters were no longer potable. Hillside springs and streams were also becoming inadequate for the growing population. Typhoid outbreaks were not uncommon. Looking ahead, the City of Portland decided that the Bull Run watershed in the Cascade foothills 26 miles away was its best source for a stable, clean water supply.

Today, Bull Run water is among Portland's most touted assets. Unlike many cities, where river water is "pre-used" by upstream communities and then treated to physically remove wastes and chemically remove contaminants, Bull Run water comes from federal forest land that has been closed to the public since 1904. Logging did take place in the watershed from 1958 to 1993; it has since stopped, however, due to growing public awareness of logging's environmental impact. The area is now protected by law from logging and related road-building activities. (For more on Bull Run water, see Walk 16.)

Despite the purity of Bull Run water, it was not without its detractors. During the planning stages in the late 1880s, Oregon Governor Sylvester Pennoyer, who did not want to issue revenue bonds to finance the dam and pipeline infrastructure, protested that Bull Run water came from glaciers (it doesn't) and would therefore cause goiter in "the fair sex." (He wasn't out in left field on this last point. Goiter, an inflammation of the thyroid, is more common in mountain areas where the iodine content of the drinking water is very low, and it affects women five times more than men. There's a simple solution, however: use iodized salt.)

Dubbed "Sylpester Annoyer" by *Oregonian* editor Harvey Scott, Pennoyer never did acknowledge the water's incredible purity. When he took the first ceremonial drink of Bull Run water on January 2, 1895, he scoffed, "No body." Perhaps he'd grown used to solids in his drinking water.

Around the upper reservoir runs an old promenade. When the reservoirs were built in the 1890s, they were designed as destinations for strollers and bicyclists. Wide walkways, decorative iron grillwork, medieval stone towers, and even steps leading down to the water level, for the adventurous, were all part of the attraction.

The chain-link fence went up and sightseers were evicted in the 1940s after the attack on Pearl Harbor, when fears of sabotage were rampant on the West Coast. Thirty years later, in the swinging 1970s, there were concerns that "druggies" would spike the reservoir water with LSD. In 2002, the City of Portland proposed to replace these open reservoirs and those on Mount Tabor with underground tanks to protect the water from environmental damage and sabotage. Citizen disagreement about the covering of the tanks led to the development of a task force to investigate the matter.

7 You'll soon come to an intersection with lots of signs. Follow the arrow toward "City Center," keeping the upper reservoir on your right, then turn right at the bend in the chain-link fence onto a little-used gravel path and stairway.

Take the forty-eight stairs along the eastern side of the reservoir to a dirt path that descends to a fine and seldom-seen view of the damlike wall across the valley. Continue carefully on the uneven, gravelly path along the fence. You'll see the lower reservoir and then a building, the Hypochlorination Facility. Just upslope from this building, stay on the path as it veers away from the lower reservoir. Carefully negotiate twelve uneven brick steps with no railing toward a road. Turn right and walk down the road.

Exit the park, and stay straight, which puts you on Madison Street, a short avenue with many homes on the National Historic Register. In front of you is a large English Tudor. In its yard grows a huge tulip poplar, a native of eastern North America. This specimen is one of Portland's Heritage Trees. Cherokee Indians used tulip poplars, with their long, straight trunks, to make 30-foot-long canoes. You're in the King's Hill Historic District now, named not for the regal heights but for Amos King, of course: King's Hill is another neighborhood created from his original 513 acres.

Perhaps you'd like a place to sit down and ponder; if so, walk down Madison one block to the intersection with SW Vista Avenue. A curved, concrete settee built into the elegant Vista Bridge awaits you. Hidden from traffic behind a

Looking northwest into Washington Park, circa 1900. Both of the park's reservoirs are visible, and above the reservoirs are terraces carved into the hillside for homes. After a landslide, the property ended up in the hands of the city, which later used the hillside as the site of the International Rose Test Garden. Photo courtesy of the City of Portland Archives.

large planter, you can sit above the canyon of the former Plank Road. This bridge leads to the Portland Heights neighborhood. (See Walks 5 and 6 for more on this neighborhood.)

By 1926, Portland Heights was home to many of the city's wealthiest families, and these families didn't like the city's idea for a plain, low-cost bridge to replace the old span over the canyon. They wanted a more elegant design, with soaring concrete arches and decorative walls and benches. Since beauty wasn't in the city's budget, Portland Heights residents agreed to pay one-fourth of the additional cost through a temporary tax assessment. A later generation of homeowners kept up the tradition. In the 1970s, when the old lights were crumbling, residents resisted the city's plan for unadorned metal fixtures. Years of fundraising resulted in the elegant cast-concrete lights you see today, complete with imported mica and quartz to give them just that extra bit of sparkle.

Coming back off the bridge, retrace your steps on Madison for half a block until you reach SW Ardmore Avenue. Turn right here and switch into a lower gear for the climb back up into the park.

8 At SW Park Place, turn left and negotiate a steep sidewalk that's been heaved up by the roots of southern magnolias. These were planted in 1962 to replace Douglas firs blown down by the Columbus Day storm. As you're chugging along, don't forget to look up at the beautiful homes you're passing. You'll also notice some apartments across the street that were built in what appears to be the Soviet style; these replaced an old chateau-style mansion. On your left, a red-brick mansion at 2370 was traded by its original owner, Aaron Holtz, to Thomas Harry Banfield, after whom the Banfield Freeway (Interstate 84) is named.

At the end of Park Place, you're staring straight up into the formal entrance to Washington Park, as envisioned by the Olmsted Brothers. At the top of the grand brick staircase, a granite memorial column rises like a miniature Washington Monument. Under it, President Theodore Roosevelt buried a time capsule of objects from 1903. In the florid style of the day, the column reads:

> *Erected by citizens of Oregon to commemorate achievements of Captain Meriwether Lewis and William Clark who with the encouragement and under the direction of the President of the United States Thomas Jefferson started from Saint Louis May 14, 1804 and through many hardships penetrated the vast continental wilderness to the Pacific Ocean at the mouth of the Columbia River and returning September 1806 gave to the pioneers a pathway and to the nation the Oregon country.*

A heroic sentence. It seems understandable that with all the pomp and honor of a presidential visit, the exact location of the time capsule was never recorded. No one realized that it was lost, however, until 2003, when Theodore Roosevelt IV, the president's great-grandson, was getting set to visit Portland to commemorate the commemoration. When searches through the records and newspapers of the day turned up no clues, and psychics and scientists couldn't help, it was decided to let the time capsule age a bit more.

From the column, looking to your left, you'll see picnic tables, slides, and old-fashioned swings. Walk straight into the park, downhill across the grass, to a 34-foot-tall bronze sculpture of Sacajawea, holding her baby, Jean Baptiste Charbonneau (nicknamed Pomp by William Clark for his "little dancing boy" antics).

This, the first statue of a woman unveiled in America up to 1905, honors the Shoshone translator whom Lewis and Clark relied on during their explorations. The statue, which also commemorates "the pioneer mother of old

Oregon," was promoted and paid for by women; sculpted by a woman, Alice Cooper (her signature is on the statue's base); and unveiled in the presence of early feminists Susan B. Anthony, Portland's own Abigail Scott Duniway, and Eva Emery Dye.

Both "Sacajawea" and "The Coming of the White Man" were unveiled at the 1905 Lewis and Clark Exposition. (For more information on the exposition, see Walk 1.) Beyond the Sacajawea sculpture is a cast-iron fountain set in an octagonal basin. This 1891 fountain, called Cupid's Fountain, was an early-day filling station for horses. After pulling their owners' buggies up the long hill into the park, they refueled here. Cupid, who pranced atop the fountain, has long since disappeared.

From the fountain take the concrete walkway to the right, cross the road at a painted crosswalk, and turn right onto SW Washington Way, the road with the white gate. Walk past the gate; you'll pass the thirty-nine steps you climbed at the beginning of the walk, and a second gate. Stay on the road. You'll see another familiar set of stairs on your left under the horsechestnut tree. On your right is a double-trunked bigleaf maple, an extremely common forest tree west of the Cascades and one of only three maple species native to Oregon out of 115 nationwide. You'll see various footpaths that lead down the slope and through the forest to Burnside Street.

9 As the road climbs, you'll come to a place with staircases on the left and right. This is your exit. Use caution: some of the steps are in poor repair. Turn right and begin to descend a flight of fifty-six steps to a landing. You're in the heart of the forest again. Turn around and look back up the staircase, which looks like an archeological relic amid the jungle growth. Forty-six more steps down lead to a dirt path. Turn left and make an immediate right onto a steep trail that appears to run into a Douglas fir. At the base of the fir is the first of thirty more steps. Take them, and go left at the bottom to the final staircase of 119 steps, which will take you back to 24th Place and Burnside Street.

The bus stop back to town is just downhill from the intersection at the Stearns drinking fountain, named for Judge Loyal B. Stearns, an early King's Hill resident who felt a fountain was needed at this very site.

Every walk merits a reward, and you have to walk only a few more blocks to find yours among the many good restaurants in the shopping district that runs north of Burnside along NW 23rd Avenue.

PORTLAND HEIGHTS TO PARK BLOCKS AND GOOSE HOLLOW LOOP

STARTING POINT SW Vista Avenue and Spring Street

DISTANCE 3 miles

ELEVATION 600 feet at the starting point; 110 feet at SW 17th Avenue and Jefferson Street

GETTING THERE AND PARKING From SW 13th Avenue and W Burnside Street, drive south on 13th. Just past Market Street is a freeway ramp for Interstate 5, Interstate 84, and Interstate 405 South. Take the ramp and stay in the right lane, which will take you to a stop sign at SW Montgomery Drive and 14th Avenue. Drive straight through the intersection, which puts you on 14th. At its end, turn right onto SW Hall Street. As Hall winds around and climbs up the hill, it becomes Upper Hall Street and then 16th Avenue. Stay on 16th to the intersection with SW Spring Street. Turn right and drive four blocks to the start of the hill walk. Park on the street.

TriMet: From downtown, take bus 51 (Vista) to the stop at SW Vista Avenue and Spring Street.

RESTROOMS AND DRINKING FOUNTAINS Restrooms and drinking fountains can be found at Portland State University in the basement level of the Smith Memorial Student Union building.

FOOD AND DRINK Vista Spring Café, located at 2440 SW Vista Avenue, is open daily for lunch and dinner; 503-222-2811. You'll find a food court in the Smith

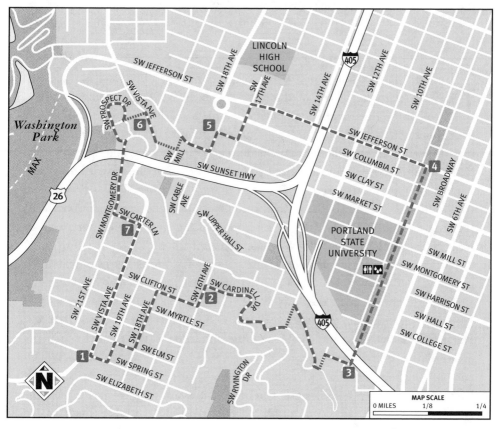

WALK 5. *Portland Heights to Park Blocks and Goose Hollow Loop*

MAP KEY

- ▪ ▬ ROUTE
- ⋯⋯ STAIRS
- ‐ ‐ TRAILS
- ╫╫╫ RAILROAD TRACKS
- ▨ PARKS/GREENSPACE
- 🚻 PUBLIC RESTROOMS
- ◈ WATER
- 🚏 BUS STOP

Memorial Student Union building. Coffee shops can be found midway through the walk in the South Park Blocks and along SW Jefferson Street in Goose Hollow.

P LAN THIS WALK FOR A SUMMER OR FALL SATURDAY when you can stroll through the outdoor Portland Farmers Market located in the South Park Blocks. This hill walk starts you out in Portland Heights, among the city's most beautiful neighborhoods of mansions and grand homes, and drops you out of the heights to stroll under a canopy of elms in the Park Blocks, a linear park flanked on its southern end by Portland State University (PSU). From there you'll follow the historic Plank Road into Goose Hollow, an old neighborhood at the base of the West Hills, and head back up the steep hillside for a tour of some of Portland Heights' most elegant streets.

Parts of this hill walk and the adjoining Portland Heights to Council Crest Loop (Walk 6) follow the route of a "Northwest Hillside Parkway" suggested by Park Commissioner L. L. Hawkins to John Olmsted in 1903. The route started from the southern end of the Park Blocks and climbed the slopes of Portland Heights to include today's SW Hawthorne Terrace at 17th Avenue, which sits on a prominent knob, and the area now occupied by SW Prospect Drive (which is along the route of this hill walk). Of these two prominences, the Olmsted Brothers said, "From no other points will it be possible to view the city so close at hand, and at the same time so high above it." Neither high point has been reserved for parkland, but the views are indeed stupendous.

1 At the intersection of SW Vista Avenue and Spring Street, you're at the heart of Portland Heights, among the city's most desirable neighborhoods for its views and proximity to downtown. Early Portland money settled here and has acted as a magnet ever since. This area was known as Carter's Addition when it was first platted out in 1878 from Thomas Carter's original donation land claim. (Carter's home, built in the 1850s, was at SW 18th and Jefferson, where the First United Methodist Church now sits.) In the early years, because the roads turned to mudslides in winter, the heights were used mostly for summer homes. In 1883 lots sold for $250, but they weren't too hot an item. That changed when the cable car began operating in 1887, providing the first practicable avenue for year-round travel up to the heights. The trestle started below the hill, in Goose Hollow, and traveled a thousand feet at a steep 20 percent grade over the ravine now occupied by SW Montgomery and up 18th Street into Portland Heights.

Looking northeast from the still pastoral Portland Heights, circa 1900. The homes clustered at the base of the hills in Goose Hollow are located where the Sunset Highway approaches now run. The large building in the center is the Exposition Building, now 19th and Burnside. The small dirt road on the hillside is SW Montgomery Drive. Photo courtesy of Don Nelson.

The trestle also carried a road for horse-drawn carriages. Cable Avenue in Goose Hollow sits beneath the path of the former trestle.

In 1903 a forerunner to today's Vista Bridge was built over Jefferson Street, enabling streetcars to climb into the neighborhood. Soon after, the cable trestle was torn down. Today the cable car's powerhouse at 18th and Mill (one street south of Market in Goose Hollow) is buried under the approaches to the Sunset Highway (Highway 26).

With good transportation up to the heights, lots sold fast. By 1910 they were going for $10,000, and this neighborhood, unlike many other inner city neighborhoods, has never seen a downturn since then. At the turn of the twenty-first century, even near-vertical lots previously thought to be unbuildable were selling for $850,000. While Portland Heights is home to plenty of mansions and grand homes, it also has a surprising number of early-twentieth-century apartment homes (called "flats" back then), many of which are now condominiums. You'll pass by several of these.

From Vista and Spring, walk one block east; turn left on SW 19th Avenue. The small brick home at 2428 SW 19th was built in 1911 to house the library of the Episcopal Bishop, whose home, the Bishopcroft, also built in 1911, was located at the corner of SW Elm Street and 19th (now a private residence not affiliated with the church). Turn right on Elm. Across from the Bishopcroft, behind two ginkgo trees, sits the F. L. Bowman Apartments building, at 1837 SW Elm. Built in 1913 as "streetcar apartments" and now on the National Register of Historic Places, this building houses eight condominiums. Each unit has a fireplace and servants' quarters in the basement.

Turn left on 18th. One block south of this intersection, at 18th and Spring, was the original turnaround of the cable car. The brake slipped one day at this location, however, and the car went careening down the hill; after that, the turnaround was moved to flatter ground a few blocks west, near the intersection of Spring and Vista. Walk north on 18th as it drops steeply downhill. Most homes on this section date from the early twentieth century, although some were built when the cable car began operating in 1887. The home at 2218 was built in 1889 for a cable car operator. Those at 2109 and 2023 were built in 1888 and are among the oldest homes in Portland Heights.

A block past SW Clifton Street, 18th reaches a dead end. If you could continue walking down the steep, overgrown hillside, you would end up in Goose Hollow near the MAX light rail stop at 18th and Jefferson. The City of Portland owns this property and may decide to develop a trail here. According to the city's Historic Resource Inventory, some pieces of the old cable line still exist downhill from 1900 SW 18th. I decided against bushwhacking through the blackberries to verify this.

Turn right on Clifton and then, in two blocks, left on 16th Avenue, a street that feeds into the western edges of the PSU campus.

2 Walk one block downhill on 16th and turn right on SW Cardinell Drive, onto a ridgeline called Gander Ridge, which you'll ride all the way down the hill and out of Portland Heights.

Keep left at the intersection with SW Rivington Drive. Just west of the house at 1295, take a set of stairs downhill. These 179 concrete steps, built in 1905, drop you into the gloom of an old maple forest heavily curtained with ivy. Hold tight to the pipe handrail; the last two flights are steep and slightly canted forward. Enjoy the nice views down SW 12th Avenue. At the bottom you're back on Cardinell, a real snake of a street. Here the roar of Interstate 405 is unpleasantly loud.

Turn right at the bottom of the steps, and walk a few blocks. Just past 1245 is a wooden staircase. Fifty-six steps lead you to the end of SW 10th Avenue, at which you'll find an authentic ruin: an antique brick gate house for a city reser-

A city staircase leading up to SW Cardinell Drive.

voir that once filled the ravine at the southwestern end of 10th. The reservoir was fed by a small stream in Portland Heights but was abandoned because the water supply was insufficient. It was part of the Portland Water Works that used West Hills water, including Balch Creek, for the city's water supply before Bull Run water came on line in 1895.

3 Walk one block on 10th, turn right onto Clifton, and turn left onto the very southern tip of SW Park Avenue. Behind you are lots of new homes built into the hill on stilts. Like girls in dresses high atop the bleachers, these houses have left their underpinnings exposed to the curious eyes of those below. The Olmsted Brothers had just this inelegant view in mind when, after consulting with Parks Commissioner L. L. Hawkins, they wrote:

> It would be very desirable for the city to acquire a few acres of land for a little local park at the southwestern end of the Park {Blocks}, which at present terminate abruptly and unsuitably against . . . private property. It would always be pleasing in the vistas looking southwest . . . through the Park {Blocks}, to have a pleasure ground with picturesque plantations for the eye to rest upon, rather than to have some crooked arrangement of private buildings.

You'll cross Interstate 405 on a relatively pleasant overpass, where wide swaths of lawn separate you from the traffic below. This is the busiest section of the Interstate 405 belt around the city's core, with 125,000 cars per day traveling under this overpass. Finished in 1968, Interstate 405 was originally known as the Stadium Freeway (named after the former title of PGE Park). From here you have a lovely view into the South Park Blocks, lined on both sides by PSU.

PSU was founded in 1946 in North Portland as the Vanport Extension Center. (See Walk 19 to learn about Vanport.) In 1952 the center moved into Lincoln Hall in downtown Portland, and in 1955 became Portland State College, a four-year, degree-granting institution. It became a university in 1969.

Once over Interstate 405, the first building on the right is the Native American Student and Community Center, opened in 2003. The building was designed by Portland architect Don Stastny, who also designed the elegant Museum at Warm Springs on the Warm Springs Reservation in central Oregon. The building's organic shapes seem appropriate given that the idea for the project and the legwork needed to stir up university and donor support grew organically, from American Indian students and alumni of PSU. More than 150 Indian cultures are represented in Portland's urban Indian community, and until this building was constructed there was no physical center to that community.

The Olmsted Brothers anticipated the aesthetic challenges of hillside development.

Walk straight into the Park Blocks. The elms creating the canopy overhead were planted soon after this land became a park in 1852. They are aggressively managed to keep them from succumbing to Dutch elm disease. (See Walk 14 for information on this disease and how the city fights it.) Sometimes, in between visits from the arborist, the trees can look a little scruffy, their long sinuous trunks sprouting numerous tiny branchlets that mar their grace just slightly, like chin hairs on a pretty woman. The street was once lined with large homes, but none remain.

At the intersection with SW College Street is the red-brick Shattuck School, a Portland public school from 1915 until the 1960s. Its playful terra-cotta accents are worth a look, especially the wise old owls on the northern and southern sides, and the pigtailed girls who gaze down with laughing eyes at each entrance. This ornamentation was likely partially responsible for the outcry over the school's exorbitant construction cost of $126,000. College Street, oddly enough, was named a century prior to the founding of PSU. There was no college on the street at that point, although there were some academies nearby, including Saint Mary's Academy, a Catholic school for girls, which still exists.

Just north of the Peter W. Stott Center, a fitness center, is the Branford Price Millar Library. Millar was the second president of PSU, serving from 1959 to 1968. You'll find restrooms and water on the first floor. The library was built in 1968 on the site of what is now the Vedanta Society (see Walk 16). A 1980 addition, with its concave wall of windows, was designed to save and celebrate the 1890s-era copper beech in front of the building. The beech drops edible nuts in the fall, each bound up inside a four-petaled involucre that looks like a small wooden flower. American Indians ate the nuts of the American beech. To save time and energy, they would leave the nut harvest to the chipmunks and deer mice, who would stash their haul in logs or holes. Once snow was on the ground, the Indians would simply look for a pile of beechnut husks, dig down, and clean out the animal's stores.

Portland Farmers Market sets up here on Saturdays from May 1 to the weekend before Thanksgiving. Vegetables, fruits, pestos, cheeses, sausages, and baked goods, all grown or made in Oregon, will tempt you to sprint back to your car and drive over to load up on the bounty. On a cold November Saturday, I warmed my hands next to a twirling drum of roasting sweet peppers, got the backs of my legs swatted by the tails of several happy dogs, and sampled enough jams, cheeses, and coffees to fortify me for the rest of the hill walk. This market represents the best of Portland: great food in a gorgeous, seminatural setting that has been preserved for all by the foresight of early citizens.

Next to the Blackstone, a 1931 apartment house with implacable Egyptians guarding its façade, is the Simon Benson House. This house, which belonged to one of the city's most beloved philanthropists, used to sit at the southeastern corner of SW 11th Avenue and Clay Street. In the late 1990s, after years of abandonment, it was moved to its present site and restored for a new life as PSU's Alumni and Visitor Center. Benson, who lived from 1851 to 1942, is known to every Portland schoolchild for his Benson Bubblers, the bronze four-bowled water fountains scattered around the downtown area. He commissioned these fountains in 1912 with the intention of providing an alternative for citizens who, without this resource, might be tempted to venture into a tavern to quench their thirst. Benson High School, the Benson Hotel, and Multnomah Falls and Benson State Recreation Area in the Columbia River Gorge are other parts of his legacy. Benson summed up his generous philosophy when he said, "No one has the right to die and not leave something to the public and for the public good."

Across from Simon Benson's house is the Smith Memorial Student Union building, where in the basement level you'll find a food court, restrooms, and drinking fountains. The diagonal sidewalks in the Park Blocks here were laid out in 1905 to thwart baseball games by local kids.

Just after you cross the streetcar tracks you'll see Lincoln Hall on the right. Erected in 1911, this building served as the second Lincoln High School, the first having been located at SW 14th and Morrison. In 1951 Lincoln High moved to its present location on the grounds of the Kamm estate at SW Salmon and 16th. At Market Street you leave PSU and enter the city's Cultural District of museums, theaters, and performance halls. On this stretch, a few more food options can be found in the ground levels of the various condominium buildings. One notable building is Jeanne Manor at SW Clay and Park, which is listed on the National Register of Historic Places.

At the intersection with SW Columbia, look one block east to the 1883 Stick-style carriage house of the Ladd mansion, which sat in the block now housing the *Oregonian* building. William Sargent Ladd was among the city's first magnates. After his death, the Ladd Estate Company sold off land that eventually became Laurelhurst, Eastmoreland, Dunthorpe, Riverview Cemetery, and, of course, Ladd's Addition. This carriage house, bigger than all but the biggest homes, has held the offices of the Junior League of Portland and workshops for the Portland Civic Theater. Today it holds office space.

Also on Columbia, at Park, is the unusual ziggurat-style Sixth Church of Christ Scientist, built during the Depression in 1931. Its architect, Glenn Stanton (of Whitehouse, Stanton, and Church), was charged with designing a church that would put as many men as possible to work for the greatest length of time. Despite the intricacy of the brickwork, it was finished in six months.

4 Walk one more block and turn left at SW Jefferson Street. This intersection is where the first plank of Portland's old Plank Road to the Tualatin Plains was laid in 1851. (See Walk 4 for more on the Plank Road.) On your right is the Portland Art Museum, designed in 1931 by the famous modernist architect Pietro Belluschi, who took early, more classical drawings for the building and pared them down to cleaner lines. Belluschi was born in Italy in 1899. After training at Cornell University, he didn't want to return to Mussolini's Italy. With help from the Italian ambassador, he stayed in the United States after completing his education, came to Portland in 1925, and began working for A. E. Doyle, who designed the first buildings at Reed College and many other buildings, such as the white terra-cotta Meier and Frank building in downtown Portland and the central branch of the Multnomah County Public Library. When Doyle died in 1928, Belluschi began managing his architectural firm. In 1950 he left the city to become dean of architecture at the Massachusetts Institute of Technology, returning to retire here in 1972. He died in 1994.

At SW 10th Avenue and Jefferson you'll find a Safeway, opened in 2003, that replaced the old Safeway across Jefferson. This is not your mother's Safeway, with suburban parents carting their toddlers around. The customers are a bit more eclectic here. Straight ahead, down Jefferson, you can see the Vista Bridge arching above the canyon; this walk will take you to within a few feet of its southern terminus on SW Vista Avenue.

At SW 13th Avenue, cross over the gash in the earth that is Interstate 405. Before the freeway came along, this area was filled with homes. Saint Helens Hall, a school for girls, once sat at SW 14th and Montgomery. Alexander Kerr, who invented the Kerr Economy Canning Jar, also had a home near here. In 1912, after his young wife Albertina died of typhus following childbirth, Kerr gave the house to a society that sheltered abandoned children, and left Portland for Chicago. Since then the mission of the Albertina Kerr Centers has evolved; these centers now serve the needs of emotionally disturbed children and provide care for teens and adults with developmental disabilities.

Once over the freeway, Jefferson descends into the Goose Hollow neighborhood, which has suffered greatly as a cohesive place due to Interstate 405 as well as to the Sunset Highway approach ramps gobbling up its streets and homes. Goose Hollow is the lowland now occupied by and surrounding the Sunset Highway approaches. Its very old homes sit next to commercial buildings and newer condominiums. In the late 1800s it held a pond with a large goose population.

The intersection of Jefferson and 17th is the low point before the land starts climbing out of the hollow. Turn left onto 17th and then right onto Clay Street. The old duplex on the corner has an untold story in its lovely stone foundation. Much of the rock used in it is not local. It appears to be granite and was probably used as ballast on a ship sailing around the tip of South America from New England. Once docked, the ballast was offloaded and in many cases used for foundations or walls. Another fine example of a ballast stone wall is at SE 27th Avenue and Hawthorne Boulevard.

The section of Clay Street between 17th and 18th Avenues is a rare block of intact, small Victorian homes, and makes for a peaceful interlude; the freeway sounds are surprisingly muted here.

5   Climb more as you turn left on SW 18th and then right on Market, where some of the city's oldest extant architecture resides. The Italianate apartment house at 1814 was a private residence when it was built in 1885, and the building at 1824 was built in 1890 as a three-story home, originally located at SW 10th and Clay. When it was moved here in 1911, the owners had to add the two lower floors to accommodate the sloping site.

These old homes sit next to a hypermodern, blocky trio of condominiums at 2020 SW Market that were built on the site of an old rock quarry. Ironically, not a bit of local stone was used in these buildings. A set of concrete steps heads uphill, across from SW 19th Street. Don't take these stairs, which are private. Instead take the next flight of steps up, across from the townhome at 1917 SW Market.

These 153 steps quickly pull you up out of the hollow and into the heights. Views are great from here, and they keep getting better. At the top of the steps you're in a cul-de-sac of SW Mill Street. On the right is a set of stairs with a gate that reads, "Although this is private property, owners permit public use." Before taking these lovely folks up on their offer, wander down Mill just a bit and stand right over the steaming lanes of the Sunset Highway as they dive into the Vista Ridge Tunnel. Rock excavated from this tunnel was dumped along the Willamette River, creating the level ground at Willamette Park in Southwest Portland. On the southern side of the freeway you can see the canyon through which the cable car rode 200 feet above the ground on its way up to Portland Heights.

The hills around you were formed by Columbia River Basalts, which originated from vents in the ground in eastern Washington, northeastern Oregon, and western Idaho. Between six and seventeen million years ago, lava flowed out of these vents in such enormous quantities that it covered 63,000 square miles of land (an area equal to about two-thirds the size of the entire state of Oregon). Countless different flows of these "flood basalts" spread like syrup. In some parts of Portland they accumulated to depths of more than 600 feet. The elongated ridge of the Tualatin Mountains, more commonly known as the West Hills, was formed by the faulting and folding of these basalts. The West Hills range from 500 to 1000 feet high, and are 20 miles long and about 3 miles wide.

Take the gated stairs toward the iron fence at Vista Avenue. Before you emerge onto this busy street, you may want to sit on the steps and gaze at the Portland panorama viewable from the vacant hillside lot here. The Fremont Bridge, Mount Saint Helens, the barrel roof of the Multnomah Athletic Club, and the green glass spires of the Convention Center are just a few of the landmarks you can pick out from this spot. The Kaiser Permanente complex in North Portland can be seen on the river bluffs just to the left of a green water tower.

Once up on Vista, turn right. The address at 1540 SW Vista is the top of the condominium trio that started on Market. On the other side of Vista, huge homes tower above you.

6 Across from the home at 1456 SW Vista are three inconspicuous stairs. Carefully cross the street here and take these stairs to a steep path that leads up to SW Prospect Drive. Like Vista, Prospect was named to signify to potential buyers that homesites came with fine views.

Looking east toward downtown Portland from SW Mill Street, atop the Sunset Highway's Vista Ridge Tunnel.

The path ends at eleven stairs that drop you off on Prospect next to a leaning, curb-eating giant sequoia. How long until this tree keels over? In this neighborhood it's a safe bet that someone is closely monitoring its tilt, and the tree will come down via chain saw before it finds its own final angle of repose. In the fall the tree litters the ground with its cones, which are surprisingly small and cute for such a beefy tree. Fire is required for these cones to open and release their seeds. In its native California, a giant sequoia can reach thirty-five hundred years old and more than 300 feet tall. This particular specimen, planted in 1910, marks a corner of the property at 1728 Prospect. The 1908 residence, built in the Twentieth-Century Classical style, was the home of David and Nan Wood Honeyman. Honeyman was the daughter of Charles Erskine Scott (C. E. S.) Wood, a nationally famous writer and lawyer. Politically she was a progressive, leading the charge in the 1920s to end Prohibition, and serving as president of Oregon's League of Women Voters. She was a supporter of Franklin Roosevelt's New Deal and a good friend of Eleanor Roosevelt. In 1937 she became the first Oregon woman in the U.S. Congress, where she served for one term.

Turn right to begin walking the Prospect loop. Prospect Drive follows the contour of a small peak, at elevations between 350 and 400 feet, giving wonderful views in three directions. The home at 1735 was built in 1923 and was once the home of Thomas Banfield, best known for the freeway named after him. His mansion on SW Park Avenue is on Walk 4. Banfield, born in 1885, ran the Iron Fireman, which manufactured automatic coal stokers.

Just before the house at 1743, you'll notice a nice view across the canyon to the Kings Heights neighborhood on the slopes below the Pittock Mansion. The home at 1743 is a 1909 Colonial bungalow owned by James Wood, Nan Wood Honeyman's uncle. Another female first, Dorothy McCullough Lee, lived in the 1906 home at 1767 Prospect. Portland's first woman mayor (1948–1952), she was a reformer focused on promoting civil rights and trying to clean up vice. She died in 1981.

The grand home at 1770 was designed in the Arts and Crafts and Tudor styles by Ellis Lawrence, a luminary in Portland's architectural firmament, for Max and Clementine Hirsch. In the 1880s Max Hirsch joined his uncle, Aaron Meier, in the family business, Meier and Frank, still one of Portland's flagship retailers. Later he bought Willamette Tent and Awning, a manufacturer of outdoor wear that was later reborn as White Stag. The White Stag deer, a huge neon icon, still prances high above the Burnside Bridge, though it now advertises for Made in Oregon, a chain of retail stores.

At the end of the Prospect loop, turn right onto SW Montgomery Drive, a truly grand avenue. Pass SW West Point Court, a dead end where homes are arrayed around another small, view-giving knob of land. At about 1782 Montgomery, as you walk over the freeway tunnel, you can see bits of the Sunset Highway through the trees.

Turn left at SW Carter Lane, named after Thomas Carter, whose donation land claim roughly encompasses the area of Portland Heights. Carter started the first store in Portland and later, in 1881, founded the Arlington Club. The Plank Road ran through his property. Carter Lane is the path his cows took each day to and from their pasture. The house at the southeastern corner of Montgomery and Carter has a window in its chimney, something you don't see too often.

7 Cross Vista and turn right so that you are walking uphill. The first house you'll see, at 1934, is a stunner. This was the site of Carter's orchard, and then the site of one of the first homes in the area. In the 1920s the old building was torn down and replaced by this Mediterranean residence, designed by A. E. Doyle for Joseph Bowles, owner of Northwest Steel Company. The Bowles family sent Doyle to Italy to soak in its architectural ambience, and this was the result. The $750,000 construction costs translated to $150 per square foot of home; in today's dollars that's about $1500 per square foot, or $7.5 million for the house alone. Walls are either paneled, draped in fabrics like silk brocade, or covered in silver and gold leaf. A fur vault kept Mrs. Bowles' collection of pelts cool, and several walls reveal hiding places for jewelry or liquor. Faucets and spigots are sterling silver. This home is on the Historic Register. It would be worthwhile finding out when it's open for its annual tour.

One block east of the intersection with SW Jackson Street is the site of Carter's barn (where a gray and white home sits on the corner of Carter Lane and Jackson). The residence at 2030 SW Vista is the Nicholas-Langer home. Built in 1885, this is the oldest home on the street.

The Colonial Revival home at 2133 SW Vista presents a beautiful argument for planting Douglas firs in city neighborhoods. The home here is quietly elegant, but the trees elevate it further, framing it as though it were nestled in a miniature city park. Another example of the Colonial Revival style can be found at 2303 and 2305, an early duplex. One identifying feature of this style is the oval window on top, with points extending north, south, east, and west. The Mediterranean multifamily bungalows at 1926 SW Elm date from 1927; seventy five years later they were still owned by the same family.

Consider ending your walk at the cozy Vista Spring Café, a neighborhood landmark, where the food, beer, and wine are most welcome after this long hill walk. The building was constructed in 1908 as a corner drug and grocery store, with four flats above. When the top burned, the second story was torn down and the building continued on in various commercial iterations. During the 1960s this building, right across from Ainsworth Elementary School, was home to an ice cream parlor and candy store. Shouldn't every grade school be situated next door to a candy store? That would keep the kids from rushing home to interface with a computer.

The café, here since 1985, is a great place to relax and is among the few commercial establishments in the neighborhood.

The cable railway that ran up to Portland Heights, photographed circa 1887. Photo courtesy of the Multnomah County Library.

PORTLAND HEIGHTS TO COUNCIL CREST LOOP

STARTING POINT SW Vista Avenue and Spring Street

DISTANCE 4.5 miles

ELEVATION 600 feet at the starting point; 1073 feet at Council Crest Park

GETTING THERE AND PARKING From SW 13th Avenue and W Burnside Street, drive south on 13th. Just past Market Street is a ramp for Interstate 5, Interstate 84, and Interstate 405 South. Take the ramp and stay in the right lane, which will take you to a stop sign at SW Montgomery Drive and 14th Avenue. Drive straight through the intersection, which puts you on 14th. At its end, turn right onto SW Hall Street. As Hall winds around and climbs up the hill, it becomes Upper Hall Street and then 16th Avenue. Stay on 16th to the intersection with SW Spring Street. Turn right and drive four blocks to the start of the hill walk. Park on the street.

TriMet: From downtown, take bus 51 (Vista) to the stop at SW Vista Avenue and Spring Street.

RESTROOMS AND DRINKING FOUNTAINS Drinking fountains are at Council Crest Park and Portland Heights Park; restrooms are at Portland Heights Park.

FOOD AND DRINK Haul a picnic up to the park at Council Crest, or better yet, just haul yourself up with some cash in your pocket and reward yourself near the end of the hill walk with a gourmet meal from the deli at Strohecker's, 2855 SW Patton Road; 503-223-7391. Sit at one of their tables or take your lunch next door to Portland Heights Park.

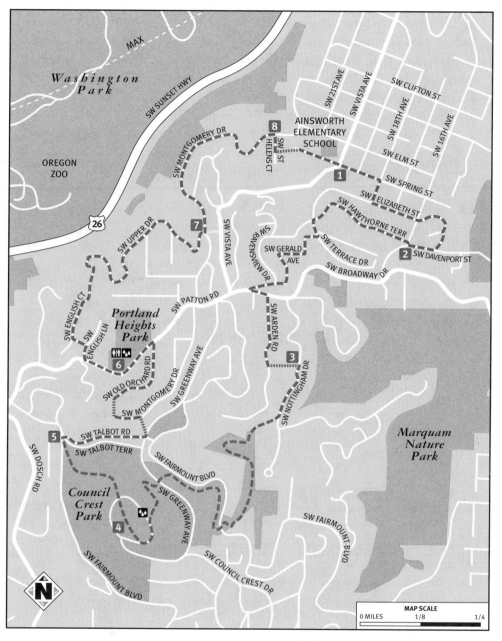

MAX

Washington Park

SW SUNSET HWY

OREGON ZOO

26

SW MONTGOMERY DR

SW UPPER DR

SW ST HELENS CT

AINSWORTH ELEMENTARY SCHOOL

SW 21ST AVE
SW VISTA AVE
SW CLIFTON ST
SW 18TH AVE
SW 16TH AVE
SW ELM ST

SW SPRING ST

SW ELIZABETH ST
SW HAWTHORNE TERR

SW DAVENPORT ST

SW VISTA AVE

SW RAVENSVIEW DR

SW GERALD AVE

SW TERRACE DR

SW BROADWAY DR

SW PATTON RD

SW ENGLISH CT

SW ENGLISH LN

Portland Heights Park

SW OLD ORCHARD RD

SW GREENWAY AVE

SW MONTGOMERY DR

SW ARDEN RD

SW NOTTINGHAM DR

Marquam Nature Park

SW TALBOT RD

SW TALBOT TERR

SW DOSCH RD

SW FAIRMOUNT BLVD

SW GREENWAY AVE

Council Crest Park

SW FAIRMOUNT BLVD

SW FAIRMOUNT BLVD

SW COUNCIL CREST DR

N

MAP SCALE
0 MILES   1/8   1/4

WALK 6. *Portland Heights to Council Crest Loop*

MAP KEY

- ROUTE
- STAIRS
- TRAILS
- WATER
- RAILROAD TRACKS
- PARKS/GREENSPACE
- PUBLIC RESTROOMS
- BUS STOP

S AVE THIS HILL WALK FOR A CLEAR, CLOUDLESS DAY when you can use the viewfinder at the top of Council Crest to identify the many Cascade peaks visible from there. This walk traverses street after street of beautiful homes in Portland Heights before and after it climbs up to the top of Council Crest. It includes several unexpected (except to the initiated) forays into right-of-ways and staircases that you won't find in your *Thomas Guide*.

The route includes a 1-mile hike through the Marquam Nature Park. Although this park is well known citywide and popular with neighbors, use discretion about walking alone in the woods.

1 From the intersection of SW Vista Avenue and Spring Street, walk east on Spring. You'll pass, at 1930 Spring, the 1910 bungalow that was home to Captain Kerrigan, the fire chief of the station next door at 1920 Spring. The 1927 firehouse replaced the first firehouse, built in 1907 on this site. Ascension Chapel, tucked into this residential street, was built in 1889. In two blocks you'll reach SW 18th Avenue. This intersection was the terminus of the cable car that ran up to the heights starting in 1887. (See Walk 5 for more on the history of Portland Heights and the cable line.)

Turn right onto 18th and left onto SW Elizabeth Street. Elizabeth is the highest street in the rectangular grid portion of Portland Heights that ignored the land's undulations. The street was named by Governor LaFayette Grover, who platted out this area in 1883, for his wife, Elizabeth Grover. East, south, and west of Elizabeth, the street layouts finally surrender to the land's mountainous topography.

The home at 1800 Elizabeth is among the oldest on the street, built in 1890. Just east of it is a dilapidated and gated staircase dating from 1895. These steps were built so that riders disembarking from the cable car that ran up 18th could walk up to the street above, SW Hawthorne Terrace. On Hawthorne the views were sweeping, and an observation tower and Japanese teahouse attracted visitors—potential homebuyers, it was hoped—to the heights. These stairs are no longer open to the public. The homes at 1704 and 1710 share a graceful, calf-building staircase that must have caused the hearts of countless moving men to sink.

Cross SW 16th Avenue, one of the main feeder streets into the neighborhood from downtown. At a bend in the road, you can savor, free of charge, the view that Portland Heights residents pay serious money for. As you walk downhill on Elizabeth, just before it meets with SW Davenport Street, you get a fine view across Marquam Gulch to Council Crest, the high point of this hill walk. Davenport east of here was once a fruit orchard run by the Sisters of the Holy

Name, who operated Saint Mary's Academy in downtown Portland. Milo McIver bought the land from the sisters and began developing it in the 1930s.

Turn right on Davenport. A homesite at 1535 was carved in the late 1990s out of a small piece of hillside that had been passed over for a hundred years. The gunite-covered wall that sits very close behind the home retains the hillside in a modern version of the basalt rock retaining wall seen throughout the West Hills. Gunite is a type of "shotcrete," cement applied by a spraying device.

2   Turn right at 16th and then immediately left onto Hawthorne Terrace, which skirts the top of one of Portland Heights' peaks. The basalts here are the youngest flows in the Columbia River Basalts. The 1927 Arts and Crafts house at 1727 has a street-side retaining wall filled with surprising elements; it is reminiscent of Rome, where builders for centuries have helped themselves to architectural doodads from ages past.

The Lewis and Clark Observatory drew Portlanders up this hillside when it was located at 1740 Hawthorne Terrace, before it was moved to Council Crest. The Olmsted Brothers noted that this spot is "a remarkably prominent view point, already well known and much resorted to by the citizens. . . . This view point is well worth preserving as a local park."

The Japanese teahouse, built in 1908, sits at 1741, though it is barely visible behind a wooden wall. The Markle-Pittock House at 1816 is in the Queen Anne and Jacobean styles. J. Carroll McCaffrey, a promoter of the neighborhood and the cable railway, had it built in 1889 as a showplace to entice others into coming and enjoying the heights. Before it was finished, McCaffrey sold it to George Markle of the Oregon National Bank. Frederick Pittock, son of Henry and Georgiana Pittock of the Pittock Mansion, remodeled the home in 1928.

At this point in the road, a walker might get a little frustrated. Though it was originally recommended that this peak be left open to the public for its stupendous views, the opposite has occurred; homeowners here aren't sharing their views, putting up one impenetrable fence after another along the road. One exception, and I do appreciate it, is a wooden fence in which the wooden slats on one panel have been thoughtfully angled so that passersby can see the views northwest to Washington Park and the Pittock Mansion.

At a stop sign, turn left onto SW Terrace Drive. The many streets angling off at this multiple intersection are all worthy of an out-and-back exploration, but to avoid too circuitous a peregrination, you may want to turn your back to their charms and make a right on SW Gerald Avenue. This street is a charmer. Tucked away onto the upper flanks of Marquam Gulch, it makes urban density look very, very good.

Council Crest Park: serenity at the top of the city.

Walk along Gerald to its end at SW Corona Avenue. Turn left onto Corona, then left at SW Ravensview Drive; head down Ravensview to a short staircase that leads to SW Broadway Drive. Carefully cross this busy road and turn left. At the first street, SW Arden Road, turn right.

Arden, which used to be called Mountain Boulevard, is among my favorite Portland streets: riding along at the 700-foot contour level in Marquam Gulch, it's a dead end with a secret escape hatch. Other plusses are that it's within walking distance of downtown, it's on the edge of the woods, and it's lined with interesting houses. The home at 2421 was built in 1926 by Caroline and Louise Flanders, daughters of pioneer ship captain George H. Flanders. Elements taken from their father's mansion at NW 19th Avenue and Flanders Street are incorporated into this house. Just past 2490 is an old concrete driveway leading to a newer concrete path. Take this route into a magical, narrow green canyon where birds flee from your approach. This path drops you down onto SW Nottingham Drive, where you'll turn right.

Another thing I like about Portland Heights is that on just about every street someone is doing a major remodel on their home. While I enjoy chatting with the many workers I see building additions, reroofing, pouring concrete, or scraping old paint, I also appreciate the abundance of portable toilets that accompany all these home improvement projects.

3 Nottingham is just as lovely as Arden. Walk down it until the sidewalk ends, just before two trailheads, one going upslope and one going downslope. Take the upslope trailhead to Council Crest, 1 mile from this point. This ravine is called Marquam Gulch. In 1968 developers planned to construct six hundred apartments here, but concerned neighbors and other citizens organized in opposition. Someone dug up the Olmsted Brothers' 1903 report to the city, wherein a 40-mile loop of parks and parkways was envisioned. The activists formed the 40-Mile Loop Land Trust, which ultimately saw the developers retreat and led to the 83-acre Marquam Nature Park, the last west side link in a system of trails that connects the Saint Johns Bridge with the Sellwood Bridge.

The trail is pleasant; the firs here are good-sized. After crossing a seasonal creek bed, watch for a large stump from this forest's virginal days. The abundant, seemingly free-floating vine maple gives a lacy look to the forest, a nice counterpoint to the solid, somber fir trunks. Vine maples were much used by American Indians. The sap was dried and eaten, and the flexible wood was shaped into snowshoes. English ivy removal is evident in the forest here, but you have to wonder if this task will someday become insurmountable, the forest floors a monoculture of this difficult weed.

The trail stays to the western side of the creek drainage. Homes that begin appearing on the slopes above are on SW Fairmount Boulevard. The trail crosses it and continues, fairly level and open above the road, until it emerges onto SW Greenway Avenue, the former path of the streetcar up to Council Crest. Cross Greenway and hike the short distance up into the park.

4 Council Crest Park and the hill it sits on were once called Talbot's Mountain, an oblong peak in the West Hills that runs northwest to southeast. This peak is the highest point in Portland's city limits, at 1073 feet. What is now the park was once part of John Beal Talbot's donation land claim and the site of his family's home, which was moved in 1908.

After the success of the 1905 Lewis and Clark Exposition, Portland seemed ripe for more public amusements, and in 1907 the Council Crest Amusement Park opened. Attractions on this hilltop included a scenic railroad, a dance hall, a rifle range, a carousel, and the Lewis and Clark Observatory, which was moved here from Hawthorne Terrace. The park was not profitable, however, and closed in 1929. Its buildings were torn down in 1941 when the land was donated to the city for a park. The observatory was razed to make way for the water tanks that are here today.

The park, with its sweeping lawns, is a nice place to throw a Frisbee or lie down and dream. The best views are to the northeast. A plaque at the monu-

The top of Council Crest as it appeared during its amusement park heyday, around 1910. The carousel building is in the foreground, the Lewis and Clark Observatory in the background.
Photo courtesy of Don Nelson.

ment on top gives you the sight lines and distance in miles to all the visible Cascade peaks. To the south is the massive radio tower on Healy Heights.

To leave the park, walk north toward the water tower. North of it, and west of a radio tower, is an asphalt path leading downhill. Take it, then turn left onto a trail into the forest. Where the trail forks, stay left; at an asphalt path, turn right and you'll soon find yourself at the intersection of SW Talbot Terrace, Fairmount Boulevard, Gaston Avenue, and Talbot Road.

5 Turn right onto Talbot Road (the lower Talbot), a road that John Talbot built in 1851 to get to his property. Walk along its unpaved shoulder, and just before the Greenway Avenue underpass, descend a flight of wooden steps that lead to a dirt path next to some homes. You're on the southern end of SW Montgomery Drive. Turn left. At 2980 is a Ranch home that has successfully morphed into a Craftsman—no small feat. Take the inconspicuous stepped path that starts to the left of the garage at 2989. It drops you down next to a garage at the end of what appears to be a very private driveway. As you saunter out the driveway onto the street, you may feel like you have emerged into some new

One of Portland's secret passageways between streets.

reality. I like these hidden portals. Like Harry Potter's Platform 9 ¾, Portland's invisible-to-the-uninitiated pathways circumvent the usual modes of transit.

You've left behind the lofty manses of Montgomery for the smaller but quite charming abodes of SW Old Orchard Road. This street was named for a cherry orchard that once grew here. Maryanna Boudinot-Seeley developed the orchard into residential lots in the 1920s, keeping the best, 2775, for herself. She was the daughter of a Mrs. Ross, whose donation land claim included Ross Island. (See Walk 7 for more on this island in the Willamette.) The home at 2725 was home to Philip Parrish, a writer who in the 1930s chronicled early Portland history.

Where Old Orchard ends at SW Patton Road, turn right and cross Patton at the marked crosswalk. In front of you is Strohecker's, a Portland landmark. Gottlieb Strohecker had his house and barn at this site in 1898. In 1902 he opened the Mount Zion store at this location, and it has been here ever since. In the 1990s Lamb's Markets bought it. I recommend stopping for a culinary reward, even though the walk's not over yet; treat yourself to some gourmet cheese or chocolate, and head over to the lovely Portland Heights Park next door. Water and restrooms are available at the park.

6 From the park, turn right (west) and walk along Patton on the paved path or bike path to SW English Lane. Take a right and then a quick left onto SW English Court, a street at the far reaches of Portland Heights. Curve right on English Court. This street looks like it ends at someone's driveway. Walk boldly on and you'll pass through some invisible barrier where the street morphs into SW Upper Drive.

You're close to the Sunset Highway here, which runs just 250 feet away from the westernmost point of Upper Drive. You're also across the canyon from the zoo; if the freeway wasn't roaring, you might hear some actual beasts. After a bit the street passes beyond the din of the highway and starts to get a lovely tucked-away-in-the-woods feeling. This cozy hillside feeling comes with a price tag, though: these very steep slopes are no stranger to landslides.

In the 1910s this street was home to summer cottages, tucked into the cool shade offered by the deep woods. The cozy cottage-like home at 2947 features one of the top five garages in Portland for style and beauty; it has more windows than many houses. The home at 2855, which sits too far back a long brick driveway to be seen, was built by Nellie Fox, described in the city's Historic Resource Inventory as an "eccentric librarian." Judging from the location of her house, "reclusive" might have been another appropriate adjective. Next to this, at 2845, is a 1931 English cottage owned by Homer Angell, who served as Oregon representative to Congress from 1938 until 1955, when he lost to Tom McCall.

At 2833 is another nifty touch: a custom screen door that is a mirror image of the main door. If you're looking for home improvement ideas, this street is a good place to start. Despite points off for noise, Upper is a very cool drive, twisting in and out of small canyons as it gently climbs. It gets more manicured and less bohemian the closer you get to the heart of Portland Heights.

7 Where Upper meets Montgomery Drive, turn left. At 2578 is a 1951 home designed by John Storrs in the Northwest Regional style. Mrs. Harold Gill lived here; she designed the garden, where native salal and Oregon grape grow under a multitiered canopy of flowering witch hazel and pine, among other lovely things. Just past the house is a set of stairs leading up to SW Alta Vista Place at Vista Avenue. If you want to circumvent the last wanderings, you can take these stairs and follow Vista to Spring Street.

At 2525 Montgomery sits a beautiful home from 1905. Its original owner was a postal clerk, James Howes, who chose this hillside location because of its access to clear spring water in the canyon below. In the 1940s a landslide destroyed much of the property. Past it, the road is too steep for houses, until you reach a Norman farmhouse at 2455. The date of its construction, 1925, is incised in one of its leaded glass windows. As the road curves into the hillside, the Frank J. Cobb home comes into view. This Jacobean mansion was designed by A. E. Doyle in 1918. The home is 15,000 square feet, and the property used to extend down the hillside all the way to Highway 26. Its stables were located just below Montgomery. If you walk along Vista you can peer down at the sweeping concrete stairs, the slate roof built by Italian craftsmen, the greenhouse, the swimming pool, the cultivated grounds, the tower that contains the library, and all the other accoutrements of one big, fancy house. The original furnishings that the Cobbs accumulated on a world tour were auctioned off in 1959.

8 Turn right on SW Saint Helens Court. Just past the home at 2526 is a sidewalk that leads to a footbridge across a forested ravine. Take the bridge to the dead end of Spring Street, which puts you behind Ainsworth School, a Jacobean-style building from 1912. Walk one block to the starting point at Spring and Vista.

HILLSDALE TO HEALY HEIGHTS LOOP

STARTING POINT SW Dewitt Street and Cheltenham Street

DISTANCE 4 miles

ELEVATION 530 feet at the starting point; 1030 feet at Healy Heights, near the Stonehenge radio tower

GETTING THERE AND PARKING From downtown Portland, drive south on SW Broadway. After you leave downtown, follow signs directing you to SW Barbur Boulevard. The last road in a series of turns is SW Sheridan Street. The next right puts you on Barbur. On Barbur, after the stoplight at SW Hamilton Street, drive 0.8 mile to a right-lane exit for Highway 10, Hillsdale, and Beaverton. Take the exit, which puts you on SW Capitol Highway. Drive through the first stoplight for SW Terwilliger Parkway, and turn right at the next light, about 0.4 mile further, at SW Sunset Boulevard. Drive one block and turn right on SW Dewitt Street. The street parking here is free but has a two-hour limit. Park here or one street up the hill, on SW Pendleton Street, for unlimited parking.

TriMet: From downtown, take bus 56 (Scholls Ferry Road) to the stop at SW Capitol Highway and Sunset Boulevard. Walk one block east on Capitol Highway, turn left on SW Cheltenham Street, and walk one block to the starting point of the hill walk.

RESTROOMS AND DRINKING FOUNTAINS You'll find restrooms and drinking fountains at the Hillsdale Library, 1525 SW Sunset Boulevard, and a drinking fountain at Healy Heights Park.

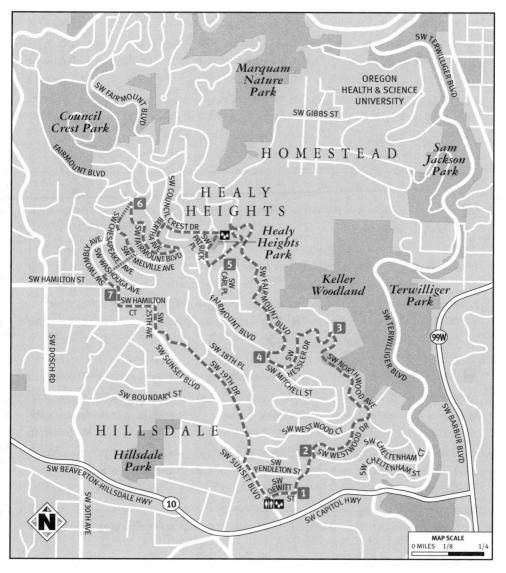

WALK 7. *Hillsdale to Healy Heights Loop*

MAP KEY

- ROUTE
- STAIRS
- TRAILS
- RAILROAD TRACKS
- PARKS/GREENSPACE
- PUBLIC RESTROOMS
- WATER
- BUS STOP

FOOD AND DRINK There's a peaceful city park at the summit of the walk, so you may want to pack a picnic to enjoy at the top. Provisions can be found at Noah's New York Bagels in the Hillsdale Shopping Center, 6366 SW Capitol Highway, just west of the starting point; 503-293-3183. Or leave your pack in the car and reward yourself after the walk with lunch at the Three Square Grill, also located in the Hillsdale Shopping Center, at 6320 SW Capitol Highway; 503-244-4467. Three Square Grill is open every day but Monday.

THIS HILL WALK UP THE SOUTHERN END OF COUNCIL CREST IS BIG: a big gain in elevation, big mileage, homes with big prices, and at the top, a big, big sky. You'll walk uphill through the Hillsdale, Hessler Hills, and Healy Heights neighborhoods. I recommend taking this walk during the spring or fall: the many gardens you pass will be performing, and you'll have the best chance of catching a classic Northwest sky of towering clouds, peaking sunrays, and distant showers and rainbows. If you plan your walk for a Sunday morning between May and October, you can end it at the Hillsdale Farmers Market.

1 Start on SW Dewitt Street between SW Sunset Boulevard and Cheltenham Street, where a library, fire station, and playground create a friendly nexus. The Hillsdale Library was finished in 2004, replacing a 1959 library building on the same site. This building is green, ecologically speaking; it is the first Multnomah County building to pursue Leadership in Energy and Environmental Design (LEED) certification, meaning that it incorporates environmental design elements to reduce or eliminate its negative impact on the environment. These elements include access to public transit, water-efficient landscaping, recycling or salvage of construction waste materials, and a commitment to purchase at least 20 percent of building materials from local manufacturers.

Walk east on Dewitt to Cheltenham. The home on the southwestern corner is a 1923 Colonial that originally sat a few blocks away at 6305 SW Capitol Highway, the site of the Fulton Park Dairy, one of many dairies that once occupied this area. Today the land is occupied by Wilson High School. Across from this home is Hopewell House, an in-patient hospice that is part of the Legacy Health System.

Turn left on Cheltenham. At 1244, tucked back from the road, is an 1893 Rural Vernacular home. On the other side of this home, a private rail line once hauled logs from SW Hamilton Road (on the western side of Council Crest) to the Terwilliger area.

Stay right at the intersection with SW Pendleton Street and then veer left at the intersection with SW Cheltenham Court. At 1020 Cheltenham Court is a circa-1865 Italianate home that in 1964 was moved to make way for Interstate 405. The ornamental iron fence is from Saint Helens Hall, another casualty of a freeway (the Sunset Highway).

2 Walk uphill on Cheltenham Court to SW Westwood Drive. Turn left onto Westwood. There are no sidewalks here, but the streets are lightly traveled; on a quiet fall morning I saw more walkers than drivers. As you walk up the southern flanks of Council Crest, you'll pass a City of Portland distribution tank. After the water has been treated, the city stores it in open reservoirs, closed ground-level reservoirs, elevated water towers, and standpipes (water tanks that are taller than they are wide). From these storage facilities, water flows directly to the end user.

While the homes on this walk span a gamut of prices, primarily related to altitude, homeowners share two things: an extremely scenic hillside setting and an admirable lack of fear about residing under tall and notoriously shallow-rooted Douglas fir trees. The homes along Westwood aren't attention-grabbers, but their considerable beauty is revealed with a close look: nestled beneath columnar black fir trunks, each in a different way embodies a classic, understated Northwest elegance, with structurally intriguing plants, subtle Japanese accents, and varied types of stonework. Westwood itself still wears its original concrete paving from the 1920s, which has held up well under the light usage on this street. Concrete is actually a stronger paving material than asphalt, but many early-day concrete roads have been repaved with asphalt because they were not designed to withstand the weights of modern vehicles, especially trucks. The city still uses concrete when extreme durability is desired, as on NE Marine Drive, which receives heavy truck traffic. Roads like SW Northwood Avenue are left alone; according to one city engineer, the expectation is that a concrete road will last forever, and many residents like their uniquely paved streets.

Where SW Westwood Court comes in on your left, stay straight. Turn left onto SW Menefee Drive, where you emerge from the wooded southern side of the hill onto the eastern slope of the Tualatin Mountains. Downslope from you 240 feet are the scenic vistas of SW Terwilliger Boulevard, a boulevard recommended for development by the Olmsted Brothers to showcase some of the city's best views. The views on this walk are even better than from Terwilliger. Walk along Menefee past one house, and then turn left back into the hillside onto SW Westwood Drive. At the intersection of Westwood and Northwood, you're at the top of a small but very steep drainage, a ravine that channels water from the surrounding slopes down to the Willamette River, 700 feet below. The home at this intersection has created a sophisticated terraced garden out of a challenging but beautiful setting.

Turn right onto Northwood, which claims to be a dead end. Don't let that deter you. Some of my favorite streets are dead ends, often leading to a pot of gold: a trail through the woods, a fabulous view, an abandoned street right-of-way, or, best of all, a staircase to another level of the city. As a pedestrian your explorations are usually looked upon genially; in your car, you're a pest. I've found that it is not considered good form to investigate dead ends from a vehicle; inevitably a gardening homeowner will stand, rake in hand, staring disapprovingly as I back my car sheepishly out, past the clearly visible dead-end sign.

Past the homes at 5252 and 5220, built in the Stacked-Box Contemporary style of the 1960s and 1970s, you'll come to Northwood's own pot of gold: Keller Woodland. The woodland is a greenspace owned by the Three Rivers Land Conservancy, which promotes and preserves open space, scenic areas, wildlife habit, and other natural and historic resources in the Portland metro area. Ira Keller (1899–1979) once owned the approximate 40 acres and sold it to the Nature Conservancy, which wanted to preserve it as an example of a maturing Douglas fir forest with healthy seasonal streams. In 2002 the Nature Conservancy transferred ownership of the land to Three Rivers.

Where the street ends, take the wide, well-used path into a tunnel of overhanging green. The hardwood forest here is marred by a carpet of ivy, which, as in the case of many urban forests, has choked out the native groundcover. The trail is a street right-of-way for Northwood, which was cut through the woods here, as can be seen by the manhole covers on the trail, the cut slope, and the wide, level roadbed. It was never developed with homesites, however.

The trail ends at a backdoor entrance to the isolated and tony Hessler Hills neighborhood. Walk a short distance to a spectacular vista of the Willamette River, Portland's east side, and the Cascades. Stay on the road; the property is private and marked with a "no trespassing" sign.

Northwood bends around a ravine. Across the ravine at 4700 is a 1956 Colonial that was originally owned by Ira Keller, who retired here after a career in the paper industry. His retirement didn't last long: Keller then founded Western Kraft Corporation to recycle waste wood chips into paper products, and served as chairman of the Portland Planning Commission during a time of intense urban renewal activity (1959–1972). The Forecourt Fountain across from the Civic Auditorium was renamed the Ira C. Keller Fountain in 1978; it's at SW 3rd Avenue and Clay Street in downtown Portland.

Just past the intersection with SW Hessler Drive is the best vantage point on the route to see the much-altered outline of Ross Island. I know of no other publicly accessible view that shows so well the island's contours and inlets. The enormous lagoon within the island's boundaries is not a natural formation; since the 1920s it has been mined to stygian depths for its recent (geologically speaking) alluvium and for the enormous boulder, gravel, and sand deposits from the Missoula Floods. (See Walks 14 and 17 for more on the floods.)

In the 1890s, *Oregonian* editor Harvey Scott described Ross Island as the location of a bohemian houseboat community where "liberated ladies played ukuleles for gentlemen who recited poetry." In 1903 the Olmsted Brothers recommended the city purchase it for a park, recognizing how unique it would be to have a wilderness island within the city limits. Sporadic interest in developing it as a park ceased in the 1920s when Ross Island Sand and Gravel purchased the land. The name Ross Island refers to both Ross Island and Hardtack Island to the east, the two having been joined in 1926 by a berm built by the Army Corps of Engineers to help Ross Island Sand and Gravel with its mining. Before gravel mining operations swallowed the center of it, Ross Island consisted of 390 acres. About 150 acres remain; the lagoon created by the mining occupies about 150 acres. The perimeter is still in a wild state. The island and lagoon are slated for reclamation and a resumption of their old life as wildlife habitat after the last mining permit expires in 2005. The processing plant adjacent to the island now processes material from the company's Columbia River site.

The panoramic view, left to right, ranges from the Cascade foothills of Washington, to the Columbia River beyond the North Portland peninsula, to the Oregon Cascades. Rocky Butte is the first, northernmost Boring Lava dome on the Oregon side. It rises from the relatively flat plains of Northeast Portland. Southeast of it, the Boring Lava formations increase and coalesce, creating a rising plateau leading up to the Cascades. (See Walk 15 for more information on the Boring Lavas.)

James Hessler laid out the streets here during the 1940s to take advantage of the supreme views along the eastern flank of the West Hills. All of the approximately forty-two lots have deed restrictions to protect homeowners' views, and all residents are automatically members of the Hessler Hills Development Corporation. One lot was reserved for community use, and this is a tennis court. Although the neighborhood is visible from much of the east side, there is only one way into it (except for the path you just took), making it one of Portland's most isolated locales.

The view from Hessler Hills. Ross Island, with its immense lagoon, is in the foreground. (A large structure is moored within the body of the lagoon.) Boring Lava domes and Mount Hood lie beyond.

3 From Northwood, turn left onto SW Hessler Drive. The home at 1202 belonged to James Hessler. It was built in 1950 in the Northwest Regional style, and a sales brochure that I picked up noted that John F. Kennedy once dined here.

The road is steep; while you're charging up the hill, don't forget to turn around for more of the fine views. As the road curves upward, a bend suddenly places the Stonehenge radio tower right in front of you. Just below it is the apex of this hill walk. Where the road takes a sharp left turn, look to your right at 1215, with its Asian-accented landscape. This 1951 Northwest Regional home occupies a rare flat spot on the hill. At 900 feet, this property has it all: flat ground and big views.

Just before the intersection of SW Mitchell Street, you are on the cusp of two watersheds. Behind you all water flows east in a fairly direct route to the Willamette, then to the Columbia, and finally to the Pacific. In front of you water has to take a more circuitous journey to the sea: it flows down the western flanks of the Tualatin Mountains to the Tualatin Plains, and from there it makes a long journey to the Tualatin River, which flows into the Willamette at Willamette Park in West Linn.

Turn right on Mitchell. Your first view of the Tualatin Valley comes at 1626 SW Mitchell, where you can peer over the home's roof.

4 Turn right onto SW Fairmount Boulevard. There is no sidewalk here and the shoulder is small, but Fairmount is a well-known, 4-mile-long walking and biking route. It circumnavigates, about a hundred feet below the summits, the twin peaks of Council Crest. Cars have been trained by the hundreds of pedestrians who hike this street and are generally respectful of your presence. I recommend not using headphones, however, as the road is twisty and you need your ears.

After your quick glance at the Tualatin Plains, you're heading back to the eastern side of the West Hills. The walk along Fairmount is a mix of incredible scenery and ivy-cloaked dullness. Walk about 0.7 mile along Fairmount to SW McDonnell Terrace and turn left. Climb this steep little street, and at the intersection with SW Council Crest Drive, look back for a view of the green-accented Convention Center and the Lloyd district, with the control tower for Portland International Airport in the background.

If you want to get as close as possible to the summit, turn left onto Council Crest and then take a quick right onto SW Carl Place, a dead end. This intersection of Carl and Council Crest, at the top of the city, seems surprisingly unkempt. With its patched, raggedy-edged streets and a weedy common area between three streets, it looks more down-home than upscale.

Carl ends at the gatehouse for the Stonehenge radio tower, owned by American Tower. This 607-foot-high antenna was built in 1990 by rock radio station KGON; it also serves as a tower for microwave antennas and for other FM radio stations. In the late 1920s this hilltop was crowned with the largest electric sign in America, a huge neon advertisement for Richfield gasoline that was visible from Larch Mountain in the Columbia River Gorge. At that time Carl Place and Bernard Drive, which you'll soon trod, were muddy, rutted roads most notable for their use as lovers' lanes.

5 Walk back down Carl, take a left on Council Crest, and then turn left on SW Bernard Drive. This is the Healy Heights neighborhood. It was developed in the 1930s by Joseph Healy, who called it, a tad grandly, the Switzerland of America. Streets were named after various Healys: Carl, McDonnell, Patrick, and Bernard.

Healy Heights is a peaceful place. On a Monday morning in fall, I didn't see any people up here. Two dogs and a cat, roaming around lazily in the quiet streets, enjoyed the tiny diversion I created and accompanied me to the park for a game of fetch. Based on crime reports by the Portland Police, this is the city's safest neighborhood, with only two crimes in 2002: a car prowl and vandalism. It's also the smallest neighborhood, home to just 221 people.

In one block, turn right onto SW Patrick Place, and you'll soon come to Healy Heights Park. With its manicured grass, basketball court, and play structures, this 1.2-acre park feels more like someone's big, luxurious backyard than public property. On one visit, I noticed a peewee basketball hoop had been rolled out and left on the court for the neighborhood tots. (Don't try this at Laurelhurst Park!) Have a drink at the water fountain, and rest your bones on the benches in the luxurious quietude. This park, at 1000 feet, sits in the saddle between the 1073-foot peak at Council Crest Park to the north and the 1040-foot peak just off Carl Place. From here the walk starts to lead you back to the starting point.

Walk diagonally across the park, toward the baseball backstop, and exit. At the island turnaround at the corner of Council Crest Drive and Patrick Place, Joseph Healy planted trees when he developed his subdivision.

Begin walking west along Council Crest Drive. Turn left on SW Bertha Avenue. Once you leave the top of the hill, the neighborhood immediately takes on a different feel: less windswept and open, more sheltered and green. At the intersection of SW Hillsdale Avenue, stay left, on Bertha, and then turn right at the intersection with Fairmount. Now you're on the western side of the Fairmount loop, with sweeping views of the Tualatin Valley. Many of the contemporary homes here have stilt foundations, with nothing but crisp Northwest air whistling under them.

6 At the intersection of SW Wapato Avenue and Fairmount, a flight of wooden stairs leads down the ravine. Take them. The brown "SW Trails 1" sign here corresponds to the excellent walking map of the Southwest Hills created by the citizen-run SW Trails group and the Portland Office of Transportation. Route 1 on that map travels from the Willamette River to Scholls Ferry Road. These sixty-eight stairs end at a path that, when wet, can be slippery. On your way down, notice the unusual home to the left, with a stone foundation and exterior wall, and two levels of deck built with a hole to accommodate a bigleaf maple. The path ends at a woodsy street: SW Chesapeake Avenue. Turn left here.

At the intersection of Chesapeake and SW Melville Avenue, turn left onto Melville. At 4224 is a one-of-a-kind home, a neo-castle built of red brick and complete with an invader-thwarting spiked wrought-iron fence. Blue windows contrast whimsically with the brick, softening an otherwise stern façade. Just past the home at 4295 is a paved driveway with another SW Trails sign. Take the driveway to a series of staircases that lead down the western slope of Council Crest.

The stairs are uneven, so watch your step. On your way down you'll cross two unmarked streets: Chesapeake and Washouga. At Washouga, stay straight, and walk down what appears to be a driveway. This leads to SW Twombly Avenue; turn left, following the SW Trails sign.

7 Walk down Twombly half a block, turn left at SW Hamilton Street (ignoring the SW Trails sign), and take a right on SW 27th Avenue. After one block, turn left onto SW Hamilton Court—you'll be walking east, straight back toward the tower on the hill. The very cute, smallish homes here date from the 1950s and 1960s. You'll come to what appears to be a dead end. Ignore that perception and keep walking up a narrow, short path that leads to SW 25th Avenue. A seasonal stream to the left of the path makes a brief topside appearance beside a home before diving under the pavement.

At 25th, turn right (your only option), and where 25th intersects with SW Sunset Boulevard and 19th Drive, turn left onto 19th. This peaceful, sunny street of midrange, midcentury homes provides great views up the flanks of the mountain. The road climbs slightly to its junction with SW 18th Place. Walk straight on 18th downhill to SW Sunset Boulevard, where you'll turn left. This is a busy neighborhood arterial used by bikers and walkers, although there are no sidewalks. Straight ahead you can see the athletic fields at Wilson High. Walk 0.1 mile on Sunset, turn left at Dewitt, and walk back to the starting point.

If your stomach isn't rumbling after this walk, you must have brought snacks along. If you are hungry, a great way to end a visit to Hillsdale is at the Three Square Grill. Since 1995 chefs Barbara and David Barber have run this neighborhood gathering spot, which consistently wins high marks from critics. The restaurant specializes in American food—with the wide range in dishes that connotes—using local, artisan-quality ingredients. A burger here won't contain the meat of a hundred different cows, and the salmon won't have gotten its pink hue from red dye no. 2. The Barbers also make their own bread, pickles, lox, and desserts. Is there a better way to appreciate the Northwest than by spending a good chunk of the day outdoors, topped off by great local food? I can't think of one.

LAIR HILL TO OHSU LOOP

STARTING POINT SW Corbett Avenue and Lowell Street

DISTANCE 4 miles, or less with the SW Condor Lane shortcut

ELEVATION 190 feet at the starting point; 600 feet at the Homestead neighborhood

GETTING THERE AND PARKING From downtown Portland, drive south on SW Broadway. After you leave downtown, follow signs directing you to SW Barbur Boulevard. The last street in a series of turns is SW Sheridan. The next right puts you on Barbur. Turn left at the stoplight at SW Hamilton Street. Drive one block to SW Corbett Avenue. Turn left on Corbett and drive two blocks north to SW Lowell Street. Park along the street.

TriMet: From downtown, take bus 12 (Barbur Boulevard) to the stop at SW Barbur and Hamilton Street. Cross Barbur and walk one block east to Corbett. Turn left and walk two blocks north to the corner of Corbett and Lowell.

RESTROOMS AND DRINKING FOUNTAINS Restrooms and drinking fountains can be found at Lair Hill Park, OHSU, and the intersection of SW Terwilliger Boulevard and Hamilton Street (just south of the hill walk route).

FOOD AND DRINK Marquam Café is located on the third floor of OHSU Hospital.

NOTE This hill walk includes two crossings of Barbur Boulevard that are made at uncontrolled intersections. Barbur is a major city arterial with a 35-mile-per-hour speed limit that is usually ignored. Don't undertake this walk unless you

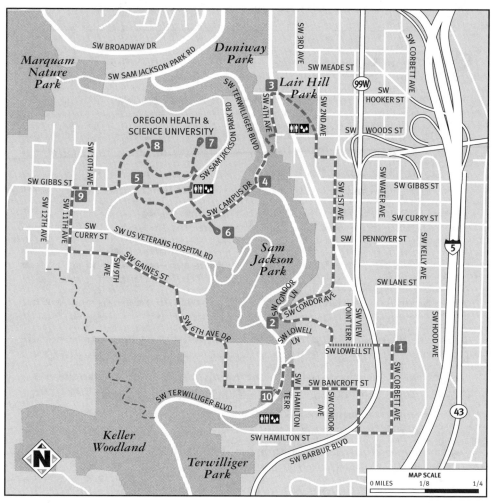

WALK 8. *Lair Hill to OHSU Loop*

MAP KEY

- ■ ▪ ROUTE
- ▪▪▪▪▪ STAIRS
- ▪ ▪ TRAILS
- ▦▦▦ RAILROAD TRACKS
- PARKS/GREENSPACE
- 🚻 PUBLIC RESTROOMS
- 🌊 WATER
- ♟ BUS STOP

Map labels:

SW BROADWAY DR
SW SAM JACKSON PARK RD
Duniway Park
SW 3RD AVE
SW MEADE ST
SW CORBETT AVE
Marquam Nature Park
SW TERWILLIGER BLVD
Lair Hill Park
99W
SW HOOKER ST
SW 4TH AVE
SW 2ND AVE
OREGON HEALTH & SCIENCE UNIVERSITY
SW WOODS ST
SW 10TH AVE
SW SAM JACKSON PARK RD
SW GIBBS ST
SW CAMPUS DR
SW 1ST AVE
SW WATER AVE
SW GIBBS ST
SW CURRY ST
SW 12TH AVE
SW 11TH AVE
SW CURRY ST
SW US VETERANS HOSPITAL RD
Sam Jackson Park
SW PENNOYER ST
SW KELLY AVE
I-5
SW 9TH AVE
SW GAINES ST
SW CONDOR LN
SW CONDOR AVE
SW LANE ST
SW 6TH AVE DR
SW VIEW POINT TERR
SW LOWELL LN
SW HOOD AVE
SW LOWELL ST
SW BANCROFT ST
SW CORBETT AVE
Keller Woodland
SW TERWILLIGER BLVD
SW HAMILTON TERR
SW CONDOR AVE
43
SW HAMILTON ST
Terwilliger Park
SW BARBUR BLVD
N

MAP SCALE
0 MILES   1/8   1/4

can confidently and quickly cross busy streets or want to take the detours noted in the text that lead to Barbur's stoplight-controlled intersections.

SAVE THIS WALK FOR A CLEAR DAY. Oregon Health and Science University (OHSU) sits high above the city. From it, views to the east, especially from an aerial walkway suspended above a canyon, are superb.

This hill walk starts in the Corbett Terwilliger Lair Hill neighborhood, an area of the city that has found itself often in the path of progress. In earlier times the homes and businesses of this neighborhood were sacrificed to major north-south arteries like Barbur Boulevard, Interstate 5, and Macadam Avenue, and to the swooping, freeway-style approaches to the Ross Island Bridge. This makes walking tours a challenge: it seems that every time you get going in a nice section of the neighborhood, you're faced with four or more whizzing lanes of traffic to negotiate. On this walk I have tried to minimize crossings of major roads, while still highlighting the area's historic streets and buildings and its hillside views. The path of progress has again cut through the neighborhood—this time, up in the air. The Portland aerial tram extends over the neighborhood, leading from a new riverfront development district up to OHSU.

Because of its proximity to OHSU and downtown, parking in the Corbett Terwilliger Lair Hill neighborhood is a challenge; most streets have a two-hour visitor limit during weekdays. When creating this hill walk, I started in Lair Hill and drove south on Corbett Avenue until I could find a place to park that wouldn't force me to run the route at top speed in order to get back to the car within two hours. I found a delightful starting point at the intersection of Corbett and Lowell; there are no time limits on parking here, and you'll find an auspicious omen in the form of a sculpture called "Admirable Bird," which soars from the roof of an 1898 Queen Anne. The sculptor is Keith Jellum, whose works can be found at the University of Oregon and in many local public places.

1 From Lowell and Corbett, walk west (uphill) on Lowell. In one block you'll run into SW Barbur Boulevard, which is unpleasantly wide and fast. Barbur is the western boundary of Corbett Terwilliger Lair Hill and the start of the Homestead neighborhood. It follows the path of a rail line that once ran from Portland to the Tualatin Valley. Walk a few feet south on Barbur until you're directly across from the end of an old iron-fenced median between the lanes. Wait for a traffic break, and then walk to the median; look carefully before you cross the last lanes of the road. Walk north a bit on Barbur to twenty-nine steps that are the continuation of Lowell Street. (To cross Barbur at a stoplight, walk two blocks south to SW Hamilton Street. Cross here, and walk back on SW View Point Terrace to the Lowell Street steps. See the map.)

The Lowell steps lead to a steep sidewalk, adjacent to the old Lowell Street right-of-way; you can still see the old curbs, now an archeological remnant, cradled on both sides by green lawn. Residents here have used the street space well: vegetable patches, lawn, and orchard trees now thrive in a sheltered nook where cars once rolled. The views behind you of the Willamette River and east side buttes are already superb. Cross SW View Point Terrace, and continue up the very steep sidewalk.

You'll emerge from the sidewalk onto SW Condor Avenue. Turn right and follow the road past a home at 3990 with elements of both Japanese and Northwest styles. Its perch does indeed have condorlike views. The road plunges into the folds of the hillside, following the contours of a ravine and giving nice views above the treetops of downtown along its southern flank. As the road begins to fold out of the hillside, look up the slope. The ravine above Condor has been filled in to support Terwilliger Boulevard, which follows the same curves slightly up the hill.

2 For a shortcut to OHSU, turn left onto SW Condor Lane. Follow it 0.1 mile to SW Terwilliger Boulevard, turn right, and walk along an extremely scenic portion of Terwilliger about 0.3 mile to SW Campus Drive. Turn onto Campus, and from there rejoin the walk at route junction 4.

Past Condor Lane, Condor Avenue begins to drop and the views become less condorlike. At the intersection of SW Lane Street, stay left on Condor as it heads north toward the towers of downtown. Its character changes here to condominiums and commercial buildings. Walk on the elevated sidewalk on the western side of the street. This part of Portland was settled by Italian immigrants and was called Little Italy in the early 1900s. The home at 3625 was purchased in 1911 by Antonio Liberto. He and his son Rosario bought the five adjacent homes and turned the hillside into a community reminiscent of an Italian village. They terraced the hill, planted gardens and vineyards, built an outdoor clay bread oven, and in the basement at 3625, processed their grapes in a 600-gallon vat. Liberto's home and the properties adjoining it share massive old stone walls.

Condor drops you down at the intersection of SW Pennoyer Street (named for nineteenth-century Oregon Governor Sylvester Pennoyer), SW 1st Avenue, and Barbur. Carefully cross Barbur again; the sight distance to oncoming traffic is good here. (To cross at a light, walk north on Barbur to SW Hooker Street.)

Begin walking north on SW 1st Avenue. You're back in the Lair Hill neighborhood; all the streets crossed from here until Lair Hill Park are named for nineteenth-century Oregon governors. As you cross SW Curry Street, note the sweet little triangular patch of flowers on the spot where it was cut off by Barbur, a good example of making lemonade from lemons.

SW Gibbs is the street over which the aerial tram line stretches. Turn left on Grover, which appears to be just a gravel parking lot, though it is marked with a sign, and then right on SW 2nd Avenue. From 3138 to 3122 are four pleasant, identical homes, vintage 1908 in the American Basic style. Cross SW Woods Street. On your right, at 3030, is the 1910 settlement house called Neighborhood House, originally owned by the National Council for Jewish Women to help immigrants from Europe find community in their new city.

The large red-brick building across the street at 3037 was built in 1918 to house nurses who worked at the Multnomah County Hospital next door. This, the city's first public hospital, was originally a mansion belonging to Charles F. Smith; Smith donated it to the county in 1909. Despite a design ill-suited for patient care, the house was used as a hospital until 1923, when the building, reputedly rat-ridden, was torn down.

In 1928 Lair Hill Park was dedicated on the vacant grounds of the Smith estate, and in 1949 the nurses' building became the Children's Museum, which resided here until 2001 when it moved to the old Oregon Museum of Science and Industry (OMSI) building at Washington Park. Today, because the building requires cost-prohibitive seismic upgrades, it is used only for storage of city documents.

Later in this hill walk you will pass Multnomah County Hospital's elegant replacement, which was built in the 1920s on the OHSU campus.

Stroll along the path that leads under old elms, cedars, maples, and redwoods to the park's northwestern corner. At 2nd and Hooker you'll see the former South Portland Library, built in 1918 with elements of the Mediterranean and Georgian styles. This was a Carnegie library, one of twenty-five hundred libraries funded by Andrew Carnegie between 1880 and 1919, not just in the United States but worldwide, including Fiji, the Seychelles, and Mauritius. Carnegie was a railroad and steel tycoon who gave away 90 percent of his fortune. The building was a library until 1954 and now houses offices of Portland Parks and Recreation.

3 At the stoplight at SW Hooker Street, cross Barbur. The park north of Hooker on the western side of Barbur is called Duniway Park, after one of Portland's most passionate women, Abigail Scott Duniway. She was born in 1834 to a family whose mother lamented the birth of each new girl, knowing the hard life she would face. Many sisters later, a brother arrived—Harvey Scott, destined to become the editor of the *Oregonian*. The rejoicing at her brother's birth made a huge impact on Abigail, as did the circumstances of her marriage. Her husband committed her without her knowledge or consent to a business deal that led to their financial ruin. Consequently, Abigail took over. As Mr. Duniway stayed home to tend the house and children, his wife taught, ran a boarding school, managed a millinery store, wrote novels, and in 1871 founded the *New Northwest*, a weekly paper dedicated to women's rights.

Duniway fought for nearly half a century for women's suffrage. When the Oregon constitution was finally amended in 1914 to provide equal rights for women, Abigail, naturally, was the first woman in line to register to vote. She died within a year, at age eighty-one. Duniway School in the Eastmoreland neighborhood is also named for her.

A few steps beyond this intersection, turn left onto SW 4th Avenue, another hidden gem of a street that's invisible to cars zipping by on Barbur. Where 4th intersects with a tiny stub of Woods Street, you'll see a narrow footpath uphill into the woods. The trail is somewhat steep and not pretty, but its width is open and not choked by the prevailing ivy—testimony to heavy use. A climb through the woods delivers you to SW Terwilliger Boulevard, just north of the main road into the OHSU campus. Terwilliger is designated a scenic parkway; it can never be expanded to accommodate more traffic. It was laid out in 1911 on an abandoned railroad right-of-way as a route that showcased many of the city's views.

4 Walk left on the paved path for runners, bikers, and joggers along Terwilliger, and then cross Terwilliger at the painted crosswalk at SW Campus Drive. Walking along Campus Drive, you'll soon pass under the 1991 Casey Eye Institute. At OHSU, architects never let something like a street get in their way; they simply build right over them. And in the case of the aerial tram, they build right over the entire neighborhood.

This area is known as Marquam Hill, named for Philip Marquam, who came to Oregon in 1851 and prospered through practicing law and buying real estate. In 1881 he platted out the first development on Marquam Hill, the Homestead neighborhood, which sits on the hillside above OHSU. Although it was here first, the Homestead neighborhood has been massively upstaged by its neighbor downslope. Located at a dead end and surrounded on three sides by forest, Homestead is hard to access. Many Portlanders have never even heard of it. You'll pass through it after leaving the OHSU campus.

OHSU, the largest employer in Portland, has a three-pronged mission. The first prong is patient care, which involves four hospitals—OHSU Hospital and Doernbecher Children's Hospital, and the separately owned Veterans Affairs Medical Center and Shriners Hospital for Children—and a panoply of outpa-

The highly engineered OHSU campus. Doernbecher Children's Hospital spans the canyon between the two hills on campus, as does the world's longest enclosed pedestrian bridge, seen at the top of the photograph.

tient buildings. The second prong is teaching, which takes place through five schools: the School of Dentistry, the School of Nursing, the School of Medicine, and the College of Pharmacy, all on Pill Hill (as this area is sometimes called); and the Oregon Graduate Institute for Science and Technology in Hillsboro. The third prong is research, carried out in buildings like the Center for Research on Occupational and Environmental Toxicology (CROET), the Vollum Institute (biomedical research), and the Mark O. Hatfield Research Center (both basic and clinical research). The university is increasingly research-based. In 2003 it received $257 million in research awards, three times the amount awarded in 1995. Most of the research money comes from the National Institutes of Health and the National Science Foundation.

After you pass underneath the Casey Eye Institute, a 0.12-mile-long aerial walkway appears between the Veterans Affairs Medical Center and OHSU Hospital. You'll soon be up there, where the views are as birdlike as you can get without paying airfare. Casey opened in 1991 and was named for James and George Casey, who as teenagers in Seattle in 1906 founded a company they would later rename United Parcel Service.

When you walk up the steep canyon on Campus Drive, the effect is majestic —so many buildings crowding the slopes above you, all devoted to the advance-

An aerial view of Southwest Portland, circa 1933. OHSU is in the top left quadrant. The Multnomah County Hospital and Mackenzie Hall are visible in a hilltop clearing at OHSU; note the forested canyon now spanned by the aerial walkway and home to Doernbecher Children's Hospital, the Casey Eye Institute, and other OHSU buildings. SW Barbur Boulevard runs along the foot of the hills, over a high pile of fill in Marquam Gulch. When this photograph was taken, the area now home to Duniway Park had not yet been filled in, and Interstate 5 had not yet cut its swath through the neighborhood. Photo courtesy of the City of Portland Archives.

ment of science and the amelioration of suffering. Even a Luddite would have to admire the engineering feats that placed all these buildings on this steep hillside. The construction seems unending, and its din is one of Pill Hill's signature sounds. Among the newer buildings is an outpatient care facility located to the right of Casey, uphill. Construction began in 2003.

Walk past the School of Dentistry and beneath the Doernbecher Children's Hospital, which spans the canyon nine stories above you. Cross in front of the Mark O. Hatfield Research Center, named for the widely admired Oregon politician who served as governor from 1959 to 1967 and as U.S. senator from 1967 to 1997. Walk toward the Hatfield Research Center, and take a wheelchair ramp on the left up to a set of twenty-seven stairs behind the Fitness and Sports Center. Walk behind the center, and take forty-three old wooden steps up to a gravel path. Walk left on the path toward the steamy hubbub of the physical plant building. Here, like the four satellite dishes turning their faces to the unobstructed southeast, you gain an open view across the canyon. The large old brick building off to the right was the State Tuberculosis Hospital when it was built in 1939. Today it is the Campus Services Building. Walk by two of the dishes to a set of sixty-three concrete steps. Climb these and some ramps to the concrete-and-glass Biomedical Information Communication Center (BICC), the main library for the campus. Walk around BICC's western side and you'll wind up at the intersection of SW U.S. Veterans Hospital Road and Sam Jackson Park Road.

Sam Jackson was the editor of the *Oregon Journal* from 1902 to 1924, in the days when there were four daily newspapers in Portland, resulting in a true diversity of perspective in news reporting. Today only one daily remains: the *Oregonian*.

5 Turn right on Sam Jackson, and walk east; pass the front of BICC, then veer right to head up the walkway into the Hatfield Research Center. Once inside, take the long hallway on the left that leads out of Hatfield and into the lobby of OHSU Hospital, which is actually on the ninth floor of that building. Turn right, and walk past the gift shop. At the end of the hall, go left, following the signs to "VA Hospital."

The aerial walkway in front of you is the longest closed, climate-controlled pedestrian walkway in the world. It was built in 1992 to transport patients, visitors, and hospital employees between OHSU Hospital and the Veterans Affairs Medical Center. Before then, patients needing treatment in one of the two buildings had to be loaded into an ambulance at hospital number one, driven down the road, and wheeled into hospital number two. The walkway facilitates not only patient and staff traffic but also the delivery of lab reports, which whiz between the two hospitals through pneumatic tubes in the exposed ceiling.

From the walkway, looking left, you'll see OHSU Hospital. Windows on its lower floors are narrow and prisonlike, reflecting the prevailing medical philosophy of the 1950s, when patients' opinions weren't a big concern. The top floors, with their expansive windows, came later and suggest a new era of health care with greater consideration for patients' preferences.

On the western side of the walkway is the Doernbecher Children's Hospital, completed in 1998. The original Doernbecher building, which you'll see a bit later on the walk, was the first children's hospital in the Northwest; today Doernbecher specializes in cancer treatment. The other children's hospital on the hill, Shriners, specializes in treatment of musculoskeletal disorders.

6 The view east from the walkway is classic Portland: Mount Hood rising above east side buttes. But in this setting this natural beauty is somehow more striking, as you contrast the vastness of the view with the unnaturalness of walking in space above a canyon. Two Willamette River bridges are seen here: on the left is the Marquam Bridge, a double-decker freeway bridge built in 1966, and to the right of that, upriver, is the Ross Island Bridge, built in 1926. To the right of the Marquam is OMSI, with its signature red smokestack and half-submerged submarine.

The Portland aerial tram is viewable from the walkway. It leads from OHSU's Patient Care Facility, just uphill and north of the Casey Eye Institute, to the South Waterfront District via the airspace over SW Gibbs Street. It rides from 77 to 165 feet above the ground and gains 498 vertical feet as it travels from river to mountain. OHSU, short on buildable space and parking, and with long-term plans to expand its research facilities, will occupy approximately 8 acres of the 120-acre South Waterfront District along the Willamette River, a former area of heavy industry. The district, which had long languished under the logistical issues of its toxic past, is being revived as the next phase in Portland's meticulously planned urban development, with narrow skyscrapers that allow for views between them, and dense commercial and residential use.

The tram has two cars, each of which can carry eighty people. The 0.6-mile ride lasts just under three minutes and is open to anyone holding a TriMet bus or MAX ticket. The tram's location, over a densely built cityscape, is a world first. Architect Sarah Graham created the winning design. Though now a resident of Switzerland and California, Graham once lived in the Lair Hill neighborhood over which the tram passes.

The tram is not the first in the city. From 1926 through 1974 an aerial tram carried sand and gravel from Ross Island in the Willamette River to the foot of SE Boise Street, where it was loaded up and distributed throughout the city.

When you're done looking around this intensely engineered scene, retrace your steps and return to the lobby. Inside the lobby is a fine exhibit that conveys Mark Hatfield's passion for making public healthcare available to all people, not just the middle and upper classes, in order to build stable, thriving societies. Without his long Senate experience and chairmanship of the Senate Appropriations Committee, many of the buildings at OHSU would not have been built.

The Marquam Café in OHSU Hospital is a good place to stop for a bite. Restrooms are also located here.

Once outside OHSU Hospital, an elevated walkway carries you above Sam Jackson Park Road. Cross the street and turn right for a stroll past the earliest campus buildings. Follow the walkway around the right side of the OHSU

Clinics (also known as the University Clinics) building. The Physicians Pavilion is on the right, the only campus building constructed with private funds. Its owner leases the building to OHSU.

7 The lovely old building with the green tile wings at the end of the courtyard is the Multnomah Pavilion. When finished in 1926, it was the second building constructed on the campus and replaced the first county hospital. The building functioned as the county hospital until 1973, when it was renamed University Hospital North, and OHSU assumed the county's role of providing care to the public. Today, 40 percent of OHSU's patients receive care for which the hospital is either completely or partially uncompensated. This compares to about 20 percent for private hospitals statewide.

The building is described in the Portland Historic Resource Inventory as having a buff-colored brick exterior with a decorative glazed terra-cotta roof cornice. It has a frieze with flowers, garlands, and cross and herringbone patterns. Its colossal entrance portico is topped by a cast-iron railing, and the three-story polygonal bays are faced with polychrome-glazed terra-cotta. *Terra-cotta*, meaning "baked earth" in Italian, refers to any fired clay. The first glazed terra-cotta such as this appeared in the 1400s; its use as an architectural accent was revived in the early twentieth century. You'll see more of this beautiful material on Mackenzie Hall.

Retrace your steps out of the courtyard. Turn right at the OHSU Clinics building, and walk uphill toward more buildings from OHSU's early days. On the right, with the green windows, is Dillehunt Hall, built in 1926 as the first Doernbecher Children's Hospital. Visiting restrictions were draconian in the 1920s: Sunday afternoons, from 2:00 to 5:00, parents only.

Doernbecher Children's Hospital was funded from a bequest in the will of Frank Doernbecher. His Doernbecher Manufacturing Company started making furniture in 1900. Doernbecher pioneered mass production within the furniture industry, and also found economies in vertical integration; he owned the timberlands that produced the wood for his factories. His plant on NE 28th Avenue, adjacent to Sullivan's Gulch, was at one time the largest in the nation.

Next is Baird Hall, where the president of OHSU has offices. Turn toward it and then up six steps to the sidewalk in front of Mackenzie Hall, the first building on the campus. It originally consisted only of what is now the east wing. Called the University of Oregon Medical School, it was designed in 1919 by Ellis Lawrence. The central block was built in 1921, the west wing in 1938.

Glazed terra-cotta carvings of pinecones and boughs provide rich elements to an otherwise plain building, as do the elaborate carvings of winged serpents, medallions, and human figures along the top. A repeated theme on Mackenzie is the staff of Aesculapius. He was the Greek god of medicine, having learned the arts of healing from the centaur Chiron. Aesculapius is often shown holding a staff with a single serpent coiled around it.

A similar emblem, the caduceus, has been confused with the staff of Aesculapius and is also used, erroneously, as a medical symbol. Featuring two intertwined snakes, the caduceus was not the staff of a healer but of Hermes, messenger of the gods. (Right or wrong, the caduceus is the emblem of the U.S. Army Medical Corps.)

Mackenzie is fronted by a lovely patch of lawn and trees, a welcome respite in this island of brick, stone, and concrete. From the front door, you can see across the West Hills to Healy Heights, with its enormous radio tower.

8 Walk in through the front door of Mackenzie, head straight through the hall, and exit through the back door into a courtyard. Here you are surrounded by, from right to left, the Medical Research Building, the Vollum Institute, and the Basic Science Building, where medical students spend most of their first two years of study. The Vollum Institute was funded by Howard and Jean Vollum. Howard Vollum cofounded Tektronix in 1945. The Vollums have contributed to many Oregon causes, including the Native American Student and Community Center at PSU.

Walk through the courtyard, past the Center for Research on Occupational and Environmental Toxicology (CROET), where researchers study the effects of pesticides and Gulf War Syndrome issues, among other things. Here is a large marble sculpture, consisting of half a human head resting atop symbols of human inventiveness and creativity. This sculpture, along with most of OHSU's campus art, was funded through a 1975 state mandate that new or renovated public buildings devote 1 percent of construction costs to public art. If the state-mandated figure had been 2 percent, one employee mused, perhaps the sculptor could have completed an entire head.

In front of CROET, take some stairs back into the courtyard fronting Mackenzie. This will put you in front of the university's first library building, now the OHSU Auditorium. In 1938 Ellis Lawrence designed this building in the Early Modern style. Its jewels include cast-bronze and art-glass light fixtures on the exterior and decorative green molded-concrete accents. The windows and doors are stunning, with bronze mullions. According to the Historic Resource

Inventory, the original terrazzo floor and decorative wood moldings continued the elegance. I could not find the terrazzo; perhaps it is under the linoleum tile.

Walk outside the auditorium and turn right. Head down a ramp to SW Gibbs Street, just below its intersection with SW 9th Avenue.

9 Turn right, walk uphill two blocks on Gibbs, and turn left onto SW 11th Avenue. This collection of streets is the Homestead neighborhood. When Philip Marquam platted it, he laid all the streets on a perfect grid, like those of the city's relatively flat east side. Either he hadn't noticed how hilly the land was or he intended to engineer it into flatness. Because of difficulties of access and topography, the neighborhood never thrived to the extent of nearby Portland Heights or Council Crest. Today many of the originally platted streets have never been built, and streets with curbs and sidewalks sit next to unpaved, unimproved lanes. For neighborhood residents, the upside to living in a residential backwater is that they are surrounded, except on the east, by open space and hiking trails. Two thirds of the housing in this neighborhood is occupied by renters, many of them students.

Turn left at SW Gaines Street, which soon takes you out of Homestead. At 9th and Gaines is Gaines Hall, built in 1930 as a dormitory for medical students.

Turn right at SW 6th Avenue Drive and leave the OHSU campus. This is a quiet wooded street, cool and welcome after the noise of the campus. It ends at SW Bancroft Street. Cross Bancroft to stay on its lower, southern section, and follow the sidewalk down to its end, where steps lead to Terwilliger.

10 Turn left onto Terwilliger and walk a few hundred feet to the intersection with SW Hamilton Terrace. Turn right. Next to this intersection is SW Lowell Lane, a dead end. At the end of Lowell is a relatively new home, located at a landmark called Eagle Point (elevation 430 feet). In the city's list of scenic viewpoints and vistas, this point was ranked as a highly desirable civic acquisition, since it is the highest easternmost point in the West Hills. Before the point could be acquired for the public, it was purchased and developed.

Walk down Hamilton Terrace. Turn left on Bancroft, a very steep downhill. This street has lovely homes; but the paucity of trees, while enhancing the view, makes it seem rather stark. Turn right on SW View Point Terrace and walk south about one block to the intersection with Barbur. Turn left, and cross Barbur at the stoplight at Hamilton. Walk downhill on Hamilton two blocks to Corbett, and turn left. Head north for two more blocks, back to the starting point at Corbett and Lowell.

Before returning to your car, you may want to check out the Contemporary Crafts Gallery at 3934 SW Corbett, two blocks north of Lowell. It was founded in 1937 by a group of women whose mission was to foster an appreciation for fine craftsmanship while providing a market for artists. The atmosphere is mellow, and the art and crafts, in both permanent and changing exhibits, are superb. Most items, except in the permanent exhibits, are for sale.

WILLAMETTE PARK TO TERWILLIGER LOOP

STARTING POINT Willamette Park: one block east of SW Nebraska Street and Macadam Avenue

DISTANCE 3.75 miles

ELEVATION 10 feet at the starting point; 500 feet at the small peak at SW California Street and 3rd Avenue

GETTING THERE AND PARKING From downtown Portland, drive south on SW Naito Parkway. After the stoplight at SW Clay Street, stay in the right lane to avoid turning onto the freeway. After leaving downtown and crossing SW Sheridan Street, take the right-lane exit for Highways 43 and 26. Immediately get in the right lane and follow signs to SW Macadam Avenue and Lake Oswego. (Macadam is Highway 43.) Once on Macadam, turn left at the stoplight at SW Nebraska Street and head one block toward the river, to the entrance of Willamette Park. Park in the parking lot. A $3 vehicle fee is charged at Willamette Park from Memorial Day weekend through Labor Day weekend.

TriMet: From downtown, take bus 40 (Tacoma) to the stop at SW Nebraska and Macadam. Walk one block east on Nebraska to Willamette Park.

RESTROOMS AND DRINKING FOUNTAINS Restrooms and drinking fountains are located at Willamette Park on the southern side of the parking lot and inside the Fulton Park Community Center during center hours, Monday through Friday and Saturday mornings.

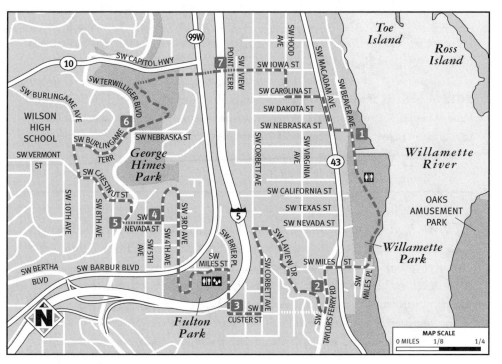

WALK 9. *Willamette Park to Terwilliger Loop*

MAP KEY
- ▪ ▬ ROUTE
- ⋮⋮⋮⋮⋮ STAIRS
- – – TRAILS
- ⊢⊣⊣ RAILROAD TRACKS
- PARKS/GREENSPACE
- 🚻 PUBLIC RESTROOMS
- ◆◆ WATER
- 🍷 BUS STOP

FOOD AND DRINK Café du Berry is located near the starting point, 6439 SW Macadam Avenue; 503-244-5551. Across the street is the Fulton Pub and Brewery, 0618 SW Nebraska Street; 503-246-9530. There is a snack bar at Fulton Park Community Center, situated midway through the walk at 68 SW Miles Street; 503-823-3180.

NOTE A portion of this hill walk is through quiet, heavily wooded George Himes Park. This park is well used, but the trails are isolated, especially when hiking in the canyon below the Barbur and Interstate 5 overpasses. Use your discretion about hiking alone.

THIS WALK PROVIDES A REAL FEELING OF ACCOMPLISHMENT. It starts at the river and climbs the eastern flank of the Tualatin Mountains to a high point at Terwilliger Boulevard, with vistas opening up at just about every level in between. Another bonus is walking in a canyon far below the whizzing Interstate 5, a rare and surprisingly beautiful experience. Take this walk in the summer or fall, when you can dip your toes in the Willamette, and then climb to the sights and smells of the charming Fulton Community Garden.

1 From the parking lot in Willamette Park, walk south along the river on the paved path. You're on part of the 40-Mile Loop, so be watchful for zipping bipeds. This park was envisioned by the Olmsted Brothers, who described it as a "beautiful stretch of low but undulating grassy land," adding that "most of the land is subject to be flooded." They noted that if this was not used as a park, the city would likely undergo the "enormous" expense of raising all the buildings and filling the streets and private lands. Both scenarios came true: the land became a park and was filled in, its undulations replaced by flat soccer fields.

Before Willamette Park was a park, nearby residents called it Carp Flats. According to Mid Barbour, a lifelong resident of the adjacent SW Miles Place, after spring high waters, carp would move into the flats to lay eggs. Neighborhood kids would catch the carp and carry them up to nearby Riverview Cemetery to sell to the Chinese gardeners. When the Vista Ridge Tunnel was excavated in the West Hills, excavation spoils were dumped here and the banks lined with riprap to prevent erosion.

Near the southern end of the park is a stand of old cottonwoods and a path down to the river's edge, where a stony outcrop just offshore invites exploration. Exit the park at SW Miles Place.

Looking north along SW Macadam Avenue, an aerial view of Willamette Park, formerly known as Carp Flats. This photo, probably taken in the 1930s, is a good illustration of the land at that time. The natural, uneven shoreline was prone to flooding before it was filled in with excavation spoils and the banks covered with riprap. Photo courtesy of the City of Portland Archives.

Miles Place is a historical and eclectic waterfront street, with many humble homes built in the days when a waterfront address didn't necessarily mean you were rich. Most Miles Place homes started out as houseboats further upriver. In the 1890s, floods lifted the floating homes off their supports and cast them adrift. To save their houses, the owners intercepted them downriver, hauled them to the western shore, and tied them to oak trees in this area. When the water receded, the homeowners squatted on the riverfront for years, and eventually bought their lots from the Ladd Estate Company, which owned the property. Each homeowner had to saw out the logs that had kept their houses afloat, and pour permanent foundations. After another catastrophic flood in 1948, many of the original homes were raised, with first floors installed below. Most

One of the old, original houseboats now founded on land on SW Miles Place. Oak trees serving as anchors saved it from being washed further downriver.

of the original houseboats have been transformed beyond recognition from the outside. I was invited into one by a friendly homeowner, and only inside were the houseboat bones readily apparent, in the small scale of the rooms, the low ceilings, and the generally unconventional layout.

The eight garages lined up side by side across the street attest to the street's early history as a houseboat moorage. The home at 7426 started out as two houseboats, which were joined in 1932. The owners of the home at that time owned the Orpheum Theater in downtown Portland. Miles Place ends at the Willamette Butterfly Park, part of the Willamette Greenway Trail system in Portland's 40-Mile Loop.

After investigating the charms of Miles Place, turn west onto SW Miles Street. Cross the railroad tracks. These tracks were built in 1888 by the Portland and Willamette Railroad Company to bring iron products manufactured in Oswego to Portland. In the 1910s and 1920s, after the smelting stopped, an interurban line carried commuters from the bedroom community of Oswego into the city. Passenger service ended in 1929, and freight service stopped in 1983. Today these tracks carry the Willamette Shore Trolley, a 7-mile run that offers a great way to tour backyards and back lots in Southwest Portland and Dunthorpe. The trolley runs spring through late summer, operated by the Oregon Electric Railway Historical Society. Rides take forty-five minutes each way, with stations at Lake Oswego and Portland. Call 503-697-7436 or visit www.trainweb.org for information about fares and stops.

Cross SW Macadam Avenue. The name *Macadam* and the word *tarmac* are both derived from John L. McAdam (1756–1836), a Scottish road builder who invented an elevated road surface made from layers of broken gravel that allowed water to drain away from the road. *Tarmac* comes from combining "tar" with "Macadam," reflecting a later improvement to macadamization, in which a layer of asphalt was applied to the top of the road surface. The Milwaukie Macadamized Road Company built this road in 1862 to a point now in the Dunthorpe neighborhood, opposite Milwaukie, Oregon. A ferry to Milwaukie at the road's end finished the trip. The ferry landing was at the White House, a roadside inn (see Walk 12), and for a time Macadam was called White House Road.

Follow signs for "SW Trails 4." After crossing over a street island, you're on SW Taylors Ferry Road. At this intersection a small community called Fulton sprang up, platted in 1888. Walk uphill on Taylors Ferry.

2 Cross the unmarked SW Virginia Avenue. You are leaving the floodplain of the Willamette River, where the land underfoot consists of alluvium from the Willamette and the Missoula Floods, and beginning to climb the eastern flanks of the Tualatin Mountains, which were formed by massive floods of another sort, the Columbia River Basalts.

Turn right at the next intersection, onto SW Laview Drive. You have a choice here: walk up steep Laview to SW Corbett Avenue, or, at the SW Trails sign, take the series of stairs, one hundred to be exact, that will lead you efficiently but much less scenically 180 vertical feet up to the intersection of Corbett and SW Custer Street.

But who could pass up a street named Laview? Besides its seductive name, Laview provides lots of reasons to stop and catch your breath as you savor its vistas. It climbs along the eastern face of the Tualatin Mountains; the area immediately downhill is too steep for streets, so the views from Laview are unobstructed.

Laview still sports its old cement paving. The homes here run a one-hundred-year gamut, and most are perched on narrow hillside slots, close to the road. Just past 7500 Laview is a view of Oaks Amusement Park across the river. (Walk 13 takes you along its seldom-walked and still-natural beachfront.) The tall building behind the park, with the faded heron mural, is the century-old Portland Memorial Funeral Home and Mausoleum. At the vacant lot at 7308 Laview is a broad view. From here you can see several Boring Lava domes, including, from left to right, Rocky Butte, Mount Tabor (above Ross Island), Kelly Butte, and Mount Scott (above Oaks Park). Beyond Mount Scott rises Mount Hood, part of the Cascade Range and the tallest point in Oregon at 11,240 feet. It is an active volcano, having last erupted in 1790.

Don't miss the house at 7185, on the uphill side. This small bungalow sits bravely and scenically on this windswept ridge amidst a grove of tall Douglas firs.

Laview ends at SW Nevada Street. If you, like me, crave new angles to view the city from, turn right and walk to the end of Nevada. From here, telephone wires dive down the face of the hill, and you can see upriver to Ross Island, the east side, the foothills of Washington, and Mount Saint Helens.

Walk up Nevada and turn left onto SW Corbett Avenue. Here you are at elevation 250 feet, halfway through the net elevation gain for this walk.

Corbett Avenue is named for Henry Corbett, a U.S. senator from Oregon in the late 1860s. This street runs from the southern edge of downtown Portland to Riverview Cemetery. In the blocks here, it is hard up against Interstate 5, and although the freeway is not visible, the noise slightly detracts from this otherwise lovely street. Across from 7128 Corbett is a hand-carved, mortarless, basalt-block retaining wall. It now borders a houseless lot that was gobbled up by the construction of Interstate 5 in the 1960s. The wall gently bulges, the load of hillside behind it pressing ever downward.

Walk three blocks on Corbett and turn right on SW Custer Street. At this intersection you're at the top of the steps that lead up the hill from Taylors Ferry. Mid Barbour recalls winter days as a child when she and her friends would slide on their bums down the snow-covered stairs after school at Fulton Park.

3 Cross SW View Point Terrace and follow the jog Custer takes to the right. Stay right on SW Brier Place, which crosses over Interstate 5. You might not have a problem figuring out how to get around in Southwest Portland, but I sure do; never having resided in that particular city quadrant, I have often been frustrated by the way the streets unexpectedly end, truncated by hill, valley, or highway. So finding Brier Place, a little gem of an egress from one level of the hills to another, simply made my day.

Turn left onto SW Miles Street, and you'll find yourself at the Fulton Park Community Center. Its age and former life as a public school are revealed in the charming terra-cotta details above the doorways. Carvings of open books, an hourglass, and other symbols lead you into a gymnasium still sporting a magnificent sheath of unpainted, 7-foot-high clear fir wainscoting. There were once classrooms on either side of the gym, each with an exit to the outdoors. Built in 1914, before cars started defining the urban landscape, this must have been a lovely, semirural place to learn.

At the driveway leading into the parking area, veer left and follow the gravel road that parallels Miles into the 2-acre Fulton Community Garden. This is one of twenty-five community gardens in Portland, open to anyone wanting to garden a 400-square-foot plot in exchange for a small annual fee. Water is available on-site. The Fulton Garden has been certified a National Wildlife Federation habitat, which means that gardening is done holistically, with wildlife in mind. Certain conventional gardening practices—use of chemical fertilizers, pesticides, and herbicides—are discouraged. Hence the slightly funky look of this garden: Butchart it's not. Portland's community gardens are real folks' gardens, warts and all. Stroll along the rows in late summer, and the thrum of bees, the glow of tomatoes, and the whiff of berries warmed by the sun give you three more reasons to love this city.

Exit the garden at SW 3rd Avenue. Cross SW Barbur Boulevard at the stoplight intersection with Miles. Jog back left to 3rd Avenue as it begins a long, steady ascent to the apex of this hill walk: a fairly symmetrical, well-defined peak at the top of this street. The house at the intersection with SW California Street, 6901, is just about at the top of the hill, elevation 500 feet. Walk east on California a few steps to its dead end for a fine view of the Willamette and the buttes on the east side. Again you can see Oaks Amusement Park. The water now visible behind it is a lake within the Oaks Bottom Wildlife Refuge that was created a century ago by the impoundment of water behind a levee built to support rail tracks. The clump of green south of Oaks Park is the heavily wooded Sellwood Park. (See Walk 13 for more information on this area.) In the Northwest, when in a strange city, you can often find a city park without a map by looking for a dense stand of Douglas firs.

After perusing the view, walk on 3rd as it curves around the northern side of the small peak. Here you get a view of Healy Heights and the distinctive red-and-white Stonehenge radio tower. The forested land drops away in front of you, bringing a momentary feeling of remoteness.

4 Somewhere along the curving road, SW 3rd Avenue turns into SW 4th Avenue, and you're heading south. Walk one block on 4th, and turn right onto SW Nevada Street. Nevada ends at SW 5th Avenue. Directly across from the intersection, to the right of the driveway at 7107, is a greenway path that leads to SW Terwilliger Boulevard. Walk down the indistinct path, a city right-of-way between two backyards, and turn right on Terwilliger.

You can either walk north on Terwilliger to the entrance of George Himes Park, or take a small loop that gets you off this busy street and into yet another hillside neighborhood.

If you stay on Terwilliger, cross SW Chestnut Street. Just north of here the Terwilliger Parkway begins, and you will walk on an asphalt path that sometimes falls below the road grade, into the woods, before leading you to George Himes Park. The route of the Terwilliger Parkway was recommended by the Olmsted Brothers in 1903. In 1909 heirs of James Terwilliger donated 19 acres of right-of-way through their property to help develop the scenic parkway envisioned by the Olmsteds.

5 To detour into the Hillsdale neighborhood, once you emerge from the greenway path onto Terwilliger, walk past two houses, and turn left on SW 6th Avenue. Turn left on Chestnut, a lovely wooded enclave of homes that encircle another peak in the hills. This neighborhood has a classic Northwest feel, with its tall firs and cedars. The blue water tanks on the left were placed high, at 570 feet, to take advantage of gravity. Ahead you can see Wilson High School, built on the site of the Fulton Park Dairy.

Turn right on SW Burlingame Avenue and then right on SW Burlingame Terrace, which leads you back down to Terwilliger. Across the road is George Himes Park, your next stop.

Far below Barbur Boulevard in a forested canyon within George Himes Park.

6 Cross Terwilliger into George Himes Park at SW Nebraska Street. George Himes came to work for the *Oregonian* in 1866 and later started his own publishing ventures. In 1898 he became the first curator of the newly formed Oregon Historical Society, a position that occupied him for the next forty years. This 35-acre park was dedicated to Mr. Himes in 1935, five years before his death. It is primarily undeveloped greenspace, save for a few trails.

As you walk into the park, take a wide trail that begins just behind the first picnic table and drops down into the woods. You're at the 460-foot elevation mark, and the rest of the hill walk drops you quickly down to river level. Stay straight when another trail enters from the left. Although many fir trees wear a coat of dead ivy, cut from the base of each trunk by volunteers, English ivy is still making serious in-roads into the native groundcover here. The native sword fern is not going down without a fight, however, as it elbows its fronds up and away from the clingy ivy embrace.

After the trail takes a hairpin turn, you'll cross a wooden bridge over a seasonal creek. At a trail junction, take the steps carved into the hill on your right. The sound on your left, on the slope above you, is the gentle whoosh of cars on SW Capitol Highway. Ahead, getting louder, is the din of Barbur Boulevard and Interstate 5, both of which soar about 80 feet above the canyon floor. The trail passes under the intricate wooden trusswork of the Barbur trestle, and then under the spare reinforced-concrete supports of the interstate bridge.

7 After passing beneath the two trestles, you'll notice several broad steps cut into the slope. Take these, which lead down onto SW Iowa Street at View Point Terrace to a Mary Poppins–esque view over the rooftops of the Johns Landing neighborhood. The freeway din is surprisingly subdued here, below the interstate grade, even during rush hour.

Walking east on Iowa, turn right on SW Hood Avenue and then left on SW Carolina Street. The Portland French Academy occupies the old Terwilliger School, a Portland public school. Walk east on Carolina and you'll pass a shop or two before coming to the shops and restaurants of Macadam. Turn right on Macadam, and try the Café du Berry or the beer garden at the Fulton Pub and Brewery for a well-deserved sit after a long hill walk. Café du Berry, under the same ownership since 1981, is a small, confidently unhip bistro with an unrushed atmosphere, wonderful food, and outdoor seating. The Fulton Pub and Brewery has been located at the corner of Nebraska and Macadam since 1926. It has always been a small neighborhood tavern, and its local flavor has remained intact since it was purchased in 1988 by the McMenamin brothers. Here you'll find pub fare and outdoor seating.

Walk east on Nebraska to return to the riverfront at Willamette Park.

MULTNOMAH VILLAGE TO VERMONT HILLS LOOP

STARTING POINT Gabriel Park parking lot: the dead end of SW Canby Street, immediately west of SW 40th Court

DISTANCE 3 miles

ELEVATION 400 feet at the starting point; 620 feet at the peak at SW 32nd Avenue and California Street; 580 feet at the peak between SW 37th and 40th Avenues; 320 feet at Gabriel Park, the low point in the walk

GETTING THERE AND PARKING From downtown Portland, drive south on SW Broadway. After you leave downtown, follow signs directing you to SW Barbur Boulevard. The last street in a series of turns is SW Sheridan. The next right puts you on Barbur. From Barbur's intersection with SW Hamilton Street, drive another 0.8 mile to a right-lane exit for Highway 10, Hillsdale, and Beaverton. This exit puts you on SW Capitol Highway. Drive through stoplights for SW Terwilliger and Sunset Boulevards and for a shopping center. At the stoplight for SW Bertha Court, stay in the left lane to remain on Capitol Highway. After passing the Mittleman Jewish Community Center, get in the left lane. At the stoplight with SW Vermont Street, veer left to remain on Capitol Highway as it starts to head south. (Staying straight would put you on Vermont.) Once in the Multnomah Village commercial district, turn right at SW 35th Avenue. In one block, turn left on SW Canby Street, drive four blocks to its dead end, and park in a parking lot at Gabriel Park.

TriMet: From downtown, take 45 bus (Garden Home) to the stop at SW Troy Street and 40th Avenue. Turn left on 40th and walk one block north to SW Canby Street, just east of the starting point.

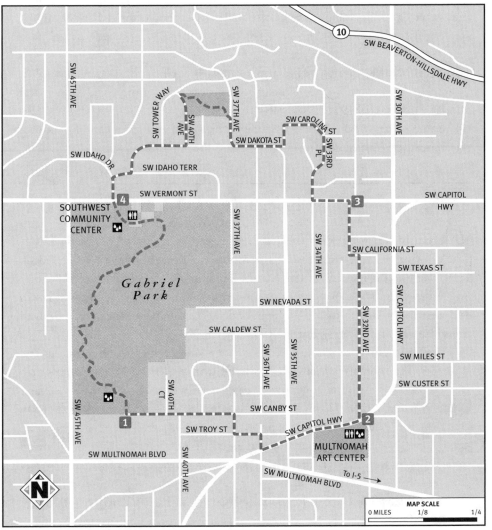

WALK 10. *Multnomah Village to Vermont Hills Loop*

MAP KEY

- ■■ ROUTE
- ⠿⠿ RAILROAD TRACKS
- ⠿⠿⠿ STAIRS
- PARKS/GREENSPACE
- – – TRAILS
- 🚻 PUBLIC RESTROOMS
- 💧 WATER
- 🚏 BUS STOP

RESTROOMS AND DRINKING FOUNTAINS Restrooms and drinking fountains can be found inside the Multnomah Art Center and the Southwest Community Center. A drinking fountain is at the southern end of Gabriel Park, near the starting point.

FOOD AND DRINK Marco's Café and Espresso Bar, located at 7910 SW 35th Avenue, is open Monday through Saturday for breakfast, lunch, and dinner, and Sunday for breakfast and lunch; 503-245-0199. Fat City Café, located at 7820 SW Capitol Highway, is open every day for breakfast and lunch, and Fridays for all-you-can-eat spaghetti dinners; 503-245-5457.

As with the Hillsdale neighborhood, this area was once dairy country, starting with the Raz family in the 1880s. These Swiss immigrants owned 93 acres just east of the Multnomah neighborhood. Their Fulton Park Dairy at 18th and Vermont later became the grounds of Reike Elementary and Wilson High School. Soon other dairies sprang up on the rolling hills south and west of the Raz farm. At the peak of the era there were seventeen dairies in the southwest hills around Portland.

The Multnomah neighborhood gets its name from the Oregon Electric Railroad's Multnomah Station, which was built in 1907 at 3535 SW Multnomah Boulevard. The station is gone; it sat across from what is now Marco's Café and Espresso Bar. Trains ran from Portland to Salem, and through this area they ran along the route of Multnomah Boulevard. In 1908, when Multnomah was developed, it was considered suburban, and it still has a semirural air, with many unpaved streets and larger lots. This rural character was part of its early attraction, as advertisements enticed new homeowners with the promise of "a little place of your own in the country to raise a garden and a few chickens."

This hill walk is relatively short, so you can spend time enjoying the considerable charms of the neighborhood's commercial district, Multnomah Village. Lined up along both sides of SW Capitol Highway east of SW 37th Avenue are shops selling antiques, art, crafts, books, toys, jewelry, clothes, coffee, and food. This is a hill walk to savor at a meandering pace. It might be best saved for a blustery day, when the east wind blows you around on the neighborhood's hilltops, and the shops in the village are a welcome respite.

1 Start at the parking lot adjacent to the southern end of Gabriel Park, once the site of a dairy. Begin walking east, uphill, on SW Canby Street, named for

General Edward Canby of the U.S. Army. In 1873 he was killed in California by Modoc Indians, who were resisting being removed to the Klamath reservation near Klamath Falls, Oregon.

Canby is an old fir-lined street of large lots, and like many streets in Multnomah, it saw new housing filling in its open spaces in the 1990s. As Portland kept its Urban Growth Boundary tightly drawn to prevent suburban sprawl, real estate developers began looking within the boundary for open lots to build on. This infill, as city planners call it, increases housing density, one of the city's goals. A great concept, but initially difficult for some longtime residents to accept when their quiet, parklike streets suddenly jump into the twenty-first century with large homes boasting three-car garages and sport courts. As a result of all the construction in the 1990s, one hundred years of age and architecture separate the homes in Multnomah.

Turn right onto SW 37th Avenue, left onto SW Troy Street, and right onto SW 36th Avenue. Don't miss the fir tree at the northeastern corner of 36th and Troy. This tree started growing in the 1920s, after the area had been logged of its old-growth timber. With its perfectly aligned triple trunks, it looks something like an enormous candelabrum. In the 1930s the *Oregonian* reported on it, calling it "the tree that grew like a harp," and even *Ripley's Believe It or Not* picked up the story.

From the tree, walk half a block to the intersection with SW Capitol Highway. This road was first paved in 1915 so that dairy farmers in Hillsdale could deliver milk to customers in West Portland, west of Multnomah. It was named Capitol Highway because it headed in the direction of Oregon's capitol, Salem. The overpass just west of here was built in 1927 after several fatal wrecks occurred between cars on Capitol Highway and the trains that used to run along Multnomah Boulevard.

This is the heart of Multnomah Village, a commercial district that offers a leisurely few hours of shopping, talking, and eating. Shops begin one block west, at the Capitol Highway overpass of Multnomah Boulevard, with the densest concentration in the six blocks northeast along Capitol to SW 31st Avenue. Although we Americans are expected to express our patriotism through the copious consumption of nonessential items, I find that malls and other venues designed to separate me from my money induce the opposite effect. Shopping in Multnomah Village feels different. These stores are owned by locals who have demonstrated a commitment to promoting artists and craftspeople. Annie Bloom's Books has been here since 1978, Marco's Café and Espresso Bar since 1983. Beyond Borders features fair-trade crafts, and Indigo Traders sells the work of women in the Middle East. Multnomah Village could be accused of gentrification, since bookstores, antique markets, and gift shops inhabit buildings where at one time groceries were sold, tools were sharpened, and fire trucks were stored, but the gentrification seems to be organic and hodgepodge rather than carefully focus-group driven, as it can be in other retail environments.

Just west of 36th, at 7875 SW Capitol, is the tiny original Multnomah Lending Library, built in 1937. Walk east and you'll encounter at 7814 an art gallery in a 1923 building constructed in the Zig-Zag Moderne architectural style. Its terra-cotta accents previously adorned a meat market and grocery. Continuing on the road, you'll come to a toy store at 7784 that was built in 1927 as the Weatherly Grocery and Multnomah Drug Store. Upstairs was the community meeting hall. Across from the toy store, at 7783, an antique shop inhabits the old Gregg Owens Chevrolet dealership. The front of the building used to have garage doors that opened wide for cars. The building next to the toy store, at 7780, was once the Multnomah Volunteer Fire Department. The fire truck would never fit in the window now located where the garage door once hung.

Marco's Café and Espresso Bar sits on the corner of SW 35th Avenue and Multnomah Boulevard, a half block south of the main strip, in the 1913 building that originally housed the Thomas Bungalow Grocery. Before Marco's, this Streetcar-Era Commercial building was inhabited by a post office, a Masonic lodge, and various retail stores. The other longtime local restaurant is the Fat City Café, located in a Streetcar-Era Commercial building that hasn't changed much since it was built in 1922. Upstairs are flats, and on the main floor, old-fashioned booths and counter service hark back to the 1940s. The food is not fancy. The walls are decorated with license plates, and the place has been described, favorably, as a "joint."

At SW 33rd Avenue is the wonderful Multnomah Center, an old Portland public school turned into a community art, music, and neighborhood center. Inside you'll find restrooms and water fountains, as well as an ever-changing shelf of bargain-priced pottery, created by students of various levels of accomplishment. Multnomah School opened in 1913 as two portables, with this Mediterranean-style building completed in 1924. When the school first opened, teachers would take the train out to Multnomah from Portland, get off at the station, and walk through deep woods to get to the school.

A large Japanese cedar on the edge of the center's parking lot is a Portland Heritage Tree. During winter the leaf color changes from green to shades of bronze or brown. This is not a sign of distress; in spring the tree greens up again. In its native Japan, the cedar, called *sugi*, is a common forest tree. Small sake brewing businesses still advertise their products in the traditional way by hang-

Looking southwest on SW Capitol Highway in Multnomah, circa 1926. The Ellis Pharmacy sits where Acapulco's Gold now resides. Other buildings remain intact. Note the wooden sidewalks and the old concrete road—the delight of roller-skating neighborhood kids. Photo courtesy of the Multnomah Historical Association.

ing a large ball of *sugi* leaves outside their shops. The fragrant wood is also used for making sake casks.

Across from the Multnomah Center is the Lucky Labrador Brew Pub, in the reincarnated Orenomah Masonic Temple Lodge. In 1915, six years before the temple was built, Capitol Highway (then called Slavin Road) was the first local road outside Portland to be paved with an experimental concrete surface. Along with stables built at the future temple site, a kitchen was set up to serve meals to the laborers. A Chinese cook banged a gong to call the men to the table.

2 Turn left on SW 32nd Avenue and begin walking up to the top of a small West Hills peak, elevation 620 feet. This street lies along the edges of two watersheds: to the east is the Willamette River watershed; to the west is the Tryon Creek watershed. The hill crests at SW Texas Street, and like so many peaks in the West Hills, it has been claimed by the Portland Water Bureau. As you walk up 32nd, the views improve and the pavement worsens. Like the Homestead neighborhood (Walk 8), Multnomah has many unimproved streets, with potholes large enough to break an axle.

Whenever a new neighborhood is developed, the City of Portland has always required the developer to put in the infrastructure—curbs, drainage, sidewalks, pavement, and so on. The developer then passes those costs on to the individual lot buyers, whose property values benefit from the improvements. When the Multnomah neighborhood was developed, however, it was outside Portland's city limits and under the jurisdiction of the county, which had looser regulations regarding a neighborhood's infrastructure. And because growth in Multnomah occurred in a hodgepodge fashion rather than in one planned development (as it did with the Eastmoreland neighborhood, for example), curbs and paving were placed on some streets and not others, depending on the discretion of each developer.

Once a neighborhood has been developed without paved streets, the onus is on the homeowners to pay the City of Portland for the engineering, drainage, and materials needed to do the job right. After that, the city assumes responsibility for maintaining the street. (Occasionally homeowners do a bit of bootleg paving, but then they bear the risk of the newly paved, unengineered street surface channeling water efficiently and disastrously into a neighbor's living room.)

Putting in a street's infrastructure after the homes are in place is a more difficult and expensive process, since improvements have to be engineered around the homes' varying elevations. Costs range from $325 to $1000 per running linear foot. That means that for a typical 400-foot-long block, improvements range from $130,000 to $400,000. Once the project is done, homeowners are assessed their share of the costs, which they can take up to twenty years to pay off. Not many choose to incur the costs. Of course, the upside to an unimproved street is that you never have to worry about people speeding through your neighborhood.

As 32nd jogs around SW California Street, the road widens and improves as it drops along the northern face of the hill. In just a few steps, the feel of the neighborhood changes from semirural to suburban. When this section of the hill was developed with Ranch homes in the 1950s, the developer paid for the full complement of improvements—a marked contrast with the other portion of the street. The view north from this intersection is of Council Crest.

3 At SW Vermont Street, an east-west collector street, turn left. Walk on the shoulder two blocks, cross the street, turn right onto SW 34th Avenue, and start climbing. Stay right at the Y in the road. You'll come to a fine view of Healy Heights and Council Crest, with their signature towers. Turn left on SW Carolina Street. It's steep here, and the pavement ends, but the road continues. There are nice, wide views of the Bridlemile neighborhood, which lies to the west of Council Crest.

Turn left on SW 35th Avenue and right on Dakota Street. This is big-sky country, with views to the distant south. Turn right on SW 37th Avenue, walk half a block, and turn left at the gate marked "City of Portland Water Bureau Vermont Hills Tanks and Building." Pedestrians are allowed here, so walk on through, and climb up to the second peak on this hill walk, elevation 580 feet.

This peak, like the one at 32nd and Texas, is used by the Water Bureau to take advantage of gravity. By placing water tanks on small peaks and promontories, the city can avoid using pumps to get the water to end users. About three-quarters of Portland water users receive water through gravity flow. On this peak, the tanks are not completely fenced off, and the city shares the fine view with pedestrians. This area is not on most people's radar, so it's quiet and feels remote, a lovely place to relax on the grass. The grounds consist of pruned lawns and mature pines, pin oaks, and spruces that accent a garden of concrete water tanks, some submerged to chest-high levels, others higher.

Around 1900 this area was farmed by a woman named Mrs. Dietrich, who kept busy as the Multnomah area's chief midwife.

Make your way over to the northwestern corner of the tank garden and the northern end of a chain-link fence. Take the path out to SW 40th Avenue and turn left. This puts you heading downhill, looking dead-on at Mount Sylvania to the south. Otherwise known as Mountain Park, Mount Sylvania is a Boring Lava dome like Rocky Butte and Powell Butte. Most of the one hundred Boring Lava buttes or cones are on the eastern side of the Willamette River, growing in number and proximity as they get closer to the Cascades. Mount Sylvania, one of the few on the west side, is a shield volcano, like the volcanoes in Hawaii. Flows from its vent cover a large area around it. (See Walk 15 for more information on the Boring Lavas.)

Turn right onto Dakota, and savor a huge western view of Beaverton and beyond, to the Coast Range. Dakota is a street of classy 1960s Ranch homes terraced on many levels into the hillside. The neighborhood strikes me as extremely egalitarian. The homes situated high up, with stunning views, are no grander or more trophylike than homes lower on the hillside.

Turn right on SW Idaho Terrace, then left onto SW Idaho Drive, which drops you back onto Vermont at the northern edge of Gabriel Park.

4   A path into Gabriel Park begins here, but detour a bit to the west and visit the 48,000-square-foot Southwest Community Center. The glass, stone, and concrete building was designed by Portland's BOORA Architects and finished in 1999. The design is both beautiful and utilitarian, and the facilities are as nice as most private clubs. The center includes a recreational pool, lap pool, hot tub, basketball courts, fitness and aerobic rooms, meeting rooms, and a great central foyer that makes a fine place to hang out, especially when the fireplace is lit. Restrooms and snacks are also available here.

Exit the center via its southern side. Turn left, and on the eastern side of the parking lot, follow an asphalt walking path into Gabriel Park. Begin walking on the trail as it heads south into the park toward some enormous and unnatural-looking grass mounds that look like something from the mind of a cartoon animator. These are excavation spoils from construction of the community center. If you climb one of these great green knobs, you'll get a view of the layout of the park, with its developed and natural areas, and a fine view to the west of the Coast Range. This northern end of the park was farmed by Henry Tannler, who operated the Multnomah Dairy here.

On the path, turn right where the trail forms a V, and follow it between the tennis courts and into the woods, where it starts dropping downhill to reach the lowest elevation on this hill walk, a creek. In 2004 invasive Himalayan blackberries were removed from the creek banks and replaced with native riparian vegetation. Cross the creek on a wooden footbridge. Once over the bridge, stay right, avoiding the stairs that climb to your left.

South of the creek, the huge pendulous branches of old western red cedars make great impromptu horses for small children to ride, and their cloak of green over a complicated wooden framework makes an exciting venue for hide-and-seek.

The western red cedar was to American Indians what plastics are today: the material of a thousand uses. The pitch was chewed as a gum, and in spring the cambium layer of bark was eaten. Bark was shredded, plaited, or braided for baskets, skirts, dresses, mats, diapers, towels, roofing, and canoe waterproofing. The wood was used for building construction, and long, straight branches were used to make ropes for whaling and anchor lines. Steamed wood was used to make canoes. Boughs were used to scrub the skin in sweat lodges. The list goes on.

The path leads across a rolling grassy lawn surrounded by a mature forest of fir, cedar, and rhododendron, a perfect place for Frisbee. Since off-leash dogs have been relegated to a fenced-in dog zone in the park, this grassy area is relatively poop-free. The park's rolling spaces were not always so open. In the 1880s a Swiss immigrant, Ulrich Gabriel, bought this forested land. With blasting powder and teams of horses and mules, he cleared it for his dairy operation of about eighty cows. Gabriel grew the cows' feed right here: corn, wheat, and vetch. Most of the park's 95 acres were donated to the city in 1950 by the Gabriel estate.

A former cow pasture, now the rolling lawns and forests of Gabriel Park.

The path continues south and passes by a bigleaf maple with an enormous burl at its base. These burls are prized by woodworkers for their fantastic grain patterns. Just past the baseball field is the parking lot, the end of the walk.

MARSHALL PARK CANYON TO CEMETERIES LOOP

STARTING POINT Marshall Park parking area: SW 18th Place, just south of Taylors Ferry Road

DISTANCE 4.5 miles

ELEVATION 350 feet at the parking lot for Marshall Park; 220 feet at the floor of the canyon in Marshall Park; 540 feet at the Ahavai Sholom Cemetery

GETTING THERE AND PARKING From the intersection of SW Terwilliger and Barbur Boulevards, drive south on Terwilliger. Turn right onto SW Taylors Ferry Road, and drive 0.8 mile to SW 18th Place. Turn left and drive 0.2 mile to an entrance to Marshall Park at the gravel pull-out (marked by a sign) on the eastern side of the road, just north of the SW Collins Court intersection. Park here.

TriMet: From downtown, take bus 12 (Barbur Boulevard) to the stop at SW Barbur Boulevard and Evans Street. At this intersection, board bus 39 (Lewis and Clark). Get off at SW 19th Avenue and Spring Garden Street. Walk south on 19th to SW Taylors Ferry Road. Turn left and then immediately right onto SW 18th Place. Walk 0.2 mile south to the Marshall Park parking area just north of the SW Collins Court intersection.

RESTROOMS AND DRINKING FOUNTAINS There are no public restrooms or drinking fountains located along this route. Restrooms are available for patrons of restaurants near the route at the intersection of SW Taylors Ferry Road and Terwilliger Boulevard.

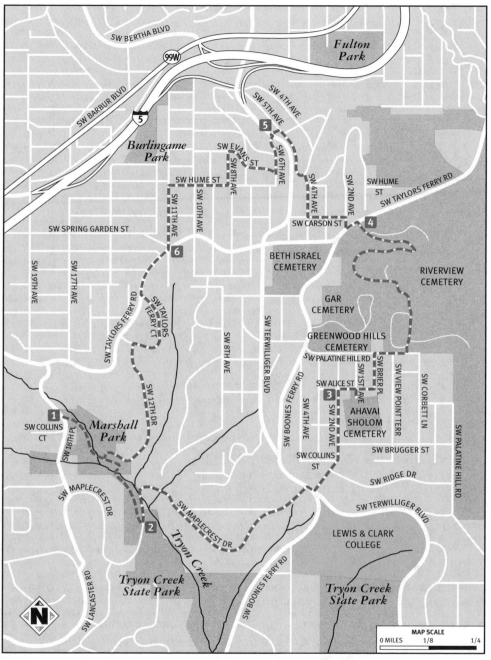

SW BERTHA BLVD

Fulton Park

SW 4TH AVE

SW 5TH AVE

99W

5

SW BARBUR BLVD

SW EVANS ST

SW 6TH AVE

5

SW 8TH AVE

SW HUME ST

Burlingame Park

SW HUME ST

SW 4TH AVE

SW 2ND AVE

SW TAYLORS FERRY RD

SW 11TH AVE

SW 10TH AVE

SW SPRING GARDEN ST

SW CARSON ST

4

SW 19TH AVE

SW 17TH AVE

6

BETH ISRAEL CEMETERY

RIVERVIEW CEMETERY

SW TAYLORS FERRY RD

SW TAYLORS FERRY CT

GAR CEMETERY

SW 8TH AVE

SW TERWILLIGER BLVD

GREENWOOD HILLS CEMETERY

SW PALATINE HILL RD

SW BRIER PL

SW 1ST AVE

SW VIEW POINT TERR

SW CORBETT LN

SW 12TH DR

SW ALICE ST

3

SW PALATINE HILL RD

1

SW BOONES FERRY RD

SW 4TH AVE

SW 2ND AVE

AHAVAI SHOLOM CEMETERY

SW COLLINS CT

Marshall Park

SW COLLINS ST

SW BRUGGER ST

SW 18TH PL

SW RIDGE DR

SW MAPLECREST DR

2

SW MAPLECREST DR

Tryon Creek

SW TERWILLIGER BLVD

LEWIS & CLARK COLLEGE

SW LANCASTER RD

Tryon Creek State Park

SW BOONES FERRY RD

Tryon Creek State Park

N

MAP SCALE
0 MILES   1/8   1/4

WALK 11. *Marshall Park Canyon to Cemeteries Loop*

MAP KEY

ROUTE   RAILROAD TRACKS

STAIRS   PARKS/GREENSPACE

TRAILS   PUBLIC RESTROOMS

WATER   BUS STOP

FOOD AND DRINK Located just one block from the route, midway through the walk at 8502 SW Terwilliger Boulevard, is Chez José, open Monday through Saturday for lunch and dinner, and Sunday for dinner; 503-244-0007. Market of Choice, a grocery store, is located right next door; 503-892-7331.

SAVE THIS HILL WALK FOR A FALL DAY when the clouds are churning and the wind is blowing. In the tree-filled canyon of Marshall Park, the winds will throw forest debris at you, reminding you of your inconsequentiality—a feeling that might return after you emerge from the canyon and enter the cemeteries, where the ambience is never better than when the day is bleak. Once atop the hills in the South Burlingame neighborhood, a wild, windy day combined with the neighborhood's big-sky view will make you feel great to be alive, inconsequential or not!

1 Start at secluded Marshall Park, on SW 18th Place. Head downhill on the wide trail. Gratification comes with the very first steps, as you descend into a forest of large Douglas firs and lacy maples, with views down into and across the canyon of a small tributary of Tryon Creek.

At the bottom of the canyon, the trail drops you off at the confluence of the two creeks. The Tryon Creek watershed is bounded to the east by Palatine Hill (home of Lewis and Clark College and Dunthorpe), to the north and west by the West Hills, and to the south by Mount Sylvania. The creek is 7 miles long and flows year-round. It starts near Multnomah Village and flows into the Willamette near State Street in Lake Oswego. It's among the few Portland-area creeks that still see the light of day (Balch Creek is another), except where it flows through culverts under roads. During winter it roars with run-off from its 4200-square-mile watershed; in summer and early fall its flow comes from aquifers that surface as springs and seeps.

Tryon Creek was named for pioneer Socrates Hotchkiss Tryon, a Vermont doctor who, after working in Hawaii, came to Oregon in 1849. His donation land claim was in the southern half of the canyon, near the confluence with the Willamette (now the Tryon Creek State Park). His home was near present-day Stampher Road in Lake Oswego. In 1874 Tryon's heirs sold their 600-plus acres to the Oregon Iron Company. Until the 1920s, Oregon Iron logged most of the old-growth forest within the watershed for charcoal to fire its pig iron foundry in Oswego.

At the bottom of the canyon, you might want to explore a bit. A footbridge to your left leads to the playground and a park exit at SW 12th Drive. This hollow was originally a quarry, as you'll see when the hill walk leads you along the fenced-off cliff just south of the playground. In 1937 F. C. and Addie Marshall retired to this spot and worked to transform the old quarry into a park. Mr. Marshall gave it to the city in 1951. Additional acreage was later purchased.

Stay right and cross the footbridge over Tryon Creek. This streambed is a virtually untouched gem. In its rocky bed, small cascades drop into smooth pools. Once across the bridge, the trail follows the creek for a brief but glorious way before turning off. After climbing a bit, it follows a fenced-off cliff. This overlooks the bottomland where the playground sits. At a trail junction, go right, and at another junction, go left, downhill. You'll see a house on the left, just on the other side of the creek.

2   The trail drops you off onto SW Maplecrest Drive in a lowland area that any proper Southerner would call a "holler." Turn left; you'll pass a home with a beautifully landscaped yard with Tryon Creek running through it. Follow Maplecrest as it climbs out of the hollow. This is one of those surprising rural nooks, just feet from a major city arterial, in this case SW Terwilliger Boulevard.

You'll see a stoplight and crosswalk at Terwilliger's intersection with SW Boones Ferry Road and 2nd Avenue. This is Portland's Collins View neighborhood. Just one block north is Riverdale High School, an educational erratic from the Riverdale School District, a school district to the south that is totally separate from Portland Public Schools. Riverdale's grade school is in the tony Dunthorpe area. When Riverdale families agreed to start a high school, they couldn't find affordable ground within their own high-priced district, so they were forced to shop around the neighboring countryside. In 2002 the Riverdale School District finally entered into a lease of the former Collins View School, a Portland public school that was closed in 1976.

Cross Terwilliger and begin climbing SW 2nd, an emphatically steep little stretch of road that lifts you quickly from 365 feet to 530 feet. Views get better and better as you climb the flanks of one of the West Hills' many peaks. There's no sidewalk, but it's a quiet neighborhood street. As you climb past SW Ridge Drive, look for the faces carved into the shrubs at the home on the corner. This humorous and creative landscape is fun to look at, especially for those of us with limited landscape design talents, and provides a good excuse to stop climbing for a moment. It's worth meandering down Ridge a bit to see a fuller extent of this home's artistic merits.

Once back on 2nd, keep climbing, but stop again at the intersection with SW Brugger Street for the view of the Tryon Creek watershed behind you. Climb a bit further and turn right onto the pavement-free SW Alice Street. At this intersection are views to the north of the charmingly seedy Greenwood Hills Cemetery. Just north of it is the Grand Army of the Republic (GAR) Cemetery, formed in 1889. Healy Heights is also visible, with its red-and-white radio tower.

3 Turn right onto Alice and then right onto SW 1st Avenue, which leads into the Ahavai Sholom Cemetery, perched peacefully at the summit of the Collins View neighborhood. This area, with its graveled, uncurbed streets, has an intriguing, time-forgotten air, accented by the hulking, rusting water tank located next door to the cemetery. Ahavai Sholom, whose name means "lovers of peace," dates back to 1869 when its 5 acres were purchased by several members of the new Ahavai Sholom congregation from J. M. Tice, who held the land as part of his original donation land claim. Ahavai Sholom merged in 1961 with Neveh Zedek to form the Conservative Jewish congregation Neveh Shalom. Located at the apex of this symmetrical West Hills peak, Ahavai Sholom enjoys a spectacular 360-degree view, a view that fifty million years ago was of ocean swells. This small peak is composed of the Waverly Heights Basalt, volcanic rock that is thirty-six to fifty-two million years old and the oldest exposed rock in the Portland area. It is believed that the Waverly Heights Basalt was part of an oceanic island that accreted itself to the North American continent. This area was then beachfront until twenty to twenty-five millions years ago, when the Coast Range accreted to the North American continent.

Millions of years ago, when fissures in the earth in Oregon, Washington, and Idaho began oozing what are now known as the Columbia River Basalts, flows worked their way around the older Waverly Heights formation, leaving these ancient rocks exposed. Covered by a mantle of soil, the rock is not visible here. If you want to see the actual Waverly Heights lava, visit Elk Rock Island in the Willamette River, where the rock is exposed.

From the cemetery, turn right onto Alice Street. Now you're looking east, and isn't it nice to be on a city street with an incredible view that isn't hogged by mega homes, released to passersby only in narrow doses? Turn left onto SW Brier Place, walk one block, and turn right onto SW Palatine Hill Road. Walk 0.1 mile to the brick and iron gate that marks an entrance to the elegant grounds of Riverview Cemetery.

Riverview was built in 1882 during the rural cemetery movement, in which landscaping was very important to a cemetery's aesthetic. Before 1831, when the first rural cemetery was designed outside Cambridge, Massachusetts, Americans living in towns or cities buried their dead in church graveyards, municipal cemeteries, or potter's fields. During the early 1800s, with increasing populations in cities, graveyards had become an issue. One concern was that they often had to be moved to accommodate increasing urbanization; another concern was that neglected and abandoned graveyards were unsightly; and lastly, in an era that was only beginning to understand the links between germs and disease, fears grew that decaying bodies contributed to epidemics such as cholera.

Mount Auburn Cemetery in Massachusetts addressed these issues while also responding to the growing American interest in horticultural pursuits, which were thought to reinforce society's moral values and reflect the new nation's vitality. Designed in a naturalistic way, with roads that followed the land's contours, and an arboretum-like lushness, this first rural cemetery appealed to people who were just beginning to get comfortable with not being able to bury their dead in close proximity. The new cemeteries, with their beauty and peace, and their ability to inspire reflection, helped ease that discomfort.

Rural cemeteries became popular places for carriage drives and strolling. One Englishman noted that cemeteries in America were "all the 'rage.' People lounge in them and use them for walking, making love, weeping, sentimentalizing and *every*thing in short." As the movement spread westward, the movers and shakers in American cities wanted their own rural cemeteries, which were seen as symbols of refinement and prosperity.

It was in this environment that Riverview Cemetery was developed. It quickly became a civic destination, and not just for the living. For early-twentieth-century Portlanders, it was *the* place to be seen once you'd died. It was so fashionable that the bodies of many early luminaries, including Governor Sylvester Pennoyer, were exhumed from Lone Fir Cemetery in Southeast Portland and deposited in this more rural, more upscale location. Among those buried here are Abigail Scott Duniway, Henry Pittock, Henry Corbett, Henry Weinhard, Harvey Scott, and pro football star Lyle Alzado.

Today Riverview is a private nonprofit cemetery that welcomes visitors, including bicyclists, who love the swooping roads that follow the contours of its hills.

Once through the gate, walk straight ahead through a newer section of the cemetery, where the gravestones are flush with the ground. Meandering is the

An elaborate monument typical of the older sections of Riverview Cemetery.

best way to soak in the beauty of this quiet place, especially when you reach the older sections with their large and beautiful monuments. If you stay in the vicinity of sections 105–109 and walk downhill, you'll end up at the Taylors Ferry Road entrance shown on the map. The map shows the route on the cemetery roads, but you are welcome to cut through the gravestones—a much more interesting path.

The cemetery has four entrances; you'll walk out the higher of two Taylors Ferry entrances. The grand entrance is on SW Macadam Avenue, which you might want to drive by after the walk. There you'll find a 1914 home, designed by Ellis Lawrence, that was originally the cemetery caretaker's home. Today it holds cemetery offices.

A view from Burlingame, looking north toward the Stonehenge radio tower at Healy Heights.

4   After passing through the gate back into the land of the living, veer left across the lawn toward SW 2nd Avenue. Taylors Ferry, by the way, originated in the 1850s at a ferry landing on the Tualatin River beyond Progress, Oregon. Cross Taylors Ferry—carefully, if you don't want to return to the graveyard as a permanent resident—and walk up 2nd to Carson Street. Turn left and begin climbing another small West Hills peak, whose summit is a few blocks west at about SW 8th and Hume. In just a few steps you've crossed about twenty million years. This peak, unlike its neighbor to the south, is only about fifteen million years old, dating back to the middle Miocene. It consists of the Basalt of Ginkgo unit of the Columbia River Basalts.

Tired of hearing about graves and old rocks? If so, walk straight on Carson to Terwilliger. Turn left, and in less than one block you'll arrive at Market of Choice, a Eugene-owned grocery that took the place of the Burlingame Market, long renowned for its great beer selection, and a victim of arson in 2001. The new store, which opened in 2003, has taken up the torch, metaphorically, and offers beers of all stripes, fabulous deli food, and seating. If you're too tired to schlep through grocery aisles, let yourself be served good Mexican fare next door at Chez José, owned since 1987 by locals Howie Schechter and Tom Midrano. A coffee shop is nearby, too.

If you don't want to eat, turn right onto SW 4th Avenue. This is the South Burlingame neighborhood, platted out in 1910. It has the same big-sky views you get in the Hessler Hills neighborhood, but at a lower price point. At SW 5th Avenue, turn left: more modest homes, more grand views.

5 At SW Troy Street, turn left and cross Terwilliger at the stoplight. This puts you walking south on SW 6th Avenue, still in South Burlingame. Walk two blocks and turn right on SW Evans Street. This neighborhood exhibits plenty of what realtors term "pride of ownership"; residents here seem to know they've got a good thing going, with their charming homes, big views, and quiet streets, all within minutes of downtown. Yet another Portland gem.

Turn left onto SW 8th Avenue. This puts you at elevation 480 feet, the top of the small peak whose flanks you started climbing at the cemetery gate. Turn right on SW Hume Street. If the wind is blowing from the west, the roar of Interstate 5, about six blocks away, might annoy you a bit, but this will quickly recede as you turn left on SW 11th Avenue and drop down the hill toward Tryon Creek. At 11th and Hume is an example of the old iron railing on the edges of street curbs, designed to protect the concrete from the wheels of horse-drawn carriages. In "19&13," as the curb quaintly notes the year of its installation, horses were already on their way out, but the iron still went in. These curbs are quickly disappearing in many old intersections, as flat, more accessible curbs are installed.

6 Cross Taylors Ferry at the stop-signed intersection with SW Spring Garden Street and 11th, and turn right. Uncle John's Market and Deli, a neighborhood institution, is located here and is your last chance for sustenance. Walk about 0.3 mile along the shoulder to SW Taylors Ferry Court, a gravel road. Turn left. Looking into the canyon behind some of the small houses, homes of long-ago country folk, makes you wonder what archeological treasures of early-twentieth-century households lie under the forest debris.

At SW 13th Avenue and Taylors Ferry, just a few steps beyond the turnoff for SW 12th Drive, was the old Whitley's Saloon. In the 1850s it was the first rest stop for horses coming up the steep hill from the Willamette on their way to West Portland and beyond.

Turn left on SW 12th Drive, the road the Marshalls used to take to reach their home. Take it to its dead end at Marshall Park. Their home was located where the park playground is sited, and the stone arch footbridge across Tryon Creek is a remnant of the Marshalls' residency.

To return to the starting point, walk across the small wooden footbridge and turn right, up the path you came down earlier.

DUNTHORPE GARDENS

STARTING POINT SW Riverwood Road and Military Road

DISTANCE 2 miles, plus walking within the Bishop's Close and Berry Botanic Garden

ELEVATION 100 feet at the starting point; 460 feet near the Berry Botanic Garden

GETTING THERE AND PARKING From the Johns Landing area, drive south on Highway 43 (SW Macadam Avenue, then SW Riverside Drive). About 1.3 miles past the Sellwood Bridge, you'll go through a stoplight for SW Riverdale Road. Get in the left lane, and a short way past this light, turn left onto SW Riverwood Road. (This turn is easy to miss; if you do, just drive to the next light, SW Military Road, and turn left.) Drive about 0.25 mile to the intersection with Military Road. Park along the shoulder on Riverwood.

TriMet: From downtown, take bus 35 (Macadam) to the stop at SW Military Road and Highway 43 (SW Riverside Drive). Walk 0.2 mile northeast (downhill) on Military to SW Riverwood Road.

RESTROOMS AND DRINKING FOUNTAINS Restrooms and drinking fountains can be found at the Berry Botanic Garden.

FOOD AND DRINK From the intersection of Military Road and Highway 43 (SW Riverside Drive), drive south on Highway 43 about 1.5 miles. The highway turns into State Street in Lake Oswego. At the stoplight, turn right onto B Avenue. This Lake Oswego district has been revivified as a shopper's mecca. On weekdays visit Gourmet Productions, located at 39 B Avenue; 503-697-7355.

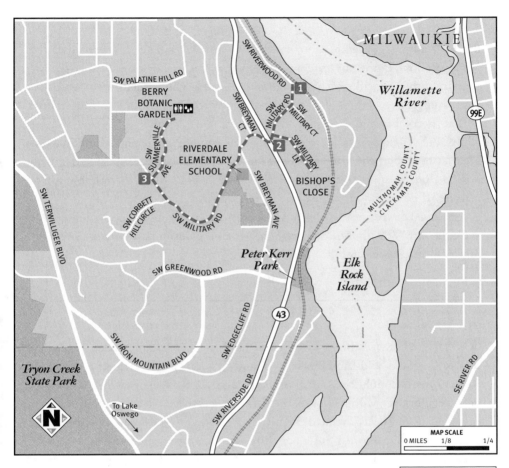

MILWAUKIE

SW PALATINE HILL RD

BERRY
BOTANIC
GARDEN

*Willamette
River*

99E

SW RIVERWOOD RD

1

SW MILITARY RD

SW BREYMAN CT

SW MILITARY CT

2

SW MILITARY LN

RIVERDALE
ELEMENTARY
SCHOOL

SW SUMMERVILLE AVE

3

BISHOP'S
CLOSE

SW CORBETT HILL CIRCLE

SW MILITARY RD

SW BREYMAN AVE

MULTNOMAH COUNTY
CLACKAMAS COUNTY

SW TERWILLIGER BLVD

SW GREENWOOD RD

*Peter Kerr
Park*

*Elk
Rock
Island*

SW EDGECLIFF RD

43

SW IRON MOUNTAIN BLVD

SE RIVER RD

*Tryon Creek
State Park*

To Lake
Oswego

SW RIVERSIDE DR

N

MAP SCALE

0 MILES   1/8   1/4

WALK 12. *Dunthorpe Gardens*

MAP KEY

▪ ▪ ROUTE

⋯⋯ STAIRS

– – TRAILS

╪╪╪ RAILROAD TRACKS

    PARKS/GREENSPACE

🚻 PUBLIC RESTROOMS

💧 WATER

📍 BUS STOP

On weekends you can take your pick from many other nearby restaurants and coffee shops.

NOTE Walking, contemplation, and nature appreciation are encouraged at the Bishop's Close, but as inviting a picnic spot as it is, picnicking, Frisbee throwing, and other parklike activities are not allowed. The gardens are open daily. Admission is free, though donations are happily received. Dogs must be leashed.

The Berry Botanic Garden is open daily. A $5 admission is requested for adults, but August visits are free of charge. As a public garden operating in a residential neighborhood, Berry is required by a Multnomah County variance to host visitors by appointment only. Call 503-636-4112 to let them know you're coming. If no one answers, just leave a message and come on over.

Getting between the Bishop's Close and the Berry Botanic Garden entails walking on SW Military Road, parts of which are busier than others. There are no sidewalks, so be careful.

I N THE 1860s, William Sargent Ladd (whose land became Ladd's Addition, Eastmoreland, and Laurelhurst) and Simeon Reed (whose bequest gave rise to Reed College) bought a chunk of property south of Riverview Cemetery for iron ore speculation. Millions of years earlier, decaying plant material layered between ancient lava flows had chemically reacted with the basalt and been compressed and transformed into hematite, an ore that had commercial value. Wealthy speculators began snapping up property in the Oswego area (now Lake Oswego) around 1861.

By the early 1890s the iron boom was over, and property owners began to look for other ways to profit from their land. In 1908 the Ladd Estate Company began to subdivide and develop its many properties. In 1916 William Ladd, son of William Sargent Ladd, began developing the family's Oswego-area property, envisioning a land of large pastoral estates. It was he who dubbed it Dunthorpe. William Ladd built his own home there in 1920 on 16 acres. Others followed, the most spectacular and accessible of which is the Frank Manor House, a gorgeous Arts and Crafts mansion built in 1925 with seven terraced gardens stairstepping down the mountain. After the Franks divorced, the estate was sold for a token amount to Lewis and Clark College as the grounds for its campus. The house is used for administrative purposes, but the grounds are open for strolling. It is located on Palatine Hill Road in Dunthorpe.

Since its beginning Dunthorpe has attracted wealth and in more recent times has become a popular neighborhood with the Portland Trailblazers, the city's NBA franchise. The team's owner, Paul Allen, is the fifth richest man in the world, having made his $20 billion fortune cofounding Microsoft. In the 1990s, despite having the highest payroll in the NBA, the Trailblazers failed to win a championship and indeed became a national joke with their attitudinal and judicial mishaps. Reform came, with troublemakers departing and salaries decreasing. But even with the more budget-minded payroll starting in 2004, the lowliest Trailblazer would still have no trouble paying for a Dunthorpe address.

1   The starting point of this hill walk is the riverside intersection of SW Military and Riverwood Roads. In the mid to late nineteenth century, this quiet intersection bustled with activity. Riverwood used to be a section of Macadam Avenue, the main road to Lake Oswego, which also doubled as the Pacific Highway, a major north-south route from California to Washington. At this intersection was a ferry landing. Across the river you can see the mouth of Johnson Creek, which is visited, at points upstream, in Walks 13 and 15.

Military Road is an old American Indian trail that once ran across the Tualatin Mountains. Farmers in the plains would bring their produce via Military to the ferry landing here, which was owned by William Torrance. Torrance was a business partner of Lot Whitcomb, owner of the Milwaukie town site directly across the river. One of their moneymaking ventures was to offer free ferry passage to any farmer who ground his grain at Whitcomb's riverside gristmill.

Just south of this intersection along the river was the 1870s-era White House, a four-story roadhouse that offered a casino, dining room, dance hall, and race-track. It burned in 1904, and the area was subsequently developed with homes.

The rail line next to the road was laid in 1888 by the Portland and Willamette Railroad Company. It now carries the Willamette Shore Trolley. (See Walk 9 for more information.)

Walk uphill on Military. In the early years of Dunthorpe, this street bordered large estates; these were later carved up into smaller parcels, often sold to family members. One such estate was located behind the superb hand-carved basalt wall that runs along both Riverwood and Military.

2   Pass SW Military Court, and then turn left at SW Military Lane. Walk down this tastefully elegant lane for 0.2 mile. Along the way, don't miss the magnificent espaliered camellia tree, two stories high, on a house at 11544. In late win-

The White House, circa 1890, located southeast of what is now the intersection of SW Military and Riverwood Roads. In the foreground at right is the racetrack. Photo courtesy of the Lake Oswego Public Library.

ter it blooms a luminous pink. The lane ends at two enormous giant sequoias that mark the boundary of Elk Rock, the former estate of Peter and Laurie Kerr. It is now owned by the Episcopal Diocese of Oregon and is called the Bishop's Close.

Close is a Scottish word referring to a road, usually with private houses, that vehicles can enter only from one end. A bishop's close is a cloister area set apart from but still accessible to the public. This is fitting at the Kerr estate, which is accessible at the end of a quiet lane and totally cut off at its southern property line by sheer cliffs dropping to the river.

Peter Kerr bought this property with his brother and his business partner in the late 1890s. He was a grain merchant from Scotland who had moved here at age twenty-six in 1888 to take advantage of America's opportunities. After the two other men married, Peter was left alone, but not for long. In 1905 he married Laurie King, and they settled in a cottage located on the northeastern end of the property. In 1914 the Kerrs began building the current home, designed by Ellis Lawrence in the Scottish Manor style. In that same year Lawrence became the first dean of the University of Oregon School of Architecture.

In the sixty-plus years he lived here, Peter Kerr indulged in his love of gardening, and the place is filled with wonderful specimen trees and plants, chosen by Kerr for their unique features or exoticism. Kerr aimed to collect every magnolia that would bloom in the Northwest climate and was still planting trees at age ninety. His large collection of magnolias blooms throughout the month of March. Various flyers at the visitor center provide lots of detail about the plants you'll encounter on the grounds. During Kerr's lifetime the estate was a paradise not just for plant lovers but also for children, with tennis courts, a swimming pool, and a golf course set among the grounds. Six gardeners were employed to keep everything in prime shape. Today, one gardener remains, and plantings have evolved from labor-intensive beds of annuals and pruned shrubbery to plants that provide year-round interest without too much human intervention.

The grounds of the Kerr estate were designed by John Olmsted, stepson of Frederick Law Olmsted, the famous designer of New York City's Central Park. Topographically, the estate occupies a flat terrace between 500-foot-high Palatine Hill and the Willamette River, 200 feet below.

Peter Kerr died in 1957 at age ninety-five. His two daughters, Ann (who married James McDonald, knighted for his service to the Queen during World War II as the British consul in Portland) and Jane, gave the property to the Episcopal Diocese of Oregon, but they wanted the grounds to remain forever open to the public. To that end, they set up an endowment to provide for maintenance. When the daughters donated the property to the church, it was envisioned that a new home would be built for the bishop as well as a freestanding chapel, and that the mansion would be used for administrative offices. Although a chapel was added to the home in 1980, no other structures have been built.

When you enter the grounds, you'll see two parking areas on the right. The upper, graveled area, marked "visitor parking," was a grass tennis court during the Kerrs' lifetimes. The carriage house here had a men's changing room on the side. Walk into this upper lot. On its western side are two century-old wisterias trellised to create a bower. From the bench underneath, earlier visitors probably enjoyed watching tennis matches. Today the massive wisterias are a worthy show all by themselves. The bower seems like the perfect spot for an exchange of vows; renting the estate for a wedding, however, is not permitted.

Walk back into the lower lot, and then head right, up a small stone staircase that leads through a rock garden. At the top terrace, stroll through an area landscaped with boxwood-edged parterres. Inside the squares of boxwood is a collection of witch hazels, which intoxicated me with their scent during one sunny March visit. This area was once occupied by a swimming pool.

Take a gravel trail that leads south, out of the upper terrace. This trail keeps you on the highest ground in the Bishop's Close. The grounds were left in a nat-

Madrona trees, young and old, near the southern point of the Bishop's Close.

ural state here; as you walk south, the hillside is dominated by madrona trees whose glowing cinnamon-colored trunks twist, arch, and crane their way toward the light over the river.

The trail takes you to the Point, where you can look down (carefully, the wall is low here) at the sheer cliffs on the Willamette. The Point overlooks Elk Rock Island, a block of Waverly Heights Basalt. (For more information on Waverly Heights Basalt, see Walk 11.) The island was also owned by Peter Kerr, who gave it to the city in 1940, stipulating that it be preserved in its natural state. A dance hall once rocked the island, during the early 1900s, but it is now among the best places in Portland to step away from the city into nature. The island is accessible on foot from the eastern side of the river during low water.

In 1955 the Kerrs gave the city another parcel, just south of the Bishop's Close property. The land, now called Peter Kerr Park, is essentially a cliff,

Pruned plants grow side by side with their wilder counterparts at the Bishop's Close.

through which a 1200-foot-long railroad tunnel runs. From 1887 until 1921, trains running from Lake Oswego had to navigate the cliff on the outside, via a high wooden trestle built over the river at the bottom of the cliff. Rockslides and the resulting fatal derailments were always a problem. If you walk a bit north of the Point, you can look back and see the face of this cliff. As the cliff wanes and the land flattens out below the Bishop's Close, you can see the train tracks and the homes along Riverwood that occupy the former racetrack.

From here, the best advice I can give is to wander aimlessly as you head back toward the house. The gardens, which grow more cultivated and more filled with specimen trees, flowers, and shrubs as you go north, are beautiful any time of year. Despite the formal design and grandeur of the estate, the Bishop's Close is not a stuffy horticultural museum where you might feel awkward sticking your nose into a cluster of *Edgeworthia chrysantha* and inhaling deeply (you should try it: it's like taking your nose on a mini Hawaiian vacation). The large area of lawn used to be a nine-hole golf course; it was installed for the benefit of Laurie Kerr, a golfer.

Among the other early spring highlights that delight a winter-weary nose are a stand of moss-encrusted daphne bushes and flowering quince. One of my favorite trees, a large *Parrotia*, stands behind the house. This tree is a native of Iran, and because of its fall color, peeling platy bark, and general gracefulness, it is often considered one of the best small specimen trees. The genus was named for F. W. Parrot, a German naturalist.

After touring the gardens, walk back down Military Lane. The barn at 11648, with a cupola on top, once belonged to Thomas Kerr, Peter's brother. In the early 1900s, Peter and Laurie Kerr sent their girls to a private school in the loft of this barn.

At Military Road, turn left. Walk through the stoplight at the intersection of Military Road and Highway 43 (SW Riverside Drive), and continue up Military 0.3 mile to SW Breyman Avenue.

You'll soon come to Riverdale Elementary School. The school district was formed in 1888, with the first school southeast of the Breyman and Palatine Hill Road intersection. The original, central part of the building was designed in 1920 by the illustrious A. E. Doyle, who designed many of the buildings on the Reed College campus.

Walk uphill on Military for 0.4 mile. Watch for cars on this twisty stretch, especially about the time school is getting out (3:05 p.m.). Normally kind and gentle mothers, determined that their child will not be late to his or her after-school enrichment activity, can be quite intimidating if you're a pedestrian.

3 Pass SW Corbett Hill Circle, which leads to a passel of streets carved out of the old Henry Corbett estate. Stay on Military another 0.1 mile, turn right onto SW Summerville Avenue, and walk toward the Berry Botanic Garden. There is no sign at the intersection, and finding your way can be a little disconcerting when you think you may be walking down someone's private driveway. Just past the home at 11603, the road heads downhill. Stay left here, and left again at the mailbox for Berry: 11505.

Berry Botanic Garden is known worldwide for its species plant collections and conservation efforts. Rae Selling Berry and her husband bought 9 acres in 1938 on land that had been logged off a half century earlier to provide charcoal for Oswego's iron-smelting furnaces. She was in her midfifties then, had raised her children, and had run out of gardening space at the family's Irvington home. For years she had subscribed to plant-gathering expeditions in Asia and Europe.

As a subscriber she received seeds that were new to the gardening world, seeds that became the basis of her lifelong study and cultivation of plants.

Rae's husband wanted the Dunthorpe house to be sited on high ground where he could see Mount Hood; Rae wanted it in the center of the property in a woodland hollow where she could overlook her garden. Mrs. Berry got her wish. The home was designed by Reuben Sinex, and the front door and fireplace were hand-carved by Fritz von Schmidt. The tree on the front door symbolizes the transition between home and garden.

Stop by the office to pay when you arrive. They'll give you a "pick of the month" chart, which lists plants currently putting on an especially nice show.

The Berry Botanic Garden is quite unlike the Bishop's Close. Berry planted her garden not with an eye for aesthetics but with each plant's needs in mind. As she once said, "You can't tell a plant where to grow. It will tell you." She studied her plants' native environments and used her garden's many microclimates to best duplicate the various conditions the plants preferred. She designed the border of shrubs and trees to showcase the many shades and textures of green in nature. The rhododendron grove is especially nice. You can stroll on paths through twisty trunks, with a canopy of leaves and flowers overhead.

Perhaps gardening is good for one's health; like her plant-loving neighbor, Peter Kerr, Rae Berry lived to be a nonagenarian, dying at home in 1976 at age ninety-six. After her death, she left the property to her children. Three members of the Portland Garden Club raised enough funds from donors to purchase the house and garden and continue Rae Berry's mission. In 1983 the garden founded the nation's first seed bank devoted to rare and endangered species. With grants from philanthropists and conservation organizations, the garden has become world-class, with a sophisticated freezer for permanent storage of millions of seeds. In 2003 the property became listed on the National Register of Historic Places.

After visiting the garden, retrace your steps on Summerville. Turn left on Military and follow it around to the grade school.

You have the option here of making a quick pass through a flat loop of about 1.7 miles, taking SW Breyman Avenue south to Edgecliff Road, Iron Mountain Boulevard, and Greenwood Road. This loop passes many lovely old estates set back from the road, some of which are on the National Register of Historic Places. Edgecliff is especially fine; this quiet road is lined with hedges that are low enough to provide privacy without creating a fortress effect.

From the school, retrace your steps back to the starting point. Once back at your car, you might want to take a drive down to the end of Riverwood, a street of extremely lovely homes overlooking a bend in the Willamette River.

SELLWOOD RIVERFRONT TO JOHNSON CREEK LOOP

STARTING POINT Sellwood Riverfront Park parking lot: SE Spokane Street and Oaks Park Way

DISTANCE 3.75 miles

ELEVATION 10 feet at the starting point; 110 feet at the top of the bluff in Sellwood Park; 40 feet at Johnson Creek Park

GETTING THERE AND PARKING From downtown Portland, drive east on Burnside Street. Turn right at the first stoplight over the Burnside Bridge, SE Martin Luther King Jr. Boulevard (Highway 99E). This becomes SE McLoughlin Boulevard just past SE Powell Boulevard. Take the Tacoma Street exit. Drive west on Tacoma to SE 7th Avenue. Turn right; in one block, turn left on SE Spokane Street. Cross the railroad tracks and the Springwater Corridor Trail, and turn right onto SE Oaks Park Way. Sellwood Riverfront Park is on your left.

TriMet: From downtown, take bus 40 (Tacoma) to the stop at SE Tacoma Street and 7th Avenue. Walk one block north to SE Spokane Street, turn left and walk three blocks to SE Oaks Park Way (you'll cross a railroad track right before Oaks Park Way). Turn right and walk to the parking area in Sellwood Riverfront Park.

RESTROOMS AND DRINKING FOUNTAINS Restrooms and drinking fountains can be found at Sellwood Riverfront Park, Sellwood Park, and Johnson Creek Park. Please note, however, that Johnson Creek Park facilities do not operate in winter.

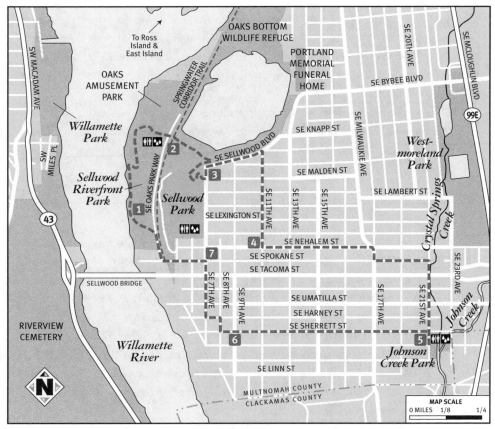

WALK 13. *Sellwood Riverfront to Johnson Creek Loop*

Map labels

SW MACADAM AVE

MILES PL

SW

To Ross
Island &
East Island

OAKS BOTTOM
WILDLIFE REFUGE

SE 20TH AVE

SE MCLOUGHLIN BLVD

OAKS
AMUSEMENT
PARK

*Willamette
Park*

SPRINGWATER CORRIDOR TRAIL

PORTLAND
MEMORIAL
FUNERAL
HOME

SE BYBEE BLVD

99E

*Sellwood
Riverfront
Park*

SE SELLWOOD BLVD

SE KNAPP ST

SE MILWAUKIE AVE

*West-
moreland
Park*

SE MALDEN ST

Crystal Springs Creek

SE OAKS PARK WAY

*Sellwood
Park*

SE LEXINGTON ST

SE 11TH AVE

SE 13TH AVE

SE 15TH AVE

SE LAMBERT ST

43

SE NEHALEM ST

SE 23RD AVE

SELLWOOD BRIDGE

SE SPOKANE ST

SE TACOMA ST

SE 7TH AVE

SE 8TH AVE

SE 9TH AVE

SE UMATILLA ST

SE HARNEY ST

SE SHERRETT ST

SE 17TH AVE

SE 21ST AVE

Johnson Creek

RIVERVIEW
CEMETERY

*Willamette
River*

*Johnson
Creek Park*

SE LINN ST

MULTNOMAH COUNTY
CLACKAMAS COUNTY

N

MAP SCALE
0 MILES   1/8   1/4

MAP KEY

- ROUTE
- STAIRS
- TRAILS
- RAILROAD TRACKS
- PARKS/GREENSPACE
- PUBLIC RESTROOMS
- WATER
- BUS STOP

FOOD AND DRINK There are lots of dining options in streets just off the route of this walk. Sellwood's commercial strip along SE 13th Avenue has enough antique stores, coffee shops, and restaurants to make a digression from the route worthwhile. New Seasons Market at 1214 SE Tacoma is a locally owned grocery store that promotes local, sustainable agriculture and has a great deli with outdoor seating; 503-230-4949. It is located near the end of the hill walk.

NOTE Use your discretion about hiking alone in the Oaks Bottom Wildlife Refuge and along the stretch of riverfront just west of Oaks Amusement Park. Both are isolated areas, although there are usually lots of walkers in Oaks Bottom.

B RING BINOCULARS ON THIS WALK, FOR TWO REASONS. First, Oaks Bottom is located near one of the city's largest blue heron rookeries, and the bird watching here is prime. Second, the fabulous panorama of the West Hills and downtown from the top of the 80-foot-high bluffs along SE Sellwood Boulevard makes it a great place to pick out city landmarks.

You might want to pack a picnic lunch to enjoy at the walk's turnaround point, Johnson Creek Park, another hidden city jewel. At this tiny 2-acre park, located at the confluence of Johnson and Crystal Springs Creeks, you can picnic at tables set next to the water. No riprap, no concrete—the only things separating you from the water are your shoes.

The first leg of this hike varies, depending on the Willamette River's water level. From about July through November, you can walk along its sandy eastern shore to Oaks Amusement Park. If river levels are too high, follow the directions in the text to the Springwater Corridor Trail.

1 Sellwood began as a separate town from Portland. Incorporated in 1887, it was named after John Sellwood, an Episcopal minister who had a donation land claim here. The town merged with Portland in 1893. This walk will take you into not only the historic Sellwood district but also five city parks, four of which are similarly named. They are, in the order in which you'll encounter them: Sellwood Riverfront Park, Oaks Amusement Park (also called Oaks Park or the Oaks), Oaks Bottom Wildlife Refuge, Sellwood Park, and Johnson Creek Park.

The hill walk starts in the parking lot at Sellwood Riverfront Park, an 8.75-acre park that provides one of the city's few sandy-beach accesses to the Willamette River (at low water levels). After parking, walk a short way north on a path through the lawn. Before the woods begin, turn left toward the river, and walk down onto the beach. One November the beach here was wide, about 50 feet, but every year is different. As fall and winter progress, it can disappear and may not be accessible until July.

If you find the beach isn't there, enjoy the river view from the platform under a stand of old poplars, and then walk back out of the parking lot to the Springwater Corridor Trail. You crossed this trail in your car, just before entering the parking lot. Walk north on the trail until you reach the rail underpass directly across from the Oaks Park entrance. Exit the trail at the underpass and rejoin the walk at route junction 2.

On the river beach, walk north. Across the river is the steep Fulton Park neighborhood explored in Walk 9. This eastern bank of the Willamette is a stretch of rare, unengineered river frontage within the city. No riprap, no sea walls, no filled-in bottomland. A cottonwood forest stands on your right as you walk on a sandy, then pebbly, beach. This is a pleasant walk for a weekday in fall, when the motorboats and jet skis are quietly moored and you can enjoy the river's quiet. River temperatures range year-round from 50 to 65 degrees Fahrenheit.

While the beach continues north for more scenic views of the river, the surrounding hills, Ross Island, and downtown, turn eastward about midway through the row of floating homes on the western side of the river. You're across the river from SW Miles Place, the quirky little street of once-floating-but-now-anchored homes discussed in Walk 9. This spot provides a good perspective of Willamette Park. Its flat riverside land used to be a seasonal wetland; it was filled in when the Vista Ridge Tunnel was excavated for the Sunset Highway. Today, where carp spawned and beavers gnawed, soccer players kick and bikers pedal.

From the beach, the trail to the east heads quickly through bushes to a walkway with iron handrails that leads to Oaks Park. This trail is indistinct from the river's edge but easy to find once you climb the beach a bit. (You can walk further north along the beach to a concrete staircase up into Oaks Park. It is adjacent to a large "clean rivers" sign.)

While most people approach Oaks Park by car from its eastern side, walkers can enter it via this trail from its picturesque river side. Oak groves, historic buildings, and riverside paths with views of the West Hills and downtown make this a wonderful place to stroll, even in winter when most of the park's operations are shut down.

Enter the southern end of Oaks Park at Groves 3 and 4. The oaks here are Oregon white oaks. Native to the area, these trees once covered the low hills of the Willamette Valley. American Indians would set fires in the valley to improve forage for deer and elk, resulting in grassy oak savannas. They also roasted the acorns and used them for flour. Because of settlement and fire suppression over the last two centuries, many white oak forests have been overgrown by conifers.

Turn left and walk north to a paved riverside path lined with old flowering cherry trees. These trees put on a grand pink show in March.

Oaks Park is one of the ten oldest amusement parks in the United States. It opened two days before the Lewis and Clark Exposition in 1905 and was owned by the Oregon Water, Power and Railway Company, which built it to stimulate rail travel on its new rail line (the linear strip that has been reincarnated as the Springwater Corridor Trail). In its heyday, Oaks Park was *the* place for full-dress family outings. The only way to get there was by trolley, foot, or boat, and it was so popular in the early days that trolley cars ran to it every five minutes from downtown Portland. The rides here still thrill children and teenagers. For parents, the low prices and natural setting of Oaks Park make it a very pleasant alternative to the hyperstimulating, wallet-sucking amusement parks more common today.

Walk along the path above the river until you see, on your right, the Oaks Park Historic Dance Pavilion, open for weddings and parties. Turn east and walk further into the park. After passing the dance pavilion, you're at the southern end of the midway. Here you'll see the Oaks Skating Rink, open year-round, where at scheduled times you can glide the boards accompanied by the live sounds of a Wurlitzer organ. The floor of the rink is built atop airtight iron barrels so that it can float above the floodwaters that occasionally inundate the site. The Noah's Ark carousel dates from 1912 and is on the National Register of Historic Places. Its hand-carved animals were made by the Herschell Spillman Company of New York, which created eighteen different menagerie animals for its carousel designs; it could keep a child busy for a while seeing if all eighteen reside in Oaks Park.

Walk toward the main park gate, and exit the park through it. Walk across Oaks Park Way and head to the tunnel under the Springwater Corridor Trail.

2   Once through the tunnel, you are out of funland and back to nature, in the South Meadow of the Oaks Bottom Wildlife Refuge.

Landfill from the construction of Interstate 405 eradicated many of the original natural wetlands here. In the 1970s, activists saved the area from being further filled and developed into ball fields. Today this 160-acre wetland is the only wildlife refuge within city limits; a hundred different bird species have been spotted in its meadows, bluffs, and lake.

The large lake was formed in the 1800s when a railroad built the embankment you just passed beneath. The Olmsted Brothers referred to this railroad path in their 1903 report, declaring that it "greatly injured the views, where it has been run over the low meadows and flats between the bluff and the river south of Holgate Street."

The water was further impounded when tons of construction refuse and dirt were placed in the area you're walking over. Prior to the embankment and fill, the entire Oaks Bottom lowlands drained and filled with changing river levels. Today there is a dam adjacent to the railroad bridge; it has a water control structure that engineers play with throughout the year to mimic the natural fluctuations in the wetland's water level.

Walk along the lake on a gravel path toward the bluffs. The large building on the bluff across the lake is the Portland Memorial Funeral Home and Mausoleum, among the nation's first crematories. When it was built in 1901, cremation was becoming increasingly popular in large cities, owing to concerns over the possible public health threat from burying the dead, and an aversion to the growing commercialization of death, with cemetery burials and their accompanying expenses. The first modern American cremation took place in 1876 in Washington, Pennsylvania. Twenty-five years later, Portland Memorial became the twenty-sixth crematory in the United States, performing twenty cremations its first year. The remains of a hundred thousand people now rest at the Portland Memorial, and nationally, one out of every four Americans is cremated.

Portland Memorial is a city gem, with original Tiffany windows, miles of marble-lined walls, and stunning views. The four stories above the bluff are only half its square footage; there are another four stories underground. It is open to visitors seven days a week during business hours.

3 At the base of the bluffs, turn left, and take a quick right next to a sign warning of fire danger. This trail will lead you up the 80-foot-high bluff to the northern end of Sellwood Park. To the south are its groves of trees, pool, playground, and paths.

The 16-acre Sellwood Park was acquired by the City of Portland in 1909. Its pool, built in 1910, is the oldest public pool in Portland. It was built to replace the city's public bathhouse, which was located in the Willamette River at the foot of SW Jefferson Street. At the bathhouse, bathers would hop in the slat-bottomed wooden tank floating in the river and cleanse themselves; after a time, however, the river became too polluted for that to be feasible. Originally, the Sellwood pool did not permit the sexes to bathe together; on alternate days, males and females frolicked behind a 10-foot-tall privacy fence.

6/14/48 AERIAL VIEW FLOOD WATERS
East Side-Vicinity Selwood Bridge

An aerial view of Sellwood during the flood of May 30, 1948 (the same flood that destroyed the city of Vanport). Oaks Amusement Park is almost totally submerged, as is Oaks Bottom, with the water almost breaching the railroad embankment. Sellwood Park is the forested area south of Oaks Bottom. Photo courtesy of the City of Portland Archives.

Before 1909, Sellwood Park was the site of the City View Park and Racetrack. Today its thickly planted grove of firs and banks of rhododendrons make it one of the city's most beautiful parks, especially in late spring when its rhododendrons are blooming. The area was a contender for the 1905 Lewis and Clark Exposition, the world's fair that put Portland on the map, but lost out because it was too far from downtown.

Walk straight across the parking lot to the intersection of SE 7th Avenue and Malden Street. Turn left on 7th, walk a short way to the top of the cliff, and turn right onto SE Sellwood Boulevard, a street of early-twentieth-century homes with some of the city's loveliest views. Healy Heights, OHSU, downtown Portland, the towers of the Steel Bridge, the green glass spires of the Convention Center, the office towers of the Lloyd district—all combine to make a backdrop for a stunning foreground view of the lake and woodlands of Oaks Bottom.

One side of Sellwood Boulevard is lined with homes, but take a walk on its wild side, at the top of the bluff. Benches here let you turn your back to everything but the great view. At the intersection with SE 9th Avenue is a spiny monkey puzzle tree. (See Walk 19 for more on this tree.)

Turn right onto SE 11th Avenue, a pleasant wooded street. On the corner of Malden is a building with a western falsefront; built in 1905 as a corner grocery, this is now a residence. The intersection with SE Lambert Street is worth a look around for the old homes and trees. In the parking strip at 1013 Lambert are two Heritage Trees, both horsechestnuts, a tree that is not actually a chestnut. Its seeds, which look like nuts, are inedible. If you've ever wanted to know how a horsechestnut differs from a real chestnut, pick up a leaf and a nut if any are available and carry them with you; in a few blocks you'll walk by two more Heritage Trees, both American chestnuts.

Continue walking south on 11th. This old neighborhood still wears its iron-clad curbs, installed to defend the concrete from the wheels of carriages, although by 1915, the year in which many of these sidewalks were poured, the horse-drawn carriage was becoming a relic.

At the corner of 11th and Lexington Street are two American chestnut trees. Their nuts are edible. This species, native to the East Coast, suffered greatly from a chestnut blight in the early 1900s and is seldom, if ever, planted today. Growers of edible chestnuts now plant hybrids that blend the superior taste of the American chestnut with blight-resistant strains from Europe and Asia. Nuts are contained in a spiny husk, and are sublime—sweet and chewy—when roasted. Cherokee Indians used the chestnut as a food source, and it has been used as a coffee substitute.

4 Turn left on SE Nehalem Street. At SE 13th Avenue you can make a detour either left or right to explore Sellwood's antique shops and restaurants. To resume the walk, stay straight on Nehalem. At the corner of Nehalem and 15th, look right. One block to the south, at 1436 SE Spokane Street, is the Sellwood Community Center. The building was constructed as a residence hotel for workers at the Sellwood Log Mill. When the hotel closed in 1920, the city purchased it and turned it into a community center.

A huge copper beech, planted in 1892, claims the sky above 1579 Nehalem. The great plant expert Michael Dirr has said of the European beech—of which the copper beech is a cultivar—that there is no finer specimen tree. I agree. Beautifully smooth gray bark, a graceful growth habit, and stunning fall color make this tree a living treasure for anyone lucky enough to live near one.

Continue east on Nehalem to the intersection with SE Milwaukie Avenue, which from this point south turns into SE 17th Avenue. Turn right, walk one block, and cross 17th to walk east on SE Spokane. Right about here, the land starts dropping toward the channel of Crystal Springs Creek. Over the years the creek has eroded the flood deposits laid down by the catastrophic Missoula Floods, creating a broad lowland that begins here and continues through the Eastmoreland Golf Course.

Walk downhill on Spokane, a street of small tidy homes, to its end where it runs into the creek, at SE 21st Avenue. Turn right at 21st, which here is a road-less sidewalk that carries you right next to the creek. Take the sidewalk one block to where it emerges onto SE Tacoma Street. Cross Tacoma carefully, and continue on 21st, which is more of an alley now, with the creek flowing along-side it. The charming little intersection of 21st and Tenino is a quiet spot where, according to a longtime Sellwood resident, a bootlegger named Moogie Myers once found a hospitable spot for his endeavors. Stay on 21st three more blocks.

Turn left on SE Sherrett Street into Johnson Creek Park, one of the few parks in the city where you can walk along a stream—and here there's not just one stream, but two. Walk on the paved path and over a bridge to the peninsula formed by the confluence of Crystal Springs and Johnson Creeks. (Walk 14 vis-its the headwaters of Crystal Springs Creek, on the Reed College campus; Walk 15 brushes up against a more easterly portion of Johnson Creek, by the Leach Botanical Garden.) Johnson is the larger of the two creeks, having run 25 miles from its headwaters in Mount Hood's foothills. A house used to sit on the penin-sula but has been torn down, and the ground has been replanted. When I vis-ited the park in February 2004, schoolchildren were planting native riparian plants like snowberry, salmonberry, and willow to help restore the land to its natural state. From here Johnson Creek flows another mile south to its conflu-ence with the Willamette River in Milwaukie.

5   Retrace your steps out of the park. At the entrance is a stand of Oregon grape, the state flower. This plant is in the barberry family, and it has the same prickly leaves of its cousins. The dark blue berries are tart but edible and were used by native peoples. Indians in Montana crushed the berries and mixed them with water and sugar for a refreshing drink. Other tribes ate them raw, roasted, or mashed, or used them in preserves. The shockingly yellow roots make a bright yellow dye.

Once outside the park, turn left on Sherrett. Follow it as it climbs away from the creek. This is a quiet street, like many streets south of Tacoma, with early-twentieth-century homes and a relaxed feel.

In the parking strip at 1653 is a big southern magnolia. This tree, native to the American Southeast, is a symbol of southern culture. Despite the cultural differences between the Southeast and Northwest, the magnolia thrives in the maritime climate here.

The Sellwood Middle School playing fields, between SE 15th and 16th Avenues, were once lined with homes. The two very old walnut trees along the street here once graced someone's front yard. Like many similarly aged walnuts seen on this walk, these trees might have come from the nurseries that operated just south of here, on land now occupied by Waverly Country Club.

At SE 14th Avenue the land starts falling toward the Willamette River. An enormous Douglas fir towers over the corner of 13th and Sherrett. When I asked the gentleman who resides in the home beneath the tree how old it was, he replied, "It was old when I first saw it seventy-five years ago." He also told me that the streetcar used to run down 13th, in front of his house, to its terminus at Golf Junction. This junction was three blocks south of here, where the streetcars met the interurban train that ran to Oregon City and Estacada. The streetcar barns at the junction were torn down in 2003.

6 Walk past Share-It Square at Sherrett and SE 9th Avenue. This neighborhood gathering spot, an unorthodox collection of structures and art that sprang up in 1996, looks as though it's situated in the public right-of-way. And it is, in fact; residents won a tussle with the city to leave their "public square" alone.

Share-It Square's communal playhouse, one of many public structures for passersby in the parking strips at the intersection of SE 9th Avenue and Sherrett Street.

175

What's more, supporters were so persuasive that in 2000 the city council passed an ordinance allowing any group of citizens to convert certain street intersections into public squares such as this one. In 1999 Governor John Kitzhaber presented the square with the Governor's Livability Award.

You can't just walk by this funky bit of grassroots creativity without investigating. You'll find on one corner a twenty-four-hour tea station, where the carafe is always hot. Help yourself. Another corner is home to a children's playhouse made of tree branches and recycled house parts. At another corner, a produce exchange encourages city farmers to share their bounty. On the last corner, you can find something to read at the book exchange, and this thought to chew upon during the rest of your walk: "Every crossroads needs a place to water the thirst of those who journey through life."

This part of Sellwood, south of Tacoma and close to the river, is funky, old, and immensely charming, with little homes that wear their age well and sleepy, untrafficked streets that take you back a few decades. Turn right on SE 8th Avenue, then left on Harney Street, where a Camperdown elm presides, like a dumpy dowager, at the northwestern corner of the intersection. (See Walk 2 for the history of these odd trees.) Turn right on SE 7th Avenue. You'll pass a home that would probably win first place if the city ever held a competition for rock cairn art.

The sweet scent in the air at 7th and SE Umatilla Street comes from the Essential Oil Company, which imports and distributes essential oils for use in soaps, aromatherapy, and other products. The company was founded in 1977 by Robert Seidel. While nothing is manufactured here, the aromas do escape, enticing you inside to the sample bar and retail outlet, open Monday through Friday.

Cross SE Tacoma Street. This is not a pleasant crossing; Tacoma is a busy road, leading to the Sellwood Bridge three blocks west of here and effectively splitting the neighborhood. Watch for cars, and cross carefully. If you want to use a crosswalk, walk six blocks east to the stoplight at 13th.

7 Turn left on SE Spokane Street. At the corner of SE Grand Avenue is the Oaks Pioneer Church. Dedicated in 1851 as Saint Johns Episcopal in Milwaukie, this is the oldest continually used church in Oregon. Oregon pioneer Lot Whitcomb helped build it; the bell in the belfry came from one of his steamboats. In 1961 the church was barged to this site. Its quaint size and setting among the oaks make it hugely popular for weddings. How precious the oaks are to the appeal of the church can be seen at the back of the building, where the roof has been notched to accommodate one of the trees.

At Spokane and Oaks Park Way, you'll see ahead of you the concrete boat launch that was once the ramp for the Spokane Street Ferry. It was replaced in 1925 when the Sellwood Bridge opened. This narrow span is the state's busiest two-lane bridge. The hills above its western approach are claimed by the lovely Riverview Cemetery.

Turn right on Oaks Park Way and follow the sidewalk that leads back to the starting point.

REED CANYON TO EASTMORELAND LOOP

STARTING POINT SE 38th Avenue and Reedway Street

DISTANCE 2 miles, plus about 1 mile of walking trails within the Crystal Springs Rhododendron Garden, but excluding exploratory forays down various trails in the Reed Canyon

ELEVATION 210 feet at the starting point; 60 feet at Crystal Springs Rhododendron Garden

GETTING THERE AND PARKING From downtown Portland, drive east on Burnside Street to SE 39th Avenue. Turn right onto 39th and travel 2.6 miles to the stoplight at SE Steele Street. Drive four more blocks and turn right onto SE Reedway Street, a dead end. Park in this block.

TriMet: From downtown, take bus 19 (Woodstock) to the stop at SE 39th and Woodstock. Walk three blocks north to SE Reedway. Turn left. The hike begins at the dead end, one block west of 39th.

RESTROOMS AND DRINKING FOUNTAINS Restrooms and drinking fountains are available at the Crystal Springs Rhododendron Garden and the Eric V. Hauser Memorial Library on the Reed College campus.

FOOD AND DRINK Just west of the Eastmoreland neighborhood, across Highway 99E, is the Westmoreland neighborhood. Here, at the intersection of SE Bybee Boulevard and Milwaukie Avenue, is a collection of restaurants and shops of all stripes.

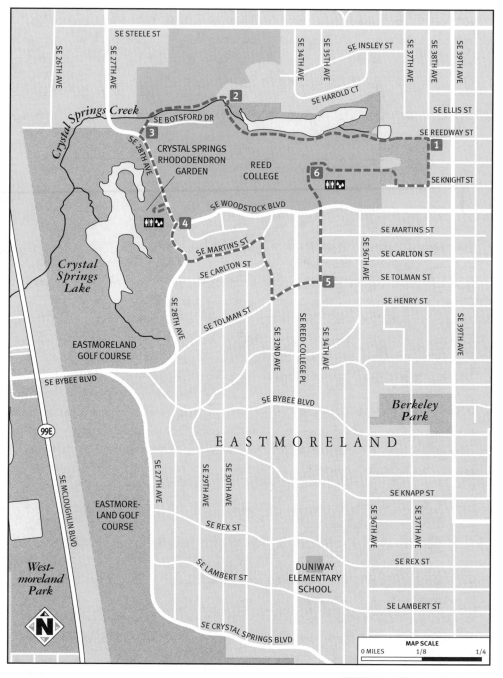

SE STEELE ST

SE 26TH AVE
SE 27TH AVE
SE 34TH AVE
SE 35TH AVE
SE INSLEY ST
SE 37TH AVE
SE 38TH AVE
SE 39TH AVE

SE HAROLD CT

Crystal Springs Creek

SE BOTSFORD DR

2

SE ELLIS ST

3

SE REEDWAY ST

SE 28TH AVE

CRYSTAL SPRINGS
RHODODENDRON
GARDEN

REED
COLLEGE

1

6

SE KNIGHT ST

SE WOODSTOCK BLVD

4

SE MARTINS ST

*Crystal
Springs
Lake*

SE MARTINS ST

SE CARLTON ST

SE 36TH AVE

SE CARLTON ST

SE TOLMAN ST

SE HENRY ST

5

SE 39TH AVE

EASTMORELAND
GOLF COURSE

SE 28TH AVE

SE TOLMAN ST

SE 32ND AVE

SE REED COLLEGE PL

SE 34TH AVE

SE BYBEE BLVD

SE BYBEE BLVD

*Berkeley
Park*

99E

SE MCLOUGHLIN BLVD

E A S T M O R E L A N D

SE 27TH AVE

SE 29TH AVE

SE 30TH AVE

EASTMORE-
LAND GOLF
COURSE

SE REX ST

SE KNAPP ST

SE 36TH AVE

SE 37TH AVE

SE LAMBERT ST

SE REX ST

SE LAMBERT ST

*West-
moreland
Park*

SE CRYSTAL SPRINGS BLVD

DUNIWAY
ELEMENTARY
SCHOOL

N

MAP SCALE

0 MILES   1/8   1/4

WALK 14. *Reed Canyon to Eastmoreland Loop*

MAP KEY

- ▪ ROUTE   ╪╪╪ RAILROAD TRACKS
- ▪▪▪▪ STAIRS   PARKS/GREENSPACE
- ‒ ‒ TRAILS   🚻 PUBLIC RESTROOMS
- 🌊 WATER   📍 BUS STOP

NOTE Parts of this walk cut through rich bird habitat. Bring your binoculars, and for maximum wildlife exposure, leave your dog at home. If you do bring a dog, Reed College requests that you use a leash while in the canyon and that both you and your dog stay on trails or boardwalks to preserve the wetland environment. If you're a tree lover you may want to visit the Trees of Reed Web site (web.reed.edu/trees), a fabulous resource that maps just about every tree on the campus and provides names, history, and a complete horticultural description.

THE HILLS OF PORTLAND'S EAST SIDE are either obvious volcanic outcrops like Rocky Butte, Mount Tabor, and Mount Scott, or gentle inclines separated by steeper pitches. The walk into Reed Canyon takes you down one of these steeper pitches, the edge of one of the Portland Terraces, a series of fine silt, sand, and gravel beds that stairstep uphill from the Willamette River. These beds were laid down by the violent, debris-laden Missoula Floods, which thundered down from Montana through the Columbia River Gorge around thirteen to twenty thousand years ago. When the flood met a bottleneck near present-day Kalama, Washington, the water backed up 125 miles south into the Willamette Valley. Ice, boulders, soil, and trees churned in a maelstrom that reached up to 400 feet deep in the Portland area and swirled more than halfway up the existing buttes and cinder cones. Today the floor of the Willamette Valley is covered with these deposits, which were later carved into terraces by changing water levels. Because the flood deposits are granular and porous, they make an excellent water-storage medium. Rain percolates down through the material; when it reaches an impervious layer, it perches atop it, creating an underground reservoir, otherwise known as an aquifer. Where the land is eroded away, as at the edge of a terrace, the aquifer meets the light of day, and voilà!—a spring is born. (See Walk 17 for more on the Missoula Floods.)

In Reed Canyon are some of the outlets of Crystal Springs, the largest concentration of springs in the Portland area. Here, springs emerge from six to eight sites, including from the bottom of Reed Lake. Other springs emerge at the Eastmoreland Golf Course and in the Crystal Springs Rhododendron Garden. Reed Canyon (a magnanimous term, given its 50-foot depth) is a valley incised into the edge of one of the Portland Terraces by the erosional force of the springs that emerge here.

Much of this hill walk takes place on the Reed College campus. Reed was founded in 1908, and its first classes were held in 1911. It is named for its benefactors, Oregon pioneers Simeon and Amanda Reed. The Reeds made their fortune in the Oregon Steam Navigation Company, which in the 1860s handled

Columbia River traffic to and from gold mines in eastern Oregon and Idaho. Simeon died in 1895. His will was altruistic but unspecific, stating a wish to "devote some portion of my estate to benevolent objects, or to the cultivation, illustration, or development of the fine arts in the city of Portland, or to some other suitable purpose, which shall be of permanent value and contribute to the beauty of the city and to the intelligence, prosperity, and happiness of the inhabitants." Amanda, after consulting with the Unitarian minister Thomas Lamb Eliot, fleshed out this rather amorphous directive by setting up a board of trustees to found an institution of learning in Portland, with no limits other than an insistence on equality and secularism. Once this was in place, Eliot used his persuasive powers to induce the Ladd Estate Company to donate to the campus 40 acres of cow pasture and orchard on its Crystal Springs Farm. Some of the old orchard trees still exist, such as the walnuts in the campus's southeastern corner, which you'll pass by near the end of the walk. The Reed campus has been nationally noted for its outstanding botanical interest, along with Dartmouth and Bryn Mawr.

Reed College has become one of the nation's preeminent institutions of liberal arts and sciences. Loren Pope, education editor of the *New York Times*, has called it "the most intellectual college in the country." It has a reputation for attracting brainy iconoclasts to its traditional and rigorous liberal arts curriculum. With annual tuition and fees in the low $30,000 range, an absence of collegiate sports, and a demanding academic environment, Reed doesn't attract the typical student. SAT scores of incoming freshman are around 1400.

Despite the fact that Reed is a private and well-endowed institution, its reach is generous. In its enthusiastic sharing of its magnificent grounds, both wild and cultivated, it seems to embody Simeon Reed's wish. See www.reed.edu for more information on the Reed Canyon history and restoration efforts.

1 Begin walking downhill on the well-defined trail behind concrete stanchions at SE 38th and Reedway. When you're halfway down the wooden steps just below the trailhead, stop and look left. What you see is the head of a natural drainage, significantly altered by human activity. When SE 39th Avenue was constructed, its route traversed up and down through several small valleys. To create a level roadbed and space for homesites, the tops of these valleys were filled in. The head of this valley originally began a bit further east of here, at about SE 40th Avenue.

After walking down the stairs, you're on flat ground. The natural valley configuration here was steep sides converging at a narrow floor. Look to your right, and you can see what created the flat ground: a man-made berm, which becomes more noticeable as you walk further down the trail. This berm appears to be an old pond embankment, perhaps built to create a swimming hole or an irrigation pond for the Crystal Springs Farm. Today the pond area is silted in, creating ground as flat as the proverbial pancake.

Keep right as the trail forks. The trail to the left leads to Reed College's Studio Art Building. Continue down the trail; below the pond embankment are the first signs of the wetlands created by Crystal Springs. Here are the headwaters of Crystal Springs Creek, which travels west through this canyon and temporarily becomes Reed Lake. From the lake, the creek reemerges via a fish ladder and then runs south through Eastmoreland Golf Course and Crystal Springs Rhododendron Garden to its confluence with Johnson Creek in Sellwood.

Surprisingly, the output of the springs does not vary with rainfall, remaining constant at 4–6 cubic feet per second. The constant dampness makes a welcome environment for common horsetail, the plumelike plant growing in the bottomland. It looks like no other plant: a single, segmented, hollow stem with needlelike leaves arrayed at each joint. Horsetail dominated the plant world 200 million years ago as giant, fernlike trees. All horsetail species have a high silica content, hence one common name: scouring rush. The highest silica content occurs in the fall, after the plant dries. Ancient Romans used these plants to scrub pots. American Indians used them to polish bone tools and fingernails. Native peoples also used the hollow stems to administer medicine to babies; and in what must have been a satisfying practice, as a puberty ritual they stuffed a hollow horsetail stem with lice from a young girl's head and tossed the plant and its hapless passengers into a stream.

An old sign near the top of the canyon notes that this is the Reed Canyon Fish and Wildlife Refuge. The area was declared a state game refuge in 1913, a designation that no longer exists. The state refuge system has been superseded by the more site-specific but less evocative environmental overlay zone designations. Back in 1913 the canyon was still in a relatively natural state. Although less corrupted by human activity then, it was, as a greenspace, smaller, with the land on the north farmed much closer to the water's edge. In the ensuing years, Reed has planted many trees to expand the canopy.

In the 1930s, Una Davis, a Reed student, inventoried the canyon plants. Absent then were many of the noxious weeds like blackberry, English ivy, and reed canary grass that later choked out much of the native vegetation. Except during the annual Canyon Days, in which various projects were undertaken to improve the canyon, either by taming it or turning it into a place for student recreation, the area was largely left alone for invasive species to colonize undisturbed. That changed in 1998 when Reed alumna Laurel Wilkening gave the

The spring-fed wetlands upstream from Reed Lake in Reed Canyon. Photo by Zeb Andrews.

college $35,000 to restore the canyon. Her gift was the catalyst that spurred the ongoing efforts to revitalize and conserve the canyon's natural state.

At the first boardwalk is a magnificent stand of blue elderberry, which bears fruit in July. While the berries can be used to make jam or wine, elderberry has had a long history of contributing in other ways to the human race. The fine-grained wood from older elderberry limbs has been used to make mathematical instruments; genteel ladies have applied elderflower water to skin "afflictions" such as freckles; and children for centuries have cut the young branches, poked out their cottony centers, and used the hollow tubes for blow guns. The plant is not without its risks: the roots, stems, and leaves contain cyanide-releasing substances.

As you descend on a gentle path into the canyon, you'll see more pools of standing water. A boardwalk on your right takes an interesting foray into marshy ground. Even in a dry July, fresh water flows through horsetail and skunk cabbage, looking as pure as Perrier. Looks are deceiving: as with any open water source, the parasite giardia is a nasty hazard, and because this water percolates from the ground surface over a heavily populated 10-square-mile area, it's got a few residual unpleasantries in it. Ocean-dwelling lampreys spawn here in the summer, after surmounting the fish ladder downstream.

Continue on the boardwalk all the way across the wetlands for a full-on view of the upper marsh, with ducks usually in residence. After passing across the marsh, you emerge at the foot of SE 37th Avenue into an old orchard that, though now owned and maintained by Reed, was formerly owned by the Wiley family. Look for cherries in June and plums in July. In the fall you'll find filberts, chestnuts, English walnuts, and even hickory nuts from an old shagbark hickory.

After you've had your fill of exploring the orchard and the marsh, retrace your steps back to the main trail. Follow it as it descends along the southern side of the canyon. For another splendid view of the marsh, take the next boardwalk on your right. A scramble over a fallen tree and uneven footing on various planks are worth the effort, leading you to a secluded peninsula anchored by an old, leaning cedar and a bench that begs you to sit a spell and let this sanctuary of quiet decay and rebirth hush the buzz in your mind.

Back on the main trail, you'll begin to see the wetlands transition into a proper lake, and you'll have fine views of Reed Lake's glassy surface, many islands, and bird life. In Portland's Johnson Creek Basin Protection Plan, Reed Lake has been called "the only naturally occurring pond (or lake) remaining in the inner city area." As you'll see, an earthen dam, built around 1900, belies this assessment, although there is speculation that beavers may have had the first crack at engineering in this canyon.

The large cast-iron pipe that spans the lake is a City of Portland domestic water main serving the surrounding neighborhoods. The occasional green number sign marks an outflow from a campus drain. Outflows are marked to monitor soil sediments flowing from open areas into campus drains, or automotive oils reaching the drains from impervious surfaces on developed parts of the campus. For stormwater disposal, newer construction on the Reed campus uses bioswales (ditches planted so that roots and soil can naturally filter biohazards and sediment), and in fact Reed Lake itself functions as a bioswale. Because of the fairly long resident time, about three days, water entering the lake moves slowly toward the outfall. This allows time for sediments to settle and contributes to the high quality of the water downstream.

Continue on the trail as it passes under a footbridge that connects dorms on the northern side of the canyon to the rest of the Reed campus. Duckweed, a native, free-floating plant, covers the lower end of the lake. Just past the bridge is a flight of stairs cut into the slope on the left. Take them, and follow the trail as it continues along the lake's edge. During a visit here one July, the only sound I could hear was the quiet snipping of a large clan of ducks, eating duckweed in order to get at its resident insects, their real prey.

Looking down on Reed Lake from the Barry Cerf Memorial Theatre and Garden Area at Reed College. Photo by Zeb Andrews.

You'll pass the Barry Cerf Memorial Theatre and Garden Area. Named for a classics professor at Reed College, this amphitheater of wooden benches was built during the Great Depression with the aid of the National Youth Administration. In 1935, with more than 25 percent of employable Americans out of a job, President Franklin Roosevelt created the Works Progress Administration (WPA) to provide useful jobs, with the aim of preserving the skills and self-respect of victims of the Depression. During its eight-year run, the WPA (and its offspring, the National Youth Administration, which Eleanor Roosevelt urged her husband to create), produced more than 650,000 miles of roads, 125,000 public buildings, 75,000 bridges, 8000 parks, and 800 airports. The Barry Cerf amphitheater was rebuilt in 1988. Until 1970 it was the site of Reed's commencement, and it still hosts the annual Greek Theatre Festival. The stonework atop Rocky Butte was also built by WPA workers, as were the barrel-vault tunnels on NW Cornell Road.

2 Past the amphitheater, the trail runs up into a maintenance area. Stay right, next to the water. Walk across the road that sits atop the earthen dam. Until recently, water was routed via a culvert that discharged to a steep waterfall, preventing fish passage. The gate on the dam marks the fish ladder that was installed in 2001 as part of the efforts to restore native wildlife to Reed Canyon.

Once over the dam, take the path to the left that continues downstream. In addition to the fish ladder, a recent addition to the canyon here is a rocky stream channel, whose authentic look belies the fact that, until 2001, this was the site of a large outdoor swimming pool. Built right in the stream channel in the 1930s, the pool was a concrete behemoth that by the 1990s had become too expensive to maintain. The quandary of what to do with the pool dovetailed with plans to restore the canyon, and the pool was demolished. A staircase up the hill is all that remains of the pool structure. While it may seem odd for a pool to have been built in this shady canyon, photographs from the 1930s show throngs of decorously clad bathers splashing on a bright hillside with only a few trees to get between them and the sun.

Since its rebirth, the stream, with its fish ladder, rocky pools, and overhanging plants, has been all dressed up and waiting for the arrival of the honored guests: coho and chinook salmon. Cutthroat trout are already at the party. A picnic table next to the creek provides a good excuse to sit and enjoy the handiwork of the college staff and student workers who artfully recreated this natural setting.

After a sojourn near the stream, go back on the main trail as it heads downstream. Past the small grove of aspen on your left, the trail crosses the creek on a wooden bridge. Just downstream of the bridge, the theater building spans the creek, a design decision that today seems ludicrous. Until planned improvements are made to the trail here, you'll have to follow the creek as it flows under the theater by wending your way around the building's foundation. Once past the building, the creek disappears in and out of lush swampy vegetation. If you could follow it, you'd see that the creek emerges from its thicket of impatiens and horsetail and is corralled into a tidy, rock-lined channel next to a private home. From there it flows into a culvert under SE 28th Avenue and emerges in the Eastmoreland Golf Course.

3 At a fork in the trail, go left. A brief climb puts you on SE Botsford Drive on the Reed campus. Turn right and walk toward busy SE 28th Avenue. Cross 28th carefully; although the sight distance is good, traffic is fast and there is no crosswalk. Walk south on a sidewalk shaded by giant sequoias. After about 0.1 mile you'll arrive at the Crystal Springs Rhododendron Garden.

The 7 acres occupied by the garden were part of the Ladd Estate's Crystal Springs Farm. The land was sold to Portland Parks and Recreation in the early 1900s, and the gardens have been a work in progress since 1950, when the Portland chapter of the American Rhododendron Society began sculpting them from the overgrown brush, blackberry, and native vegetation on the site. While the garden is part of Portland Parks, the plants have been donated and most of the work has been performed by volunteers, who also keep the gardens elegantly maintained. This is a popular wedding venue. Spring is the best time to schedule a visit, but the garden is worth a stroll any time of year. A small fee is charged to tour Crystal Springs Rhododendron Garden on certain times and days; at other times there is no charge. Call 503-771-8386 or visit www.parks.ci.portland.or.us for details. Restrooms are available.

4 From the garden parking lot, walk south on 28th along the golf course to the stop sign at SE Woodstock Boulevard. Cross to the other side of 28th, and then cross Woodstock. Continue south along 28th, the western edge of the Eastmoreland neighborhood.

Like the rhododendron garden and Reed College, Eastmoreland was established on Crystal Springs Farm. After the Ladd Estate Company had donated land to the college, it began to develop the surrounding area, and marketed the Eastmoreland neighborhood as similar in appearance and quality to verdant neighborhoods surrounding universities back East. Initially, home sales in Eastmoreland were disappointing, probably due to its distance from the city. To sweeten the pot, the Ladd Estate Company donated another 150 acres to the city for the Eastmoreland Golf Course.

At 2840 SE Woodstock, just a few steps from the intersection of 28th and Woodstock, is a 1929 Arts and Crafts home. At 10,000 square feet, it reputedly was the largest home on Portland's east side when it was built.

Turn left in one block onto SE Martins Street. Eastmoreland is among the most heavily treed neighborhoods in Portland, and by good luck and liberal applications of fungicides, many of its American elms have been spared the Dutch elm disease, a fungus that has wiped out most elms in the country. Even so, every year an average of thirty-five American elms are cut down in Portland and replaced with hybrid elms that are more resistant to the disease. Dutch elm disease was first isolated in Europe in 1920; the first case in Portland was found in 1976, probably brought by travelers from Idaho carrying diseased wood west for firewood. The fungus invades a tree's vascular system, preventing water movement up the tree. It is often spread by beetles, which move from diseased to healthy trees, carrying the fungal spores on their backs. Once any disease is found on a tree, the entire tree is cut down and the wood carefully disposed of. Every three years the remaining elms in Portland get a dose of fungicide, which is pumped into holes drilled into the base of the tree.

As you climb Martins it becomes a deep green tunnel, with elms on both sides of the street arching and twining together. On a hot summer day the effect is magical. Although this neighborhood was first platted out in 1910, its slow pace of development led to many lots, such as those here on Martins, not being developed until after World War II.

Emerge from the elms onto SE 32nd Avenue. The large intersection here once had a traffic island. Its removal during the Great Depression kept ten jobless men busy for five days. The total labor cost of this WPA project was $189, less than $4 per day per man. Turn right and walk one block to the intersection of 32nd and SE Carlton Street, where a small Art Deco home holds its own among its grander neighbors. Walk one more block past Carlton to SE Tolman Street. Turn left for a tour past a mix of architectural personalities. The obvious care these homes receive creates a harmony that weaves together their diverse ages and styles.

In one block, cross SE Reed College Place, whose center median is edged by two lines of bigleaf lindens. On the other side is another elm bower. Here, as Tolman rises, levels, and rises more to the east, you can see evidence of the Portland Terraces. The relative steepness of the street here is the transition between terraces. The land levels off again at about 35th and Tolman.

5   Turn left onto SE 34th Avenue. Walk a block or so; in the yard at 6025 grows a large, spreading saucer magnolia whose hand-sized pink flowers bloom in April. Just past it in the parking strip is a venerable rose bush growing up a utility pole. (See Walk 4 for information on the history of parking strip roses in Portland.)

Cross Woodstock and take the sidewalk that angles into the Reed campus past some giant sequoias. The building to your right is the Eric V. Hauser Memorial Library, designed in 1930 by Pietro Belluschi, who was then working for A. E. Doyle. Belluschi's usual modern style was subdued here in an attempt to create a library that would harmonize with existing buildings on campus, such as the Old Dorm Block and Eliot Hall, the two long, English-Manor-style brick buildings you can see ahead and to the left. These had been designed by Doyle, who died in 1928.

The trees on your left with the knobby, blobby trunks are London plane trees, a cross between the American sycamore and the Oriental plane tree. The first printed record of this tree was in 1663, when the hybrid was found growing in London, where it has been so widely planted that it has taken the city's name. Also just west of the library are two of the city's largest ginkgo trees. They are both female trees, whose seeds are encased in a squishy, smelly capsule. The library's main entrance sidewalk used to pass right between the two trees. With hundreds of students treading on the seeds on their way to study, the capsules were ground to a malodorous mash. When the library was renovated in 1980, the main entrance was moved to the northern side.

6 Where the path ends, turn right, toward the bike racks located in front of the library's main entrance. There's a drinking fountain in the plaza here, and restrooms inside the library. The library also houses the Douglas F. Cooley Memorial Art Gallery, open afternoons, Tuesday through Sunday; admission is free. The plaza in front of the library is a lovely place to contemplate life. Resting here in the bosom of academia, it's easy to hark back to your own halcyon days before bills, children, jobs, and house payments.

After your rest and reverie, walk under the breezeway between the library and biology buildings, and turn left. On your left is a large coast redwood, the world's tallest tree species. Stay on the path as you walk by the psychology building (also designed by Belluschi, in 1949), past a row of sugar maples and European beeches planted unusually close, in a sentinel-like formation. These trees are remnants of nursery stock that was never thinned, from the days when the campus was a working farm. As you cross a campus roadway, the blue-roofed Studio Art Building (built in 1979) stands in front of you. Walk toward it, and then take the asphalt path that climbs uphill to its right. To the right of the path is a beautiful 1952 Northwest Regional home, once the residence of

Professor Dorothy Johansen, who worked at Reed from 1938 to 1969. It now houses Career Services.

Walk on the paved path through an orchard of walnut trees. A bit further on is an enormous black walnut whose muscular limbs swoop gallantly down before you, offering easy pickings. This tree is native to the eastern half of the United States. Its nuts were an important food source to native peoples; Iroquois, for example, would crush the nutmeats and add them to corn soup. The tree must have had some insecticidal properties, too; many native peoples scattered the

Looking west at the Reed College campus and Eastmoreland in 1915 from near the present location of the Studio Art Building. Note the farm with nursery stock in the foreground at right. The first of Reed's buildings, Old Dorm Block and Eliot Hall, are visible beyond the nursery stock. Photo from Special Collections and Archives, Eric V. Hauser Memorial Library, Reed College.

leaves around their homes to repel fleas, and Apaches gave juice from the nuts to dogs to dispel worms.

Where the asphalt path ends, stay straight, and in about a hundred feet veer left onto a short bark-chip path into the woods that runs along some houses. This path is the SE Knight Street right-of-way and leads to the intersection of Knight and 39th Avenue. Turn left on 39th and walk two blocks to Reedway. Turn left and walk one block west on Reedway to your starting point.

LEACH BOTANICAL GARDEN
TO MOUNT SCOTT LOOP

STARTING POINT Leach Botanical Garden parking lot: SE 122nd Avenue just south of the garden (6704 SE 122nd Avenue)

DISTANCE 4 miles, not including trails within Leach Botanical Garden

ELEVATION 230 feet at the starting point; 800 feet at the top of the Willamette National Cemetery on Mount Scott

GETTING THERE AND PARKING From Southeast Portland, travel east on SE Powell Boulevard. At the intersection with SE 50th Avenue and Foster Road, veer right onto Foster. Drive east on Foster to SE 122nd Avenue. Turn right and drive 0.2 mile to the bridge over Johnson Creek. Just past the bridge, park in the lot for Leach Botanical Garden visitors. If the lot is full or nearly so, park on the shoulder of SE Brookside Drive, just uphill from the lot, so that you will not be occupying a parking space that could be used by a garden visitor while you are on the hill walk.

TriMet: From downtown, take bus 10 (Harold) to the stop at SE Foster Road and 122nd Avenue. Walk 0.2 mile south on 122nd to the garden's entrance.

RESTROOMS AND DRINKING FOUNTAINS Visitors to Leach Botanical Garden can use the restroom located in the house, and restrooms and drinking fountains are located inside the welcome center at the Willamette National Cemetery.

FOOD AND DRINK There are no restaurants located along this route.

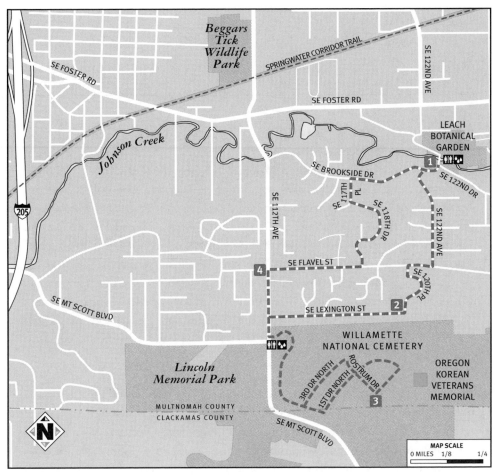

WALK 15. *Leach Botanical Garden to Mount Scott Loop*

MAP KEY

- ▪ ▬ ROUTE
- ⋮⋮⋮⋮ STAIRS
- – – TRAILS
- ⊬⊬⊬ RAILROAD TRACKS
- PARKS/GREENSPACE
- 🚹🚺 PUBLIC RESTROOMS
- 💧 WATER
- 🚏 BUS STOP

NOTE The Leach Botanical Garden is open Tuesday through Sunday and closed Mondays and holidays. Entrance is free, but the Friends of Leach asks for donations to help pay for the garden's upkeep.

The Willamette National Cemetery is open daily. Pets are prohibited, as are picnicking and jogging.

THIS HILL WALK STARTS IN A COOL, SHADY HOLLOW and climbs 570 feet to a 360-degree view from the summit of the Willamette National Cemetery on the northern flank of Mount Scott, one of about a hundred Boring Lava formations. The Boring Lavas are a group of volcanic vents, domes, and cinder cones that erupted between a hundred thousand and six million years ago, as the Portland Basin was pulled apart by tectonic forces. Named for the town of Boring, Oregon, 20 miles southeast of Portland, where they cluster in great quantities, the Boring Lavas are tied to the same uplifting forces that created the Cascade Range. Mount Scott is a huge example of the formation, much larger than Rocky Butte and Mount Tabor, other Boring Lava cones explored in this book.

Because the views in the cemetery are glorious and the grounds are dotted with deciduous specimen trees, save this walk for a clear day in the spring, summer, or fall.

1 From the parking lot, walk north on SE 122nd Avenue, taking the bridge over Johnson Creek to the entrance into the Leach Botanical Garden.

This garden is a legacy of Lilla and John Leach, who lived here from 1931 to 1972, when John died and Lilla moved into a care facility. John was a pharmacist whose Phoenix Pharmacy was on nearby Foster Road. Lilla was a botanist. For ten years, from 1928 to 1938, the couple spent summers exploring the Siskiyou Mountains in southwestern Oregon. The most famous of Lilla's five botanical discoveries is a small flowering shrub in the heather family named *Kalmiopsis leachiana* (the species, *leachiana*, is named for her). This laurel-like bush has the distinction of being the only plant for which a federal wild area has been named: the Kalmiopsis Wilderness encompasses 76,000 acres in the upper Chetco River drainage in the southwestern corner of Oregon.

The Leaches bought the 5 acres of their estate, called Sleepy Hollow, in 1931, when Lilla was forty-five. The property had been part of a donation land claim belonging to Jacob Johnson, a sawmill operator who furnished lumber for Portland's early homes. His mill straddled Johnson Creek near here. This was a sunny spot when the Leaches purchased it, thinned from decades of logging, but today it is a deeply shaded hollow located in the Powellhurst-Gilbert neighborhood.

After John Leach's death, this land was almost turned into a suburban development. John and Lilla had willed the property to Portland Parks with the condition that it be used to educate the public about plants; absent that use, the property would go to the YMCA, which could use it for any purpose. In 1972 the parks department did not have the resources to develop the site for the public, so for eight years it sat unused, becoming an increasingly viable target for vandals. A group called Friends of Leach formed to try to maintain the property while lobbying the city to develop the site. In 1980 nature came to their rescue. Mount Saint Helens erupted in May, and the YMCA's camp at Spirit Lake, high up on the flanks of the peak, was entombed under the debris. In need of a new camp, the YMCA informed the City of Portland that it intended to claim the Leach land, sell it to a developer, and use the funds to purchase another campground. That is when the Friends of Leach made their eleventh-hour pitch. They brought Charles Jordan, the new Portland Parks commissioner, out to see what the city was about to lose. He proclaimed it a "jewel" and ordered funding to be found. It was found, and the Leach Botanical Garden remains among the most unique gems in the city's collection of greenspaces.

Visitors are welcomed at the front gate by a massive Atlantic cedar, a native of Algeria and Morocco. The stone cabin visible on the southern side of the creek was the first dwelling the Leaches built. They lived in it off and on until the Manor House was finished in the early 1930s. The roof tiles came from remnants of the slate roof at Reed College's Eric V. Hauser Memorial Library. The terrazzo flooring was laid by Italian stonemasons, and John Leach incorporated pieces of petrified wood he had found on his hikes around the state. At times the Leaches' faithful burro, Pansy, who packed their equipment on botanizing forays, was housed here too. Today the cabin is accessible when the creek bridge is lowered in place, during periods of low water.

A dawn redwood grows near the cabin. This tree species was thought to be extinct until the early 1940s, when living specimens were found in China. It was introduced to the U.S. nursery trade in 1947. Like the larch, it is a deciduous conifer whose needles turn a pinkish brown before dropping in the fall. The tiny cones have the same woody symmetry as other redwoods.

The paved turnaround in front of the Manor House was lawn during the Leaches' lifetimes. Another ancient plant, a ginkgo tree, sits at the front entrance, along with a Japanese maple, and at the front door is a bed of plants from the Siskiyou Mountains, home of the Kalmiopsis Wilderness and *Kalmiopsis leachiana*.

The just-right-for-a-wedding courtyard behind the Manor House at Leach Botanical Garden. In early March the cornelian cherry dogwood in the foreground is in full bloom.

The Manor House is perched on a terrace above Johnson Creek. The steep hillsides above and below the house have been tamed with about 1.5 miles of trails, most of which the Leaches built themselves; the various areas, from boggy shade gardens to sunny alpinelike rock gardens, are planted with specimens that suit their microclimates. The Leaches planted more than a thousand different plant specimens around their home. A gift shop and an area with plants for sale satisfy the urge to take home a souvenir.

One day in early March, as I walked behind the house, I was stunned by a cornelian cherry dogwood (*Cornus mas*), with its profuse yellow blooms on branches still naked from winter. This tree has been cultivated since ancient times, but, as plant expert Michael Dirr has pointed out, it isn't used often enough in modern gardens. It is a showstopper, its early, vivid flowers appearing at a time when few plants are in bloom. A magnificent Lavalle hawthorne (sometimes called a Carrier hawthorne) also stands in the courtyard behind the house, showing off its membership in the rose family with voluptuous, red, hiplike fall berries that make it more brilliant than a fully decked holly. It is a hybrid, but like all hawthorns, its fruit is edible. The courtyard adjacent to the house has been renovated with trellises and benches, and makes a fabulous setting for an outdoor wedding.

Once you're done exploring the gardens, begin the hill walk by turning left on 122nd at the garden's entrance. Walk about 0.4 mile to SE Flavel Street, and turn right. Take the first left, at about 0.1 mile, onto SE 120th Place, laid out in 2004 as a street of high-end homes. Many of the buttes in Southeast Portland and Gresham have seen their flanks developed into "view properties," and here is a prime example.

2 Walk uphill on SE 120th and turn right onto SE Lexington Street. Here you're walking up hills and down dales on the mountain's flank, between 500 and 600 feet in elevation, with great views to the north and west, to the West Hills and downtown.

From Lexington turn left onto SE 112th Avenue, and walk 0.1 mile to the entrance to the Willamette National Cemetery.

The National Cemetery Administration is run by the Department of Veterans Affairs. In 1862 the first fourteen national cemeteries were opened to deal with casualties of the Civil War. Up until then the international practice during warfare had been to leave the bodies of common soldiers where they had fallen, or at the very most to provide a hasty burial. During the Civil War, soldiers were buried hastily, but an effort was made to mark the graves with a wooden headboard that provided identification. After the war the government made the unprecedented decision to re-inter 300,000 common soldiers with honors in national cemeteries. The next decision, to mark the graves of all soldiers, no matter the rank, with simple markers in plainly adorned fields, provides the national cemeteries with a deep and humbling sense of democracy. At the time, in the 1870s, this was a radical departure from the rural cemeteries then in vogue, in which large and ornate monuments drew attention to the status of the deceased.

Today there are 131 national cemeteries in thirty-nine states and in Puerto Rico. The most famous cemetery in the system is Arlington National Cemetery in Virginia, which is not administered by the Department of Veterans Affairs but by the U.S. Army. Fourteen other cemeteries are located near battlefields and are maintained by the Department of the Interior. The Calverton National Cemetery on Long Island is the busiest cemetery in the system, with 7000 burials a year. The Willamette National Cemetery has 3500 burials per year. By

In 1939 WPA workers graded and cleared the slopes of what would become the Willamette National Cemetery. The ground had been cleared of trees by Harvey Scott around the turn of the twentieth century. Photo courtesy of the City of Portland Archives.

2002 more than 116,000 Americans had been interred here. Willamette is the nation's sixth busiest national cemetery, based on the number of interments in 2000.

Willamette National Cemetery, 269 acres in all, is one of three national cemeteries in Oregon. The others are in Eagle Point (near Medford) and Roseburg. Washington has just one, in Kent. Located on the northern and western slopes of Mount Scott, this land was purchased in 1889 by Harvey Scott. In 1899 the entire peak was named for him. In 1909 Scott sold his land, which he had had cleared over the preceding twenty years, to the Mount Scott Cemetery Corporation. From 1935 to 1936, WPA workers graded, by hand, the slopes of what was then known as the Soldiers, Sailors, and Marine Cemetery. (For more on Harvey Scott, see Walk 16.)

Prior to World War II, this land was given to the State of Oregon. In 1941 veterans groups lobbied the U.S. Congress to provide a national cemetery in the Northwest. Although legislation was passed in December 1941 authorizing the cemetery, the onset of World War II quickly preoccupied the nation, and the cemetery did not open until 1951, on land that Oregon then deeded to the federal government.

A young visitor at Willamette National Cemetery.

In 2003 the National Cemetery Administration ruled that recreational pedestrians were not welcome in national cemeteries. However, if you do wish to visit these public lands, there is a way. Simply combine a little public service with your recreation: stop at the welcome center and pick up a comment card. As you walk the grounds, take note of your surroundings, offering thanks to the local folks for their excellent work, or helpful suggestions regarding tree maintenance or potholes that need fixing.

Once past the cemetery gate, stay right, following signs to "Locations 2-3-4." Pass the welcome center and climb the main road, Outer Drive. Just past 3rd Drive North, you'll step for a short bit into Clackamas County.

The wide-open spaces of the cemetery are due in part to the relatively young age of the trees, but the plainness of the site is also intentional. When the new national cemeteries were planned in 1870, the Olmsted Brothers advised the U.S. government to keep the designs "studiously simple," remarking that "ambitious efforts of ignorant or half-bred landscape gardeners should be especially guarded against."

Pass 2nd Drive North, and turn left on 1st Drive North. This will walk you back into Multnomah County as you climb the last little bit to the summit of this northern peak of Mount Scott. The larger peak, at 1090 feet elevation, is visible to the southwest. SE Mount Scott Boulevard runs in the saddle between the two peaks.

3 Turn right onto Rostrum Drive and walk to the 810-foot-high summit. Here are somber rows of stone seats in an amphitheater dedicated in 1970. This area, designed for contemplation, is the site of services on Memorial Day and September 11. It can also be rented by veterans groups and service organizations for reunions or other gatherings. The carillon bells here were donated in 1975 by the Oregon State Federation of Garden Clubs. The bells play on weekdays at 9:00 a.m., 4:00 p.m., and 5:00 p.m., and on weekends every hour on the hour until 5:00 p.m.

To continue the hill walk, proceed north through the rows of seats and around the central platform to Center Drive, which heads northeast off the summit. Turn left onto 1st Drive North. Just past a bench is a good view, from left to right, of Council Crest (across the Willamette River), Mount Tabor, Kelly Butte, and Rocky Butte. To the northeast is Powell Butte, and south and east of it are more buttes of the same Boring Lava formation.

Turn right on Rostrum Drive. At its curve sits one of four Committal Shelters in the cemetery. Because graveside services are not permitted in national cemeteries, these shelters are designed for families to hold brief committal services.

Turn right onto 3rd Drive North and follow it back down to Outer Drive. Turn right and retrace your steps to the cemetery entrance at SE 112th Avenue.

4 Once on 112th, walk downhill 0.3 mile to Flavel. The shoulder on the western side is wide enough for pedestrians, but walk carefully, as traffic is fast here. Turn right on Flavel, another street with a shoulder to cling to.

After 0.3 mile, turn left onto SE 118th Drive, a lovely, quiet old street that offers a steep descent along a ravine. It ends at SE Brookside Drive, which runs along Johnson Creek. Turn right on Brookside, and in 0.2 mile you'll hit 122nd and the parking lot for Leach Botanical Garden, your starting point.

WALK 16

MOUNT TABOR NEIGHBORHOODS AND PARK LOOP

STARTING POINT SE 60th Avenue and Stark Street

DISTANCE 4.25–5 miles, depending on route

ELEVATION 280 feet at the starting point; 480 feet at Mount Tabor's northern peak, SE Pine Court and 68th Avenue; 640 feet at the top of Mount Tabor

GETTING THERE AND PARKING From downtown Portland, drive east on Burnside Street, and cross the Burnside Bridge into Northeast Portland. At the intersection of NE Sandy Boulevard, NE 12th Avenue, and E Burnside, stay in the right two lanes, which will keep you on Burnside. Drive east on Burnside to the stoplight at SE 60th Avenue. Turn right. The first stoplight you'll see is SE Stark Street. Park along Stark in the vicinity of this intersection.

TriMet: From downtown, take bus 20 (Burnside/Stark) to the stop at SE 60th Avenue and E Burnside. Walk 0.2 mile south to the intersection with SE Stark Street.

RESTROOMS AND DRINKING FOUNTAINS Several restrooms and drinking fountains can be found at Mount Tabor Park.

FOOD AND DRINK Pastaworks at 3735 SE Hawthorne Boulevard is a good place to stop for gourmet picnic food; 503-232-1010. There are many small restaurants and coffee houses along Hawthorne, from SE 50th Avenue running west.

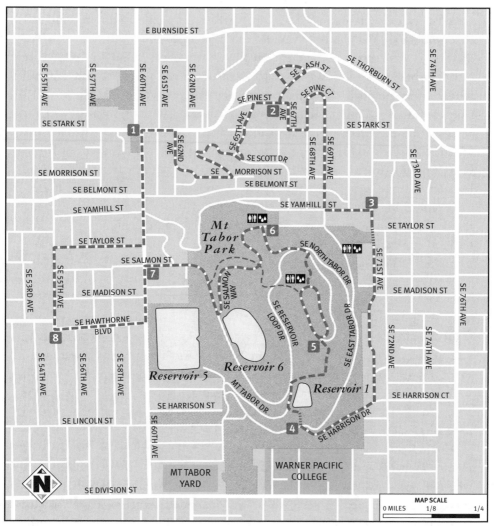

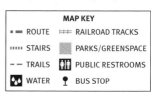

WALK 16. *Mount Tabor Neighborhoods and Park Loop*

MAP KEY

- ■■ ROUTE
- ⫶⫶⫶ STAIRS
- – – TRAILS
- 💧 WATER
- ▦ RAILROAD TRACKS
- PARKS/GREENSPACE
- 🚻 PUBLIC RESTROOMS
- 🚏 BUS STOP

NOTE Mount Tabor Park is a city treasure. After you trek to the top, plan to stay a while to enjoy the views. Bring a daypack, because before you start the hill walk you may want to stop at a nearby grocer for picnic food. I recommend Pastaworks on Hawthorne. Among the last family-run grocers in town, Pastaworks has been owned and operated by the de Garmo family since 1983. It carries two hundred cheeses, fresh pasta made on the premises, and organic, locally grown produce. Everything in the deli case is made in-house.

It's best to visit Mount Tabor Park on a Wednesday, when it is closed to motor vehicles, and the relative silence enhances an already lovely place. The park has long been a dog mecca, with its wide-open spaces and trails. No longer. If you bring your dog, be sure to leash it. I once overheard one very bummed-out dog lover lamenting the $150 ticket he had just received for letting his dog run free.

In late spring Mount Tabor is visited by thousands of birds migrating along the Pacific flyway. Along with Rocky Butte, another prominent forested outcrop in the city, Mount Tabor functions as a "migrant trap" for birds: a familiar place to stop, eat, and rest.

THOUGH RATHER LONG, THIS WALK IS ONE OF MY FAVORITES. Many people, including me, visit Mount Tabor via its Salmon Street entrance and so are more familiar with its western neighborhoods and approach. This hill walk will take you on all four sides of the peak, with forays into the neighborhoods on all but the southern side. You'll see all three of Mount Tabor's famed reservoirs, which received National Historic Landmark status in 2004.

Mount Tabor was settled at about the same time as Portland, by farmers who planted orchards and other crops to feed the voracious appetites of gold miners who had swarmed to California starting in 1848. Around 1849, Dr. Perry Prettyman built a log cabin on his 640-acre donation land claim, at what is now SE 55th and Hawthorne. He planted an orchard and cut a 3-mile trail to the Willamette River from his home—a precursor to SE Hawthorne Boulevard. Other orchards were soon planted. There were big profits to be made feeding the miners: apples were nearly $2 per pound, about the same price they are today. Throughout the 1850s, most of the fruit shipped out of Portland came from the slopes of Mount Tabor, destined for the stomachs of the 250,000 men who had come to California looking for gold.

Before the orchard trees went in, however, the land had to be tamed. And it was wild. In an interview with journalist Fred Lockley around 1900, Mrs. A. E. Hunt told of the early days on Mount Tabor: "In the fall of 1851 we moved to

Yamhill Street along the northern boundary of Mount Tabor Park.

a place on the western slope of Mount Tabor. Our place was located in the heavy timber and I can remember how frightened we children were when wolves came around and howled at night, or when we heard cougars screaming." Not all of Mount Tabor was timbered by that time. In 1846 an enormous wildfire wiped out much of the forest from Mount Scott north to the Columbia River. The denuded land was much easier to settle, a fact probably taken as an omen by the new settlers.

The northern side of Mount Tabor was claimed by Newton Gilham, who had led a wagon train to Oregon in 1852 and settled on Mount Tabor the next year. The mountain was named around 1853, when early settlers were organizing a church. Plympton Kelly named the peak in honor of Mount Tabor in northern Israel, thought to be the site of Jesus's transfiguration. Like Portland's Mount Tabor, Israel's Mount Tabor is a relatively low peak that dominates the level landscape around it, has beautiful woods, and is popular with hikers.

Farmers were the primary Mount Tabor residents until the 1880s. In 1880 the first neighborhood was platted out, but growth didn't take off until 1889, when a trolley line ran up SE Belmont Street to a terminus at SE 69th Avenue. Soon after, a line ran out Hawthorne, ending at SE 54th Avenue. From then until World War I, the area rapidly developed with "streetcar subdivisions," neighborhoods with closely built, garage-free homes.

In 1905 Mount Tabor was annexed to Portland.

1 Park in the vicinity of SE 60th Avenue and Stark Street, a commercial area that was once the spiritual heart of the early Mount Tabor community, the point at which the donation land claims of four early settlers, Prettyman, Davidson, Gilham, and Nelson, came together. All were Methodists, and here they started the Mount Tabor Methodist Episcopal Church, on land donated from each of their claims. Today the church is the Tabor Heights United Methodist Church, at 6161 SE Stark. By the 1870s the area at or near this corner was a cluster of civic life, with a store, school, post office, fire station, and another church, Mount Tabor Baptist.

The building at the southwestern corner of 60th and Stark was built in 1917 as the Mills Open Air School, a public school for victims of tuberculosis and other diseases. When Mills was founded, Mount Tabor was still rural, and it was thought that the air atop its flanks was more healthful to breathe and would promote healing. In those days tuberculosis was treated by a rigidly imposed regimen of absolute rest and fresh air. The school was designed with many windows; as part of the curative regimen of the day, they were left open, winter and summer. Currently the building houses a YMCA childcare facility, whose director told me she once received a visit from a former Mills student who reminisced about being led outside after lunch for a healthful nap under the fir trees.

Walk east on Stark. The old building at 6031 has columns salvaged from the 1905 world's fair held in Northwest Portland. In the pavement on the porch the original owner stamped his name, "T. Graham," the date of construction, "1910," and the use to which the building was put, "Drugs." It was a drugstore. At 6049, now much disguised, is the first firehouse on Mount Tabor, built in 1910. If you look at its bones and not its skin, you can see its two large doorways. Another interesting artifact from its early days is the grooved cement in front of the doorways. The grooves gave the horses traction as they burst through the doors to respond to a fire.

Turn right on SE 62nd Avenue, and then, at the first intersection, turn left on SE Alder Street. Turn left at SE Morrison Street, then left at SE Morrison Court, a small, untrafficked street. These streets switchback up the smaller of Mount Tabor's two peaks. Turn right onto SE Scott Drive, named for Harvey Scott. This road, at 420 feet, sits on the side of a small canyon between the peaks. The yards on the southern side of the road drop steeply down to the canyon bottom, at 380 feet. The main peak, at 640 feet, is in the park south of here; the smaller peak, at 480 feet, is to the north on the route of this walk.

At 6500 Scott is a view across this small canyon into the park. The hill walk route turns left onto SE 65th Avenue, but just a bit further east on Scott Drive are some grand homes. At 6687 is a large Tudor residence, built in 1922 by A.

G. Ramsey, who brought masons from Scotland to build the rubble retaining wall at the sidewalk level. The residence then was part of a large estate; as the property was divided, homes were built, but the retaining wall remained and continues to grace many nearby homes.

Turn left onto SE 65th Avenue, walk two blocks, turn right onto SE Pine Street, and turn left onto SE Ash Street. This gem of an area is hidden away on Mount Tabor's northern flanks, far out of the traffic stream. In early 2004 a small subdivision was platted for this last undeveloped section of Mount Tabor. Follow Ash Street around to Ash Court and then Ash Place. The streets, built upon in the 1970s, are laid out on relatively flat ground on a north-facing ridge, giving unobstructed views of Mount Saint Helens, Mount Rainier, and Mount Adams.

2 Follow Ash Place back to Ash Street. Turn left on Pine, right on 67th, left on Stark, and left on 68th. Follow 68th as it circles around Mount Tabor's 480-foot northern peak. The Olmsted Brothers recommended using this secondary peak as parkland. Fortunate Portlanders now live here instead.

Follow 69th, which leads slightly downhill off the northern peak, crosses the saddle between the two peaks, and rises again as it continues south toward an entrance to Mount Tabor Park. The two homes at 531 and 603 date from 1892, some of the earliest built on this side of Mount Tabor. Around the intersection of 69th and Belmont are commercial buildings and streetcar flats that once sat

The saddle between Mount Tabor's two peaks, along SE 69th Avenue.

at the terminus of the Belmont streetcar line, the first streetcar on Portland's east side.

Turn left at SE Yamhill Street, a beautiful street that hugs the northern boundary of the park. At 6810, just a few steps west of the intersection, is a 1906 Arts and Crafts home originally owned by James Morris, a civil engineer who helped design Mount Tabor Park. The stone of the porch piers, base, and retaining wall was recycled from the Tennessee Building, part of the 1905 Lewis and Clark Exposition.

3 Walk two blocks east on Yamhill and turn right on SE 71st Avenue. In one block you'll reach some stairs, which lead you into a corner of the park. Once up the stairs, stay left; within half a block, 71st picks up again and you're out of the park. Walk south on 71st all the way along the eastern flank of the mountain, savoring the incredible views. The road peaks at about 400 feet in the 1500 block and provides unusual views to the east and southeast—note the Cascades with the Boring Lava domes in the foreground. Unless you live in this neighborhood, you may not have seen Portland from this angle before. Where the views are best there is a fortunately placed vacant lot, so you don't have to take the views in gulps between houses. Off the southern side of Mount Tabor, 71st begins to drop again, and you lose much of the elevation you just gained.

Turn right at SE Harrison Street, and you'll soon enter Mount Tabor Park on its quieter southern side. Inside the park, the road climbs steeply. A park playground and Warner Pacific College are visible on the hillside below the road. Warner Pacific is a liberal arts college affiliated with the Church of God; it has been at this location since 1940.

4 At the first intersection, take the stairs up the slope. Eighty-one steps put you right in front of thimble-shaped Reservoir 1, the oldest reservoir in Portland's municipal water system. It was built in 1894 in anticipation of Bull Run water coming on line. (For a short history of the Bull Run watershed, see Walk 4.)

The water in the reservoirs is cold, between 35 and 50 degrees Fahrenheit—colder than the frigid Pacific off the Oregon Coast. Its source is rain, fog drip, and snow from the watershed, which is located in the foothills of the Cascade Mountains. The highest elevation in the watershed is about 4700 feet. Most (about 70 percent) of the city's Bull Run water passes through this or one of Mount Tabor's other reservoirs on its way to other city water storage tanks or directly to an end user's sink.

Portland's water is soft for two reasons: first, it hasn't spent time underground leaching minerals from rock, and second, the geologic formation underlying the reservoirs in the Bull Run watershed is Columbia River Basalt, an igneous rock that does not leach minerals to the extent that a sedimentary rock such as limestone would. The water's low calcium and magnesium content means that Portlanders don't have to buy distilled water to run through their steam irons and can spend less time scouring the gunk out of their bathtubs.

Because the Bull Run watershed is protected from development, Portland's water system is among the few in the nation in which the water meets federal standards without being filtered. Other major cities that share this distinction are New York, Boston, San Francisco, and Seattle.

The water is chemically treated, however. Chlorine is added near the source to disinfect it and protect users from intestinal parasites like giardia, and ammonia is added to ensure the disinfection remains adequate throughout the distribution system. Sodium hydroxide is also added to increase the pH to about 7.5. This pH adjustment helps control lead and copper leaching and reduce pipe corrosion. While lead is not found within the water distribution system, it can be present in the plumbing of older homes. In the coming years the city will have to add another layer of treatment to meet new federal regulations regarding cryptosporidium. This parasite, whose hard shell makes it resistant to chlorine disinfection, lives in every region of the United States and can cause diarrhea or other health problems, especially in people with compromised immune systems.

Rarely, when turbidity levels rise, the city shuts down Bull Run and taps its water wells, located on the south shore of the Columbia River between Interstate 205 and Blue Lake Park. Turbidity increases when heavy rainfall in the mountains sluices down larger than normal amounts of sediment into the Bull Run reservoirs. When the sediment settles or flushes out, the Bull Run taps are turned on again.

The open reservoirs were originally designed to be civic destinations, and while scenic, they are far beyond state of the art, and would never be built today. The Portland Water Bureau has worked off and on for years to cover the reservoirs, which are expensive to maintain and difficult to keep secure. After the events of September 11, 2001, this became a high priority, but neighbors remained unconvinced of the need. Once open to strollers, the reservoirs were blocked off with chain-link fence in the 1940s and may still go underground. Until they do, security cameras are trained on them twenty-four hours a day.

Walk to the left of the reservoir and climb an asphalt road. When it intersects with SE Reservoir Loop Drive, keep to the right. Take the wide cinder path that comes in on your right, just across from a drinking fountain and a view of Reservoir 6. This path affords wonderful views, upward into a second-growth forest of native chokecherry, Douglas fir, and bigleaf maple, and downward into Reservoir 1. In a 1935 make-work WPA project, men with mattocks, shovels, and wheelbarrows cut back the steep slope on the northern end of the reservoir and hauled it off. The slope is still quite steep here. Where the path curves, three prongs lead to the left. Take the middle (steepest) path through the lacy forest.

The large, rounded cobbles of rock in the path look like smooth river rock, and that is exactly what they are. Despite the fact that Mount Tabor is a volcano, it is not a homogeneous hunk of igneous rock. Most of the peak is composed of the Troutdale Formation, ancient flood sediments. When Mount Tabor began erupting, it swelled upward from beneath these sediments, but it did not cover them. (For more information on the Troutdale Formation, see Walk 1.)

5 Near the top of the path are concrete stairs leading to a park road and the statue of a scowling Harvey Scott, the curmudgeonly man who served as editor of the *Oregonian* for forty-five years, from 1865 until his death. He was also brother to Abigail Scott Duniway, herself a newspaper publisher, who fought for women's rights, specifically the right to vote. The siblings quarreled bitterly over their opposing views. (See Walk 8 for more on Duniway.)

Harvey died in 1910 but stands immortalized here, midstride, his brow furrowed and his mouth turned down in disdain as he points imperiously with one hand, the other clenched in anger. What's he so mad about? Perhaps he was sculpted, midquarrel, shouting something like, "Damn it, Abigail, get those suffragettes out of my house!" While Harvey Scott was a man of great intellect and drive, in the words of his biographer, Lee Nash, "he lacked human sympathy." When he died, Abigail had this to say about her brother: "He left his children immensely rich and his wife a millionaire. Well. She earned it, living with *him*."

On the eastern side of the base is the sculptor's name: Gutzon Borglum. Borglum, the son of a Danish Mormon bigamist, became famous by sculpting famous Americans. After sculpting a bust of Abraham Lincoln, which President Theodore Roosevelt exhibited in the White House, he began work on the Confederate memorial at Stone Mountain, Georgia. Here he developed techniques he would use in 1927 as he began carving the 60-foot-high heads of four presidents in the face of Mount Rushmore in South Dakota. While Borglum worked at Mount Rushmore until his death in 1941, there were long periods when he was not needed on-site, and at such times he would travel around the country to complete other commissions. It was in 1933, during his work on Mount Rushmore, that he sculpted the statue of Harvey Scott.

Stairs to the left of the statue lead to the grassy summit, a long, narrow oval with picnic tables scattered around under very tall fir trees. Views of downtown Portland and the Cascades reveal themselves through the trees in a pleasantly understated way. The road shooting west, away from Mount Tabor and toward the KOIN Tower (the Bic pen lookalike) downtown, is Hawthorne Boulevard. The medical cluster of OHSU sits halfway up the West Hills, beneath Council Crest—hill walks for another day.

Now is the time to lay out the picnic. Benches face the view and beg to be sat upon; once you have one, you'll not want to leave. Wherever you ramble on the summit, the views and the setting are sublime. When you're ready to leave, head north to the highest point, near a large, multitrunked bigleaf maple. This species has the largest leaves of any maple in the world. Its tendency to produce huge burls at its base makes it prized by woodworkers. West Coast Indians used the tree as a food source, sprouting the seeds and then eating the tender green shoots, as is done with bean sprouts today.

Near the maple lies a City of Portland benchmark: a brass survey marker. In a classically circuitous bureaucratic style, the marker is not stamped with the elevation, as would seem logical, but with an identification number: 1876, in this case. With this number in hand, you can do a benchmark search via the Office of Transportation Web site (www.trans.ci.portland.oru.us) to find the elevation here: 641.295 feet.

A home and stable once existed here. In 1903 the Olmsted Brothers recommended that these structures be removed and that a public shelter be built in their place, "with arrangements . . . made for the sale of the purest possible milk . . . as nothing is better for many of the hot weather troubles of infancy than absolutely pure milk and plenty of fresh air."

From here, walk north on the grass. Cross the loop road, take some stairs, and head down the hill. Keep the buried water tank, topped by a concrete lid, on your right. Soon you'll see a playground. Cross the road, jog a bit left, and follow the path into one of the city's most beautiful playgrounds, with assorted equipment scattered like colorful flowers under a towering canopy of Douglas fir, and Mount Saint Helens shining through the trees.

6 Further down the hill are a bathroom, a parking lot, a maintenance building, and the park amphitheater. Walk into the amphitheater, which was excavated at the site of the volcanic vent. Until 1912 no one knew that Mount Tabor was an extinct volcano. When workers were mining rock to build the park's roads, cinders were found. Over the ensuing years the cinders were excavated and used to surface park and city roads, resulting in the man-made crater visible today. The walls of the amphitheater show a cross section of the material, scoria, lava, and lava bombs. Today the amphitheater is used for concerts and basketball.

Get back on the main park road, and take it as it follows the land's contours around a ravine. You can follow it all the way to the park entrance at SE Salmon Street, or take the following shortcut: Come to a crosswalk painted on the road. Behind concrete stanchions is a path. Don't take it; instead, take the path next to it with nine shallow wooden steps leading downhill to a trail. The trail is nice and straight, and ends at the main park road, just inside the park gates. Turn right and exit the park.

At 6115 Salmon, a proper 1912 Colonial sits serenely beside a 1936 Mediterranean at 6015. Even in architecture, a May-December pairing can be successful. At 60th and Salmon, in the yard of a large 1910 Arts and Crafts home, grows an old deodar cedar whose sinuous limbs look like elephants' trunks swaying in the air, seeking a peanut.

7 You could turn right on 60th and cut the hill walk short by walking north to the starting point. If you continue the route, however, you'll walk through the Prettyman donation land claim and see the site of this very early Mount Tabor resident's homestead. Besides, the homes on the western side of the slope are gorgeous.

Turn left on SE 60th. At 1207, another 1910 Arts and Crafts home, lived the first woman in Oregon to be issued a driver's license. The largest giant sequoia in Portland sits in the fenced yard at 1225. From the area's orchard days is a home at 1242, a Rural Vernacular from 1886 that once belonged to Niels Simmonson, a fruit grower. As you walk south, you are beside the lowest of Mount Tabor's reservoirs, Reservoir 5, built in 1911.

Turn right on SE Hawthorne Boulevard. At 5524 is an 1884 Italianate home that was once an inn for travelers on the old Sommerville Road between Vancouver and Oregon City. The intersection of 55th and Hawthorne is the site of the Perry Prettyman cabin. One of Dr. Prettyman's claims to fame is that he brought the dandelion to Portland—not because he planned to sell herbicides to generations of lawn owners, but for its medicinal purposes. The Georgian Revival mansion now occupying the site was built in 1906 for Henry Buehner; his son Philip later lived there. Their ironworks firm built the first pipeline from the Bull Run watershed to the Mount Tabor reservoirs. Since 1944 the grounds have been the home of the Baptist Western Seminary.

Looking west in 1909 at orchards on Mount Tabor in the area where Reservoir 5 now sits. Photo courtesy of the City of Portland Archives.

8 Turn right onto SE 55th Avenue, a grand boulevard with lovely, large homes. You'll walk past the Vedanta Society at 1157. Vedanta is an ancient religious philosophy based on the Vedas, sacred scriptures of India. It has had a Portland chapter since 1925. In 1928, after receiving the cold shoulder from Lake Oswego, it moved its headquarters to the South Park Blocks at the site of PSU's Branford Price Millar Library. When PSU purchased their property in 1958, Vedanta moved to this location.

Turn right on SE Taylor Street. Many of the homes on this part of Taylor date from the 1890s and are in the Queen Anne Vernacular style. One latecomer to the party is the home at 5720, a 1950 tract house. At 5850 is an 1892 Arts and Crafts home whose upper story sports an unusual finish of stucco panels embedded with stones and pebbles.

Turn left on SE 60th. Just south of Belmont, at 911 SE 60th, is an elegant brick apartment house, the Mount Tabor Park Apartments. It was built in 1932 during the streetcar era, when the streetcar ran up Belmont to SE 69th from downtown.

Continue north on 60th to the starting point.

ROCKY BUTTE BASE TO PEAK

STARTING POINT NE 92nd Avenue and Skidmore Street

DISTANCE 1.25 miles each way

ELEVATION 140 feet at the starting point; 612 feet at the summit of Rocky Butte

GETTING THERE AND PARKING   From downtown Portland, drive east on Burnside Street, and cross the Burnside Bridge into Northeast Portland. At the intersection of NE Sandy Boulevard, NE 12th Avenue, and E Burnside, stay in the left two lanes and veer left onto Sandy. Drive east on Sandy to the stoplight at NE 82nd Avenue. Drive about 0.1 mile further and turn right onto NE Skidmore Street. Drive 0.3 mile to the trailhead, where Skidmore intersects with NE 90th and 92nd Avenues.

   TriMet: From downtown, take bus 12 (Sandy Boulevard) to the stop at NE Sandy Boulevard and 92nd Avenue. Walk 0.2 mile south on 92nd to NE Skidmore Street and the trailhead.

RESTROOMS AND DRINKING FOUNTAINS   There are no public restrooms or drinking fountains located along this route, but both are available at the Grotto, just west of the trailhead at the corner of NE Sandy Boulevard and 85th Avenue.

FOOD AND DRINK   The Grotto is located at NE Sandy Boulevard and 85th Avenue, just a few blocks west on Skidmore from the starting point of the walk. Its snack bar is open daily, with closing hours varying with the time of year. For a wider selection, when you're done with the walk, check out one of the many locally owned restaurants, bars, cafés, and coffee shops nearby on NE Fremont Street between NE 50th and 41st Avenues.

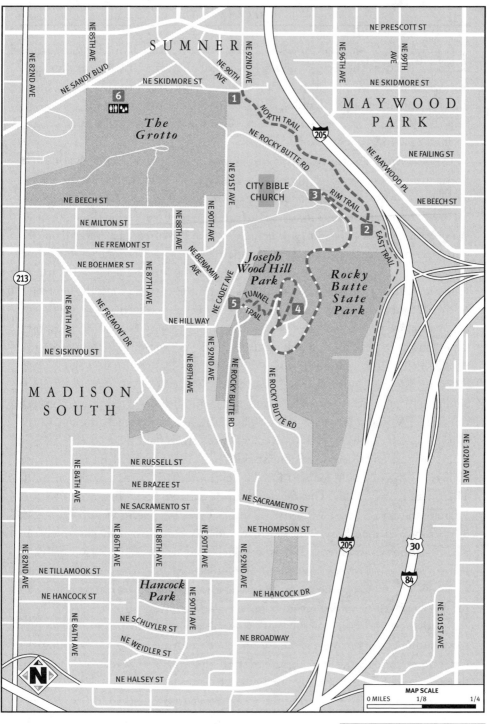

WALK 17. *Rocky Butte Base to Peak*

MAP KEY

- ▪▬ ROUTE
- ┉┉ STAIRS
- ‑‑ TRAILS
- 🌊 WATER
- ┼┼┼┼ RAILROAD TRACKS
- ▨ PARKS/GREENSPACE
- 🚻 PUBLIC RESTROOMS
- 📍 BUS STOP

I N ITS 1988 *Scenic Views, Sites and Drives Inventory*, the City of Portland listed Rocky Butte as the second most scenic overlook in the city. It's the only rock in town that offers a 360-degree view of five mountains, a river, a gorge, and a flood of human endeavor lapping at its flanks. As seems fitting for such a setting, Rocky Butte is crowned by a rock tiara of magnificent stonework created by the Depression-era WPA.

Despite these assets, Rocky Butte is not touted as a scenic overlook in Portland's tourist literature. If you're a visitor from Kansas, chances are you've never heard of Rocky Butte, and what's more, your Portland hosts have probably never been up there themselves. But after years of neglect, and having faced the possibility of its summit park being destroyed to discourage vandalism, the butte has come back. Neighbors, recognizing the butte's unique geologic past and historic pedigree, have restored the park at the top and achieved National Historic Landmark status for both the park and the roadways leading up to it.

In 1921, at the dawn of the auto age, Rocky Butte was seen as a major tourist destination for people looking for a Sunday outing. Sandy Boulevard, just north of the butte, was the city's major eastern portal. As the first promontory east of Portland along the Columbia River, the butte was planned to be a destination on an auto touring route that led from Sandy Boulevard to Troutdale, where it would hook up with the newly completed Columbia River Highway through the Gorge. Without a road to the top, however, few visitors heading out to the Gorge made the arduous trek up Rocky Butte's steep flanks.

In 1932, after a decade of tourist dollars had driven right on by, business owners on the east side lobbied for the development of a road to the summit. Their timing was apt. The newly formed Oregon State Emergency Relief Administration and the WPA saw the project as a long-term way to keep a lot of unemployed men busy. The WPA was ideally suited to manage projects in which manpower and raw materials were in abundance, as was the case at Rocky Butte. Its location in Portland also contributed to making the project attractive to the WPA, as many unemployed workers wanted to stay with their families instead of traveling to distant government work camps.

Starting in 1935, the WPA took over the project from the state. For fifty cents an hour, workers began quarrying stone from the butte and building the fortresslike park at the top, complete with stone parapet walls, bastions connected by a balustrade of basket arches, and a grand baroque staircase. Workers also built, mostly by hand, the two access roads (north and south) to the top, with their massive European-style stone walls (some more than 40 feet high), low retaining walls, and balustrades. The rock for the walls, road, and park was quarried from the eastern side of the butte, the cut stone from the northeastern

An aerial view of Rocky Butte, looking west, circa 1933. The airway beacon (installed in 1931) is visible to the left, and roads have been graded, but stonework by WPA workers is not yet complete. The bucolic lowland in the foreground is now occupied by Interstate 205. The treeless slopes on the eastern side of the butte are where the quarry was active. Hill Military Academy buildings are located on the butte in the center of the photo. Photo courtesy of the City of Portland Archives.

side, and the gravel from the southeastern side, in an area that would later house the county jail.

Work at the butte was completed in 1939. The total cost was $500,000, making Rocky Butte the second most expensive WPA project in the state. (Timberline Lodge on Mount Hood was the most expensive, at a cost of $695,730.) The project was a huge success; in the 1940s, daily traffic counts averaged more than four thousand cars in the summer visiting the top of the butte. In the ensuing fifty years, little more was done to the butte. Its cachet flagged and it became known as a place to party. In the 1990s the citizen-led Rocky Butte Preservation Society began to polish this neglected diamond in the rough. Thanks to them, the park at the top of the butte has been cleaned up and restored, with more amenities than it had even in its glory days.

As a greenspace, Rocky Butte has not yet been tamed with manicured trails and regular sweeps by maintenance crews. While it is seamed with "social" trails made by rock climbers and neighborhood kids, many of these are incredibly steep, somewhat confusing, dangerously close to cliffs, and totally unofficial. This hill walk takes you up the butte on an old trail with a manageable, though steep, grade.

The greenspaces on the butte are owned by a panoply of government agencies—Oregon Department of Transportation, Oregon State Parks, and the City of Portland—each of which laments the fact that it has neither the time nor the resources to develop the site. Because of the lack of a decent trail system, this hike is an out-and-back adventure on the one good trail I found. Despite the trail redundancy, however, you gain a totally different perspective when you descend the butte than when you ascend it.

I don't recommend hiking this route alone, even though I have seen only one suspicious character on my trips here. The isolation and the higher-than-average garbage factor indicate that some people may make the butte's wild areas their home. (That said, considering the area's popularity with climbers and the fact that no services are provided, it is surprisingly clean. Neighbors and the Rocky Butte Preservation Society, good old American activists, regularly pick up the litter.)

You could always skip the walk, buckle up, and drive to the top, but you'd be missing the full-on butte experience. To get a feel for its impressive mass, I recommend exploring Rocky Butte from the bottom up, from the base of its flood-sculpted, boulder-strewn cliffs to its sun-bleached, windy apex.

1 This walk starts at the northeastern corner of Rocky Butte. Park along the road at the triple intersection of NE 90th and 92nd Avenues and Skidmore Street. This is the western sliver of Maywood Park, a neighborhood that turned itself into a city in 1968 to fight the freeway planned within its midst. They lost, as you can tell by the roar of Interstate 205, which accompanies you at the beginning of the hike. Most of Maywood Park—which did become a city with its own mayor, despite its size (three hundred homes) and despite being totally surrounded by the city of Portland—is nestled quite scenically in a grove of firs on the other side of Interstate 205 and is accessible via Prescott Street. The freeway created a moat around Rocky Butte's eastern side, effectively cutting it off from the neighborhood's easy access, except at this point.

At the trailhead here, begin walking toward the butte on a wide dirt trail. You'll soon see lots of paths used by dirt bikers and climbers. Climbers love the butte; its hard, fine-grained volcanic rock and vertical routes are a challenge made even more difficult by the thundering roar of the freeway, which can make communication ("Rope!") difficult.

Like most of the thirty-odd cinder cones and shield volcanoes that emerge from the relatively flat terraces of Portland's east side, Rocky Butte is geologically classified as a Boring Lava. (See Walk 15 for more information on the Boring Lavas.) Because the Boring Lavas consist of basalts similar to those of Mount Hood and other Cascade peaks, their uplift is believed to be tied to the uplift of the Cascades. As millennia passed, these basalts resisted erosion by the various floods and changing river channels. That changed about thirteen to twenty thousand years ago, at the end of the last Ice Age, with what may have been the world's largest flood events.

When glacial ice sheets blocked the path of the Clark Fork River in Montana, ice dams caused the formation of the 2000-foot-deep, 200-mile-long Lake Missoula in southwestern Montana. When the dams collapsed (geologists believe they collapsed and were rebuilt several times), the Missoula Floods came thundering down the Columbia River Gorge at speeds up to 90 miles per hour. Rocky Butte, standing directly in the path of the flood as the water erupted from the narrow gorge, saw its northeastern side sheared away by the fury of the debris-laden water. Around the northern and eastern sides, the flood created plunge pools, cavities where the land was scoured away by the churning of water. The homes just west of you, in the triangle formed by NE Ward, 90th, and Skidmore, sit serenely in one of these plunge pools, a gentle depression in the land's topography that was once the site of intense geologic violence. A larger pool on the lower flanks of the western side of the butte is also worth a visit after you've finished with the hill walk. It is bounded by NE Fremont, 88th, and Russell, and is owned by the City of Portland. Rose City Golf Course, about a mile west of the butte, is another large closed depression created by scouring. (See Walk 14 for more on the Missoula Floods.)

Almost immediately as you enter the forest you can see the cliffs of Rocky Butte in front of you. The houses above are on NE Cliff Street. Here, and following the trail along the base of the cliff, is the site of one of the old rock quarries. Rock from this site was used to construct much of the finest early stonework in the Portland area, such as the First Baptist Church in downtown's South Park Blocks.

Turn left where the trail splits. You'll see the hills and valleys of a dirt bike course on your left. You may want to explore some of the many smaller trails that lead up to the base of the cliffs. The jumble of boulders you'll encounter appears to be spoils from the old quarry. Here, at the base of the butte, a forest of young bigleaf maples offers pleasant dappled shade. Stay on the main trail as it leads slightly away from the butte, toward the racket of Interstate 205, and then veers back again. As you walk, you'll see some slopes of a uniform steepness at the base of the vertical cliffs. These are talus slopes, formed over the millennia as rock sloughed off the cliffs and slid down to its angle of repose. As the trail climbs, Interstate 205 becomes visible. Shortly after the point where you can see a freeway sign for Exit 22, the trail narrows and rises above the freeway grade.

2 In about 0.1 mile, take a well-defined trail to the right that leads upslope. This trail was used by students of the old Hill Military Academy. As part of their daily schedule, cadets would lead the school's cows and sheep to pasture down this trail, ending up in the bottomland that is now occupied by Interstate 205. The lowland where the freeway now roars was described by the Olmsted Brothers as a well-wooded "romantic ravine."

If you were to continue walking south along the butte's eastern side, you would come to the site of the old Multnomah County Jail, which Interstate 205 bisected. It was built in 1941 east of another quarry on the butte's flanks. An accident occurred at the quarry in 1940 when a 1900-pound dynamite charge went awry and threw rock 2500 feet in the air, damaging homes nearby. The quarry closed in 1956 partially because of citizens' complaints about the blasting.

In the 1960s, once the freeway went in adjacent to the jail, its din was deemed inhumane to both the jail's inhabitants and its employees. In 1983 the jail was torn down. It's hard to believe that the old jail, with its medieval stonework and dungeonlike overtones, was built in the same half-century as its replacement, the euphemistically named Multnomah County Detention Center, a 676-bed, maximum-security jail housed within the elegant Justice Center at 1120 SW 3rd Avenue in downtown Portland. *Newsweek* magazine described the Justice Center, with its sparkling beveled-glass façade and sandstone sculptures, as "a radical experiment in civility."

The hand-hewn rock that was salvaged from the jail has been used to restore walls and bridges on the Historic Columbia River Highway, east of Portland, another site for viewing fantastic stonemasonry and phenomenal vistas.

The trail up the butte's flanks is moderately steep but quite walkable. The cliffs are now on your left, as you're heading north. The trail levels out near the top and, oddly, enters a pedestrian tunnel under NE Rocky Butte Road. This is your first look at some of the WPA rockwork. The tunnel was used by Hill Military Academy students, who, as I noted earlier, shepherded animals down to pastureland at the base of the butte. But why the builders created this tunnel is a mystery, because you can access the trail just a bit further west on this same road without using the tunnel. Despite its superfluity, it's a lovely tunnel, although some of its stonework facing has been covered by fill and it is missing the original details along its top. Walk through it and you will emerge from the woods onto the campus of the old Hill Military Academy, with its fortresslike dorms, complete with crenellated walls. Founded in 1901 by Joseph Wood Hill at NW 24th Avenue and Marshall Street, the academy moved to Rocky Butte in 1930, when Joseph's sons, Joseph Jr. and Benjamin, took over the family business. In 1959 the academy closed and the property was sold to Judson Bible College. Today it is owned by City Bible Church, the large dome on your right. The church also operates City Christian High School and Portland Bible College here.

3   Emerge from the tunnel, and begin walking uphill on the road. It is 0.7 mile to the summit of the butte. At this point you're on a road recognized by the National Park Service as part of the Rocky Butte Scenic Drive Historic District. There is a wide shoulder here, a low traffic volume, and a good sight distance to oncoming vehicles. This is the northern approach to the summit of Rocky Butte, accessed via NE Fremont Street and 82nd Avenue. The southern approach to the summit heads north from NE Halsey Street and 92nd Avenue. It is far windier, with a spectacular 375-foot-long tunnel. The tunnel is actually a switchback, hand-dug through basalt inside the butte (the only way the engineers could devise to keep the road at a workable grade). Its barrel vault became a model for other local tunnels such as the Cornell Road and Barnes Road tunnels in Portland's West Hills.

Along the roadside here and there are bollards, large blocks of hand-hewn rock shaped like a pyramid with the top lopped off. These date from the WPA era. Many have been incorporated into homeowners' landscapes, while others have simply been pushed over the side of the cliffs. Also part of the WPA-era roadside architecture are low stone walls and basalt-lined drainage canals.

The tiny, quaint house at 3511 has a big vista that might inspire a pang of view-envy if you're a homeowner. Owned by City Bible Church, it was originally built as the residence of one of the Hill brothers.

4   At the top, walk up the gravel path into Joseph Wood Hill Park. In 1935 Joseph and Benjamin Hill donated this land to the city in memory of their father. Benjamin Avenue, on the western side of the butte, was named for Benjamin Hill. Among the other street names on the butte that were inspired by the Hill Military Academy are Cadet Avenue, Academy Street, and Hill Way.

The tower in the middle of the park is a historic relic listed on the National Register of Historic Places. It's an airway beacon, installed around 1931, whose rotating, lighthouse-like lamp guided early aviators through the Columbia River Gorge. In the early days of flight, with no radar or radio communication, pilots flew using road maps, and by peering out their cockpit windows for visual landmarks. This worked fine in the daytime, but because the U.S. Postal Service's airmail operated around the clock, a night system of landmarks was needed. In 1921, to test the feasibility of such a system, one airmail pilot flew all night from North Platte, Nebraska, to Chicago, finding his way across the dark prairie via bonfires lit by helpful farmers and other interested parties. By the early 1920s, electric airway beacons were being installed across the country, each with enough candlepower to be seen for 40 miles in clear weather.

In this system of dead reckoning, aviators theoretically could navigate from one beacon to the next. As the beacon light turned, other lights in white and green flashed a location number in Morse code so that pilots could identify their position. With the invention of ground-to-air radio transmission, the airway beacons were ultimately phased out. The beacon on Rocky Butte was decommissioned in the 1960s (it's still lit, although with less candlepower), and the last beacon in the United States was decommissioned in 1973. The Rocky Butte beacon was not, as many young Portlanders used to believe, a searchlight aimed at thwarting escapes from the old Rocky Butte jail!

From the top, the view is panoramic. To the east is the Columbia River Gorge. On a clear day you can see Vista House, a 1917 visitor center built atop Crown Point in the Gorge, about 18 miles from here. The highway running to the east is Interstate 84, which starts in Portland and follows the path of the Columbia River for 160 miles—among the most scenic stretches of freeway in the nation. After it leaves the Columbia, Interstate 84 continues southeast through Oregon, Idaho, and Utah to its terminus in Salt Lake City.

The view to the north, of Portland International Airport, is great if you have children who like to watch jets take off and land. Across the Columbia River is Vancouver, Washington. To the west are views of downtown Portland, the West Hills, and the double-decker Fremont Bridge. Far off you can see the elegant spires of the Saint Johns Bridge, the tall white cranes at the shipyard docks of the Port of Portland, and the confluence of the Columbia and Willamette Rivers.

The southern view is less clear, as it is partially obstructed by Rocky Butte itself. The nearest butte directly south is Mount Tabor, another Boring Lava formation, with a fabulous, busy park at its top underneath the canopy of fir trees you can see here. To the southeast is a clump of Boring Lava domes that include Powell Butte (612 feet), Mount Scott (1090 feet), and Mount Talbert (740 feet). Imagine this same orderly scene thirteen to twenty thousand years ago, as a wall of water erupted from the tight confines of the Gorge, smashed into Rocky Butte, and raced past it, filling the Portland area and the Willamette Valley like a bathtub.

The style of the stonework in this viewpoint fortress has been called Oregon Rustic; it is similar to the stonework on the Columbia River Highway. As with the highway, the design is sympathetic to the natural materials found at the site, and the viewpoint's curving walls fit the topography like a custom-made hat. The railing at the top of the fortress, with its basket-arch design, mimics the low stone walls along the approach roads.

Lights around the perimeter wall were in the original plans but were not installed until 1995. For sixty years their absence made the park a perfect place for trysts of all kinds, especially before the homes were built near the top of the butte. After nine years of fundraising, the Rocky Butte Preservation Society installed the lights and planted the central circle around the base of the airway beacon in flowering currants and roses. The flamboyantly hipped *Rosa rugosa* planted here is a very hardy rose that doesn't mind strong winds or freezing temperatures; it's often used along freeways, an environment that would wilt a lesser rose. At the fortress walls, look down; the Preservation Society is also responsible for the exuberant wildflower field on the slopes below. A restored bronze marker points out the five Cascade peaks that are visible here.

This park is known as "the castle" to local climbers, who come here to practice bouldering, rappelling, and top-roping, especially on the sloping rock walls along the western side of the fortress. One sunny June day, I saw a young couple teaching their six- and eight-year-old girls the basics of rock climbing here.

At the park's northern end is a sweeping, baroque stone staircase. Its massive stone treads are so smooth and even that it's hard to believe they were hand-hewn. Take the stairs and begin walking left at the bottom.

5 You'll soon see the top of the southern approach road to Rocky Butte, which, like the northern approach, is named Rocky Butte Road. If you're feeling adventurous, take a side trip down the steep trail that begins just behind the rock wall at the top of this road. I recommend this short, steep, sweet walk for two reasons. First, it puts you right next to a spectacular WPA wall that is used for practice by climbers. In this day of machine-made, cement-block retaining walls, this wall, with its massive hand-hewn basalt blocks, qualifies as a work of art. Second, the trail leads down through the woods to the entrance to the amazing looping tunnel. From there, after you've looked around, turn around and come back up.

This side of the butte cries out for some well-designed trails. The only access from the neighborhood below is an almost vertical trail used by neighborhood kids that leads from NE Cadet Avenue to the tunnel. Unless you want to slide down on your bum, don't take it. The City of Portland discourages people from using unofficial trails such as this because they are not maintained and using them can cause erosion.

Back at the top of the butte, walk around the western side of the loop road back to the southern entrance of Joseph Wood Hill Park.

From the entrance to the park, retrace your steps on Rocky Butte Road to the pedestrian tunnel. It's rather inconspicuous from the road, so you'll want to keep an eye out for it: watch for it just after a tall rock wall on your left. Once through the tunnel, if you walk left you'll be on a network of trails used by rock climbers. Along the unfenced top of the cliffs here, the ground is tramped bare by the staging of countless climbs. Use extreme caution if you walk here: the drop-off is deadly, and the trails are unmarked.

Take the trail down to the bottom of the butte and retrace your steps to the trailhead.

6 If you're not too tired, walk or drive the short way down NE Skidmore Street to the entrance of the Grotto. There is a large parking lot for visitors. The land for the Grotto, officially known as the National Sanctuary of Our Sorrowful Mother, was purchased by Father Ambrose Meyer in 1923 from the Union Pacific Railroad. As a member of the Servite Order (a Roman Catholic order from 1233 officially called the Friar Servants of Mary), he had been looking for a site on which to build a tribute to Mary. The Union Pacific property was slated to be sold to residential developers, but Father Ambrose, even with an extremely low bid, was able to secure the land.

Like Rocky Butte itself, the Grotto is surprisingly unknown to many Portlanders. One employee told me that when she tells people where she works, they think she's talking about the Fish Grotto, a restaurant in downtown Portland. Regardless, the Grotto is well worth a stop. It occupies 62 acres of thick forest. On its lower level is a church and Our Lady's Grotto, a rock cave carved into the base of the cliff with a replica of Michelangelo's *Pieta* inside. When weather permits, Sunday Mass is held outdoors here among the massive Douglas firs. The lower level also includes a gift shop, welcome center, rest-rooms, and snack bar. For a well-spent $3, you can take the 110-foot elevator to the top, where the atmosphere can best be described as serene. The grounds on the terrace above the cliffs are laced with trails, and the landscaping rivals the best of Portland's parks. The 180-degree view from the glass-walled Marilyn

A climber on one of Rocky Butte's magnificent hand-hewn basalt walls, just below the summit.

Moyer Meditation Chapel (which is visible from Interstate 205) is spectacular, and the walk around the gardens in front of the elegant Servite Monastery, where the brothers live and work, feels like a true refuge.

WALK 18

ALAMEDA RIDGE LOOP

STARTING POINT Intersection of NE Sandy Boulevard, Sacramento Street, and 52nd Avenue

DISTANCE 4.75 miles, but can be shortened by looping back at any point on the ridge

ELEVATION 200 feet at the starting point; 140 feet at the closed depression at NE 32nd Avenue and Stanton Street; 250 feet at the highest point on Alameda Ridge

GETTING THERE AND PARKING From downtown Portland, drive east on Burnside and cross the Burnside Bridge. Get into the left lane. At the intersection of NE Sandy Boulevard and 12th Avenue, veer left onto Sandy. Drive approximately 2 miles to the stoplight at NE 50th Avenue. Turn right onto 50th, and turn left at the first street, NE Thompson Street. Drive two blocks to NE 52nd Avenue and Thompson. Park in this vicinity; the walk begins one block north of this intersection at NE Sandy Boulevard and Sacramento Street.

TriMet: From downtown, take bus 12 (Sandy Boulevard) to the stop at Sandy and Sacramento.

RESTROOMS AND DRINKING FOUNTAINS There are no public restrooms or drinking fountains located along this route. Restaurants, with restrooms for patrons, are located at the start of the walk and along NE Fremont Street east of NE 42nd Avenue.

FOOD AND DRINK Two eating establishments are located at the starting point of the walk. Violet's Café at 5204 NE Sacramento Street is open Thursday through

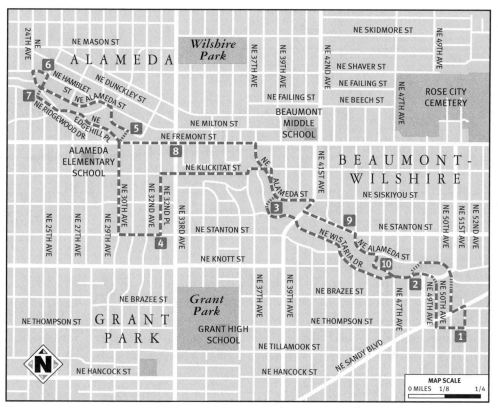

WALK 18. *Alameda Ridge Loop*

MAP KEY

- ▪━ ROUTE
- ⋯⋯ STAIRS
- ‐ ‐ TRAILS
- ┿┿┿ RAILROAD TRACKS
- PARKS/GREENSPACE
- 🚻 PUBLIC RESTROOMS
- 💧 WATER
- 📍 BUS STOP

Monday, closed Tuesdays and Wednesdays; 503-281-7933. The Rheinlander German Restaurant and Gustav's Bier Stube, located at 5035 NE Sandy Boulevard, are open every day; 503-288-5503.

THIS HILL WALK TAKES YOU UP AND DOWN Alameda Ridge, a geologic anomaly in this land of basalt. During the Missoula Floods, the ridge was created as floodwaters swirled around monolithic Rocky Butte, and then slowed and deposited gravels and cobbles into a 4-mile-long, 80-foot-high swath of granite. Another, related byproduct of these floods are large granite boulders, called erratics, that have been found throughout the Willamette Valley wherever the ice rafts they were trapped within came to rest. (Many of the erratics have been removed or depleted over the years as people chipped away at them for souvenirs, tombstones, or landscaping.) See Walks 14 and 17 for more on the Missoula Floods.

Because of the granite, some homes on Alameda Ridge and in other parts of Northeast Portland contend with radon, a heavy radioactive gas that is colorless, odorless, and tasteless. It is generated by the radioactive decay of radium present in some spring water, soil, and rocks, such as granite. Radon can seep through building foundations or pipes and accumulate inside poorly ventilated homes. The Environmental Protection Agency considers it to be the second leading cause of lung cancer, just behind smoking. Researchers at PSU have found that seven Portland zip codes have a high radon risk; six of these are along Alameda Ridge and north to the Columbia River, areas in which flood deposits accumulated. Fortunately, radon abatement isn't a complicated matter: simply open the windows.

This is a good walk for spring and fall because the neighborhoods you'll pass through—Beaumont, Hollywood, and Alameda—are thickly planted with specimen trees and shrubs that put on seasonal color shows.

1 Park in the vicinity of NE Thompson Street and 52nd Avenue. Some streets are marked "no parking," but there is plenty of free, unrestricted, off-street parking at the margins of the commercial strip along NE Sandy Boulevard. Walk north on 52nd to its intersection with Sandy and NE Sacramento Street. At this quirky little crossroads is an intriguing line of businesses, from Violet's Café, with its good coffee and atmosphere, to a caterer and a glass shop. It's one of those areas where the commercial bleeds seamlessly into the residential.

Cross Sandy at the stoplight and turn left. Take a right onto NE 51st Avenue, next to the Rheinlander German Restaurant and Gustav's Bier Stube, founded

A welcoming bungalow at the top of Alameda Ridge.

by sixth-generation chef Horst Mager in 1963. This city landmark, now operated by Horst's daughter Suzanne, serves consistently delicious German food and *bier*. Midway through this short block, the street turns from commercial to very quaint and residential. At the street's woodsy dead end, take the staircase of eighty-eight steps up to the top of the ridge, at NE Wistaria Drive. Go left, and at the intersection with NE Alameda Street, curve left onto Alameda. At 5020 is a lovely hilltop home sitting in a small grove of old Douglas firs and cedars. You'll see more great homes at 4848 and 4836. The latter has a shady, parklike front lawn that contrasts with the back, which is open to the warmth of the south. From Alameda Street north to Fremont you're in the Beaumont ("beautiful mountain") neighborhood. Not for long, though; turn left at a twisty little section of NE 48th Avenue that drops you off the ridgeline back onto Wistaria. This small street feels European, with its concrete pavement, stone walls, and yardless homes on hillside perches.

2   Turn right on Wistaria, which the route follows for the next ten blocks. This street follows the contours of the ridge and is loaded with charm. The homes are not large—in fact some could be called cottages—but they are tucked into their hillside in a cozy way that makes you long to be invited in for a cup of tea. Above Wistaria, on the top of the ridge, loom larger homes. In front of it

Under the elms on NE Wistaria Drive, sheltered on the southern side of Alameda Ridge.

and at a slightly lower elevation are the homes of Hollywood. No matter how well tended and appointed, these homes occupy a tidy, efficient grid pattern that is less lyrical than the Wistaria homes, whose locations follow the lead of the land. For example, check out the little house tucked way back on the lot where NE 45th Avenue meets Wistaria—a cozy nook that a standard 50-by-100-foot lot just couldn't duplicate.

At NE 44th Avenue, elms begin to create a leafy tunnel along the street, which curves in obedience to its underlying geology. If you want to climb the ridge and gain a wonderful view of the West Hills, a set of stairs leads up at 4317 Wistaria to 4438 Alameda; another one, at 4206 Alameda, will bring you back off the ridge to rejoin the hill walk at 4211 Wistaria. Then again, this walk is probably long enough without running up and down extra stairs like a triathlete.

In the 4200 block are homes built in the Northwest Modern style of the 1940s. The house at 4121 is a very cool modern home that looks like it could've been the cover girl for a 1950s *Sunset* magazine. Cross Wistaria before it begins to climb so that you won't have to cross at the blind corner of NE 39th Avenue.

At the confusing intersection of 39th, Wistaria, and 41st, veer left to stay on Wistaria. You'll pass a Tudor castle, complete with circular tower. It is reputed to have been built in 1928 by its owners, the Hummels, to replicate their home in Germany. Across from this medieval structure is an ultramodern home that's all angles and glass. While new homes are rare in this neighborhood, this one seems to fit right in.

This section of Wistaria, from 38th to 45th, was part of the original Beaumont subdivision platted in 1910. Written into its first deeds were two caveats: no home could cost less than $3000 (the modern equivalent, about $60,000, wouldn't even buy you a lot in this neighborhood), and stables were forbidden. To entice people to move this far into the hinterland, a streetcar providing city access was a necessity. It ran up NE 42nd Avenue, the current bus route.

Turn right onto NE 38th Avenue and then take the stairs across from 3041. After the fourth of six flights, you begin to clear the treetops and get a great view of downtown and the large radio tower at Healy Heights. The smaller tower to the right is at Council Crest Park; just left of it you can see an unnaturally square group of tall Lombardy poplars hiding the water tank up there. At the top of the seventy-eight stairs you can see the Fremont Bridge and the Montgomery Park building in Northwest Portland, and beyond them, the unspoiled hills of Forest Park.

3 A sidewalk leads through manicured lawns into the heart of big-home Alameda. Turn left. House after house in this tightly packed stretch maximizes its view, which means that pedestrians have to settle for glimpses from the unclaimed airspace above the stairways.

At the intersection of NE Klickitat Street, Alameda, and 38th, turn left onto Klickitat, which will drop you quickly off the ridge again via a street of late 1920s bungalows, Tudors, and one big mansion. Beverly Cleary, a children's book author beloved by several generations of kids, grew up just south of here in the 1920s, near 37th and Klickitat. Her parents wanted to live in the shelter that Alameda Ridge provided from the fierce east winds of the Columbia River Gorge. Ramona Quimby, the mischievous heroine of many of Cleary's books, lived on a fictional street called Klickitat; she has been memorialized in bronze at nearby Grant Park, along with her pal Ribsy the dog.

A wonderful alley starts just past 3606 NE Klickitat. Unmapped, this street was once known as Mooses Alley. Starting at 3624 is a row of tidy Tudors, lined up and enjoying their downtown view. The Barnes Mansion sits at 3533; this Colonial Revival home was built in 1914 by Frank and Isabella Barnes.

Before you cross NE 33rd Avenue at the painted crosswalk, turn around for a nice vantage point from which to view the morphology of the ridge. After crossing 33rd, turn left onto NE 32nd Place. Unlike closer-in neighborhoods like Hawthorne or Sunnyside, which were built to take advantage of streetcar lines,

Alameda was built with the car in mind, with most homes having driveways and garages.

NE 32nd Place is an extremely pleasant, quiet, tidy Tudorland. Two homes sitting across from each other, 2931 and 2940, have exuberant freeform gardens that seem to be encouraging each other's gentle defiance of the street's decorous atmosphere.

4 Turn right at NE Stanton Street. A wisteria at this corner has borrowed the trunk and limbs of a dead but still stout cherry, creating a one-of-a-kind "wischerria."

Since this is a hill walk, you may be wondering why you've been routed off the high points of the ridge and onto the flats. It's because of the interesting landform in front of you at NE 32nd Avenue and Stanton, a closed depression probably caused by the Missoula Floods. Just as water swirls around a stationary object at the ocean shore, creating depressions in the sand, the floods swirled around Rocky Butte and the ridge of rock they deposited: Alameda. The hill walk route has been descending toward this low spot since leaving the ridge; at this intersection, streets in every direction climb away from it.

The lacy trees in the parking strip here are flame ash, a species much used on Portland streets. The outer edges of the leaves turn a stunning coppery red in fall. Turn right onto NE 30th Avenue. Another quiet, tidy street, 30th had me humming that old Monkees classic, "Pleasant Valley Sunday."

As I have walked the hills of Portland, I have been struck by the scarcity of Douglas firs in many neighborhoods. Scattered here and there are a few vestigial firs from the city's forested past, but some Portland neighborhoods seem to have forgotten their Northwest roots. The intersection of 30th and Klickitat is an exception, with its stately fir, tall and proud. This tree graces and complements the homes it towers over instead of hiding them behind a screen of foliage, as so many street trees do, genetically selected as they are to never reach more than two stories high.

There is a partial reason for the relative scarcity of firs in some city neighborhoods. Douglas fir, though the essence of northwestern Oregon, is not a well-behaved street tree (a tree recommended by the city for use in parking strips). While young, a fir or other evergreen cannot be pruned for visibility purposes without essentially denuding the tree. And as it grows, the tree requires frequent pruning to avoid running into overhead wires. Mature firs also have a very effective self-preservation technique: in windy or icy conditions, they readily shed large limbs, which can fall onto power lines. This explains why firs are not found in parking strips, but I still wonder why people don't plant them in their yards.

The intersection of NE Fremont Street, Edgehill Place, and 30th Avenue is a nice spot to gaze upward at the homes perching on the ridge at its various heights.

5 Cross Fremont, and just to your right, at 3011, is a staircase of many tiers. The staggered flights and landings give the steps a cascading, pool-and-drop effect. After ninety-five steps, you're on NE Alameda Terrace. Turn left. This street has a European feel; homes on steep lots hug the street, leaving very little front yard space. At 3115 sits a bungalow on steroids. Past 3078 is a good view, across the river, of the OHSU campus, with the Healy Heights tower above it. The home at 3056 is beautifully sited; it sits on the curve of the ridge, and from under its deep, cozy eaves, residents enjoy a panoramic view framed by columns of Douglas fir trunks.

At the corner of Alameda Terrace and Alameda Street, a Camperdown elm rises dolefully above a stuccoed wall. (See Walk 2 for more on this tree.) Turn left onto Alameda Street. At the intersection of Alameda Street, Alameda Terrace, Hamblet Street, and 29th Avenue, stay on Alameda Street. This area is the heart of "the Alameda," developed in 1909 as an exclusive subdivision. *Alameda*, a Spanish word, refers to a public walk shaded by trees—presumably by *alamos*, or poplar trees, although these trees favor watery locations and are unlikely to have actually grown on this ridge. The homes here are uniformly beautiful and uniformly distinct from each other. The homes at 2834 and 2815 are examples of English cottages, although that term is loosely used in the case of these giants.

6 The home at 2611 Alameda was built for the founder of the Alameda Land Company, Edward Ferguson, in 1914. Presumably he had the pick of the lots on the ridge, and he chose this one.

In the triangular block starting at 26th sits the regal Autzen Mansion, bounded by Alameda, Hamblet, 24th, and 26th. This Arts and Crafts home was built in 1926 for the president of the Portland Manufacturing Company, Thomas Autzen. When the company was sold in 1952, his grandson, Thomas Edward Autzen, established the Autzen Foundation. One of its largest grants was to the University of Oregon football stadium, which today is named Autzen Stadium. On the grounds of the mansion, two Heritage Trees—canyon live oak and European beech—add to the grandeur. This is the turnaround point.

Walk around the mansion to Hamblet. From Hamblet turn right onto 26th. Cross Alameda to NE Stuart Drive. To the east of the house at 2532 Alameda is a staircase. Before you take the plunge off the ridge top, look back. The Olmsted Brothers, who proposed a scenic boulevard along the top of the bluff here, and the developers of the Alameda subdivision would probably be immensely pleased to see this site, with home after beautiful home, mature trees, and hired landscapers busily mowing away.

7 Seventy-five steps lead you past a bamboo forest and onto NE Ridgewood Drive. Turn left and stay on Ridgewood through a multistreet intersection. From here you can look upward into the steeply terraced and severely retained backyards of the homes you walked by on Alameda. Tucked into the base of the ridge, Ridgewood has the same sheltered-nook aura of Wistaria Drive.

At NE 28th Avenue you can see the Alameda School just down the hill. This elementary school began as a one-room schoolhouse at the corner of 25th and Fremont in 1915. It later moved to 27th and Klickitat. The present Colonial-style building was constructed in 1922, with various additions made between 1948 and 1955 to accommodate the baby boomers. This neighborhood remains popular with families. In 2004, 631 children attended school here, making it the largest public grade school in the city.

Walk uphill a bit and merge onto NE Edgehill Place. It's interesting to see how people deal with a near-vertical backyard, and from here you can see various approaches. Some go for the "master of my domain" effect, suppressing the hillside behind stiffly vertical retaining walls. Others take a more relaxed "this should do it" approach, their slopes retained by a casual mix of boulders and ivy.

Edgehill drops you off at Fremont Street. Turn left for a march back up the ridge on this steep, trafficky, attractive street. In the late 1800s, Fremont was known as Gravelly Hill Road.

8 Near the intersection of Fremont and 33rd is the site of the old gravel quarry. It was filled in by the early 1900s, but the fill in places was evidently not compacted well; I once visited a friend here whose floors sloped so much that anything round would quickly find its way to one corner of the room.

Walk about six more blocks on Fremont to the intersection with Alameda Street and turn right. This section of Alameda, because it has no view, was developed with smaller homes. Past Klickitat, the homes and views are big again. When you reach NE 41st Avenue, cross it (before it curves around a blind corner) and turn right. Turn left at NE Beaumont Street. On this tiny avenue of large homes, you'll see a Mediterranean-style house at 4120 that was designed in 1927 by its owner, an architect. The home at 4159 once belonged to Russian-born Jacques Gershkovitch, founder of the Portland Junior Symphony and conductor from 1924 to 1954. At 4190, Beaumont ends, and you're back on Alameda.

9   In the next block of Alameda are examples of the alto and baja schools of arboreal theory. Baja is represented at 4330, whose parking strip is lined with a row of uniform, mature flowering plum trees. Even though these trees are fully grown, pedestrians have to stoop a bit to look past them, and they hide the home from the view of passing cars. Perhaps that is their function. The alto school is represented at the next house, 4420, whose parking strip is planted with tall, mature oaks. Here the home is not hidden behind its street trees but framed by them. The oaks sway, whisper, and lend a gracious elegance to the home. With homes as lovely as these, why hide them behind a hedgey row of bushes on legs?

The next home is a castle. The 6-inch-thick walls at 4438 Alameda were made from basalt quarried at Rocky Butte. It was designed in 1926 by Lee Dougan, who also designed the beautiful monastery at the Grotto on Rocky Butte.

10   Walk a bit further on Alameda and then turn right onto NE Wiberg Lane, a wonderful little hillside street that drops like a slinky down the face of the ridge. At 2772 is an Early Modern home, built in 1940. A fine southeastern view of Mount Tabor pops out at 2771. Wiberg ends in one block. Turn left at the intersection with 47th Avenue and walk along the southern side of Wistaria. Take a flight of steps down to 49th and turn left; this is lower Wistaria. It leads to a staircase with a mysterious air that drops you down on 50th, a lovely, private-feeling dead end of bungalows. From here walk south two blocks to Sandy Boulevard, and reward yourself with a meal at the Rheinlander German Restaurant or Gustav's Bier Stube.

Cross Sandy Boulevard at the pedestrian light at 50th Avenue to return to the starting point.

ALBINA RIVERFRONT TO HILLTOP LOOP

STARTING POINT N Williams Avenue and Russell Street

DISTANCE 4 miles

ELEVATION 50 feet at N Interstate Avenue and Russell Street; 200 feet at N Mississippi Avenue and Skidmore Street

GETTING THERE AND PARKING From downtown Portland, drive east on Burnside Street. Turn right at the first stoplight over the Burnside Bridge, SE Martin Luther King Jr. Boulevard (Highway 99E), a one-way street heading south. Get immediately in the left-hand lane to turn left at the first street, SE Ankeny. Turn left at the next light, SE Grand Avenue, a one-way street heading north. Stay on Grand. It becomes a two-way street and rejoins MLK at the intersection with NE Hancock Street. Drive five more blocks on MLK to the stoplight at NE Russell Street. Turn left on Russell; drive two blocks, and turn right on N Williams Avenue. Park on Williams in the block north of Russell, where parking is unrestricted.

TriMet: From downtown, take bus 40 (Mocks Crest) to the stop at N Williams and Russell. Alternatively, take the MAX Yellow Line to the stop at Albina and Mississippi. Walk one block to Russell, and begin the walk from there.

RESTROOMS AND DRINKING FOUNTAINS Restrooms and drinking fountains can be found at the Matt Dishman Community Center, 77 NE Knott Street, and Title Wave Used Books, 216 NE Knott Street.

FOOD AND DRINK Various cafés and coffee shops can be found near the beginning of the walk along N Russell Street and along N Mississippi Avenue, north

Sumner/
Albina Park

N ALBINA AVE

99W

N GOING ST

N BLANDENA ST

N WILLIAMS AVE
NE CLEVELAND AVE
NE RODNEY AVE
NE MALLORY AVE
NE GARFIELD AVE

99E

NE PRESCOTT ST

4

N PRESCOTT ST

5

N SKIDMORE ST

NE 6TH AVE
NE 7TH AVE
NE GRAND AVE

N LONGVIEW AVE
N INTERSTATE AVE

N MISSOURI AVE
N MICHIGAN AVE
N MISSISSIPPI AVE
N BORTHWICK AVE
N ALBINA AVE
N KERBY AVE
N COMMERCIAL AVE
N HAIGHT AVE

N MASON ST

NE SHAVER ST

N GANTENBIEN AVE
N VANCOUVER AVE

NE FAILING ST

NE MARTIN LUTHER KING JR BLVD

*Unthank
Park*

B O I S E

*Overlook
Park*

N GREELEY AVE

5

N BEECH ST

BOISE-ELIOT
ELEMENTARY
SCHOOL

NE FREMONT ST

NE IVY ST

6

NE COOK ST

ALBINA
YARD

N COOK ST

3

N COOK ST

N WILLIAMS AVE
N RODNEY AVE

NE MONROE ST

*Dawson
Park*

NE STANTON ST

N KERBY AVE

EMANUEL
HOSPITAL

N GRAHAM ST

MATT DISHMAN
COMMUNITY
CENTER

7

NE KNOTT ST

NE 7TH AVE

N KNOTT ST

2

N RUSSELL ST

1

*Lillis
Albina
Park*

E L I O T

NE SACRAMENTO ST

30

405

N RAILROAD ST
N RIVER ST

N THOMPSON ST

N TILLAMOOK ST

N FLINT AVE
N VANCOUVER AVE

30

NE TILLAMOOK ST

NE THOMPSON ST

NE HANCOCK ST

FREMONT BRIDGE

N WHEELER AVE
N INTERSTATE AVE
N LARRABEE AVE

*Willamette
River*

NW NAITO PKWY

N

NE BROADWAY

NE WEIDLER ST

NE GRAND AVE

To Broadway
Bridge

MAP SCALE
0 MILES   1/8   1/4

WALK 19. *Albina Riverfront to Hilltop Loop*

MAP KEY

▪▬ ROUTE   ▦ RAILROAD TRACKS
▪▪▪▪▪ STAIRS   ▨ PARKS/GREENSPACE
‒ ‒ TRAILS   🚻 PUBLIC RESTROOMS
🌊 WATER   ● BUS STOP

of N Fremont Street. Toward the end of the walk, along MLK, are Billy Reed's Restaurant and Bar, 2808 NE MLK (503-493-8127), and Bridges Café and Catering, 2716 NE MLK (503-288-4169). Both are just north of NE Knott Street.

THE BOISE AND ELIOT NEIGHBORHOODS in this hill walk were first known as Albina, a city platted out in 1872 by Edwin Russell, William Page, and George Williams, all of whose names live on as streets. The city was named after Albina Page, William's wife. Once rail service arrived in the early 1880s, immigration to the West Coast increased, and Russians, Germans, Swedes, Norwegians, and Danes settled in Albina to work in the waterfront dockyards, lumber mills, and railroad yards. The city of Albina was incorporated in 1887, but independence lasted only four years before it became part of Portland. It was bounded roughly by Russell to the south, Mississippi to the west, Alberta to the north, and 15th to the east. As the main commercial street, Williams Avenue was planked from Russell north to Alberta. Along this stretch were stores such as Geist Shoe and Department Store, Trupp Shoe Repair, and Weimer's Hardware and Furniture Store. One historian described it as the center of a business district second only to downtown Portland. Later, a streetcar line on Williams connected Albina, via the Steel Bridge, to downtown Portland.

Albina was a thriving community primarily composed of laborers and was the most densely populated part of Portland, a population that was, like the rest of the city, mostly white. Through policies both stated and implied, Portland had developed a reputation for being unfriendly to nonwhites. At the start of World War II, the city counted fewer than two thousand black residents. That soon changed. In 1941, upon entering the war, the nation was vastly underequipped to fight on two fronts. Mobilization of men and materiel had to happen fast, including the building of an entire fleet of war ships. Henry Kaiser, an industrialist who had made his fortune in dam and highway construction beginning in 1914, quickly opened shipyards in Portland and Vancouver. With hundreds of thousands of men fighting the war overseas, a person's race and sex suddenly became secondary to simply getting the job done, and Kaiser recruited nationally for people of all ethnicities to come work in his shipyards. During the war the shipyards produced ships in as little as four and a half days.

Thousands of African-Americans, along with other newcomers, came to Portland to do just that. Vanport (named for Vancouver and Portland, the two cities it lay between) soon sprang up to house them. Located along the Columbia

River on what is now Delta Park, Vanport was the largest public-housing project in the nation and the second largest city in Oregon. By late 1943, forty thousand people were living in a place which one year earlier had been vacant bottomland. It was designed to be temporary: after the war ended, workers were meant to go back where they came from. But people, once settled, are hard to displace, and when the war ended, Vanport lived on. Approximately eighteen thousand people resided there when the entire city was destroyed by a flood on May 30, 1948.

With no homes left, the people of Vanport moved into the city, but redlining (an informal practice in which realtors and banks steer targeted groups into prescribed neighborhoods) kept black residents from moving anywhere except into Albina. The area settled by the black community extended south to around NE Broadway. Williams Avenue south of Broadway was the area's commercial district. Albina continued to thrive as a home to working-class Portlanders, but this prosperity lasted just a short time before the neighborhood began suffering the assaults of highway construction and public-works projects. In the late 1950s, churches, businesses, and 476 housing units were leveled at the southern end of the district to make way for the Memorial Coliseum. In response, Albina's commercial core moved north to the intersection of Williams and Russell.

Interstate 5 was constructed soon after, excising another swath of homes and businesses from the district. The civil unrest of the 1960s dealt another blow to Albina, leading to riots and destruction similar to what was happening in many urban cores. The last blow came in 1970 when Emanuel Hospital razed thirty-three blocks in the center of the neighborhood, including the commercial district, for the Emanuel Hospital Urban Renewal Project. The project, whose stated goal was "to remedy substandard housing and substandard environment by expanding the hospital and construction-related facilities, parking, employee housing, offices, and housing for the elderly," got only partway off the ground. When federal funds ran out, Emanuel could not complete the plan. The hospital thrived, but the neighborhood suffered, and many of these blocks remain vacant. Albina entered a twenty-five-year period of commercial decline, in which outside investors stayed away.

East side neighborhoods, starting with Irvington in the 1970s, began to be reinvigorated by young homeowners who were attracted to urban life and good quality homes. Albina's turn came in the 1990s when many home prices rapidly went from affordable to unaffordable (for many). With the addition of the MAX Yellow Line in 2004 and corresponding investment from the City of Portland further paving the path, the neighborhood has once again become a place for economic opportunity.

A busy intersection of N Williams Avenue, near Russell Street, circa 1930. Photo courtesy of the City of Portland Archives.

1 The hill walk starts on N Russell Street and Williams Avenue in what used to be known as Lower Albina. The section of Russell stretching from the Willamette River (former site of a ferry slip) to MLK (named Union previous to the late 1980s) was once frequented by dock workers, mill workers, and laborers in the nearby railroad yards. A century ago, thirty saloons operated in this stretch. Only one remains.

Walk downhill on Russell toward the river. Adjacent to Harriet Tubman Middle School, at N Flint Avenue, is Lillis Albina Park. Like much of North and Northeast Portland, the underlying soil here is coarse sand and silt deposited by the catastrophic Missoula Floods. The land's gradual drop to the river a few blocks west of here is a result of the Willamette River eroding the flood deposits over the last ten thousand years.

Emanuel Hospital's Ronald McDonald House sits on the right side of Russell at N Commercial Avenue. It was built in 1997 and is one of 223 Ronald McDonald Houses worldwide. The houses are an affordable, homelike lodging alternative for the families of seriously ill kids who live more than 50 miles from the hospital. The average stay is ten days, and the house is usually full, with an 86 percent occupancy rate.

Pass under the freeway and you'll come to a block of old buildings unmolested by urban renewal. Many of these are classified in the Historic Resource Inventory as Streetcar-Era Commercial buildings from the turn of the twentieth century. Most had storefronts on the first floor and apartments above for Portland's new immigrants. The red-brick building at 703 N Russell is the old Lewis Moyer department store. At 733 is a 1906 Streetcar-Era Commercial retail building that appears to be teetering between salvation and the wrecking ball. The 1890 Davis Block, occupying 801 through 813, has seen its retail roots revived, with a wine shop and a hair salon. Painted on its side is "Sam Moy & Company Men's and Women's Furnishings—Special Weave Cloth," a ghostly sign from its long-ago past. It also had apartments on the upper floors.

Across the street at 816 through 820 is the 1894 Frederick Torgler Building of retail shops and apartments, now home to Mint, a thriving restaurant with swanky cocktails. Next to this is the White Eagle, the sole survivor of the scores of taverns that once lined Russell Street. Like another bird, the starling, the White Eagle has successfully adapted to fits its surroundings. Over the years it has evolved from an immigrant refuge, to a Prohibition-era ice cream parlor, to a hard-hat retreat, to a rock music venue, to a revered elder (conferred upon it by the McMenamin brothers, masters of saving and reviving landmark buildings).

In 1989 Kurt and Rob Widmer bought the McKay and Simpson block at the corner of Russell and N Interstate Avenue. The buildings have been reborn as the Widmer Brothers Brewery.

2 Turn right on Interstate. The area west of Interstate today is a fairly impenetrable industrial neverland, but this riverfront area was the heart of Albina's early days, before people and businesses moved further up the hill. The only street access is via N Tillamook, but pedestrian access to the river doesn't exist. The end of Russell was once a ferry landing, but the site is not accessible today.

Prior to the 1950s, Interstate Avenue was the primary thoroughfare to Vancouver, Washington. It was supplanted by Interstate 5, and its fortunes dwindled until 2004, when the avenue was reborn as an urban renewal district surrounding the MAX Yellow Line.

From Interstate and Russell is a good view of the Fremont Bridge. This interstate highway bridge opened in 1973 and completed the Interstate 405 loop around the city. Its enormous arch rises 381 feet above the water and is visible from many points in the city. The graceful design sits in counterpoint to the strictly utilitarian Marquam Bridge, the upstream freeway bridge that is part of the same Interstate 405 loop. After the Marquam was finished in 1966, Portlanders began to voice complaints about its appearance. (The Marquam is visible from the route of Walk 8.) The Oregon Department of Transportation, when planning the Fremont, asked the Portland Arts Commission to weigh in with design ideas. The design chosen, a steel tied-arch, is the same as the Passerelle Debilly, a pedestrian bridge under the Eiffel Tower.

Just north of the Fremont Bridge and across Interstate Avenue are the Union Pacific Rail Yards. Rail service to the East came to Portland in 1883. The Albina Yard smokestack, visible here, went up in 1885. The railroad was the first mode of transport to use Sullivan's Gulch, a natural ravine eroded out of flood deposits through which Interstate 84 and a MAX line now run. Until Seattle came on line with rail service a few years later, Portland was the premier port of the Northwest, and the Albina Yard thrummed with activity.

This is the lowest elevation on the hill walk.

Turn right on N Knott Street. On your left is a vacant lot. A cherry tree, two pines, and a pair of cedars that stand as sidewalk sentinels are all that remain of a home that no longer exists.

In one block, turn left onto N Mississippi Avenue. Pass under the stout concrete pillars holding up the Fremont Bridge's approach ramps, and walk under Interstate 5 again as the road climbs. It is surprisingly pleasant to be a pedestrian enjoying the air and the views of the West Hills while strolling along the rushing, smelly, isolating interstate highway system.

3　Once the freeways are behind you, turn left on N Cook Street. At its end, turn right and climb N Michigan Avenue, a delightful mix of ultra-new sleek and ultra-neglected creepy. Turn right on N Fremont Street, and pass the graceful 1923 Georgian apartment building that sits at 932. The Fremont Bridge was named after this street; it was originally thought that the bridge's eastern approach would be via Fremont Street, but this was never implemented. Ahead is the Boise-Eliot Elementary School. Walk one block on Fremont before turning left on Mississippi.

Lots of new commercial lives are being led here, among them a furniture builder, a pizza pub, a building materials recycler, a nursery, a café, and a coffee shop. It is a pleasant block that has benefited from the attention of the Portland Development Commission.

The intersection of Mississippi and Shaver is a nexus, with a coffee shop and the Native American Youth Association. The latter is located at 4000 Mississippi in a Mediterranean-style building. Constructed in 1929 as an all-in-one community center, the building originally housed shops, offices, apartments, and an assembly hall. The hall, now the Mississippi Rising Ballroom, is still home to ceilis, concerts, and public meetings.

Turn left on N Mason Street, just before the crest of the hill (916 Mason), and then turn right on Michigan. At 4134 is a gorgeous 1896 home on a huge park-like lot, with towering trees that drew me in from a block away. Carvings in the stairs leading to this old home proclaim that it belongs to "W. L. Bantam," the original owner. Note the cool fish-scale shingles on the house.

Cross N Skidmore Street. On your left is the freeway overpass that leads into the Overlook neighborhood, another fine place to stroll for views atop the Willamette River bluffs. Stay on Michigan as it jogs around N Prescott Street.

4 In one block, turn left on the unmarked N Going Street, adjacent to the old red-brick Patton House. This house was established in 1887 by the Albina Union Relief Society, which wanted to create an alternative to the poorhouse for unfortunate people who had "nowhere to lay their heads." The land for the site was donated by Matthew Patton (an early pioneer, of Patton Road patronage). In those linguistically blunter days, it was called the Patton Home for the Aged and Friendless. Now Patton House is a community service of Ecumenical Ministries of Oregon and offers housing to sixty-three low-income Portlanders in a drug- and alcohol-free environment.

Going Street is truncated by Interstate 5. Turn right, walk behind Patton House, and turn right again onto N Blandena Street, where you'll walk by a community garden. Before leaving the grounds, you might want to scoop up a nut or two from the huge European chestnut in the front yard; this tree was planted in 1891. Across from Patton House, at 4548 N Michigan, is a monkey puzzle tree. These are among the world's oddest-looking trees. Native to Chile and Argentina, they are the oldest conifers on the planet and were introduced to Portland at the 1905 world's fair in the South American Pavilion. The size of this tree indicates that it probably dates from around that year. Monkey puzzles are dioecious, meaning that males and females are different. This specimen, with its large, round, heavy cones, is a female; male trees have longer, cucumber-shaped cones. Monkey puzzle trees can take up to forty years to produce the first cone, so despite the fact that the seeds are edible and similar in taste to pine nuts, they aren't commercially grown. In Portland these trees are usually planted not in a grove but as individual specimens. Without wind fertilization from a nearby tree, seeds are usually hollow.

Walk east on Blandena for two blocks, and turn right onto N Albina Avenue, where you'll find a thriving commercial scene. At 4543 Albina sits a very cool three-story tavern dating from 1895. It made the Historic Resource Inventory because of its beautiful stepped, curvilinear gable. Just before you hit the first cross street, N Prescott, veer left of the tiny triangle park. Walk straight uphill

A restored 1895 tavern building on N Albina Avenue.

on an alley that runs next to the John Palmer House, an 1898 home whose lavish ornamentation reminds me of a toddler who's gotten into her mother's jewelry box. At this point you're at an elevation of 200 feet, one of the highest points in the vicinity. Continue on the alley as it leads you down the knoll to Skidmore.

5 Turn left on Skidmore, right on Albina, and walk south through a leafy stretch of beautifully preserved homes. At the corner of N Mason Street and Albina is a church built in 1926 as the Finnish Mission Congregational Church. In this area, signs of gentrification are everywhere: new fir front doors, multi-hued paint schemes, "for sale" signs with "sold" stickers slapped across them, and contractors' trucks on every block.

Turn left on N Shaver Street and right on N Kerby Avenue. The large building on the left is the Center for Self Enhancement. Its mission is to help inner city youth realize their potential. It opened in 1996.

Turn left on N Failing Street, and take the first right onto N Commercial Avenue, which is not at all commercial in this exceedingly pleasant block of homes. At 3715 is a home that has retained its Rose City roots via its venerable parking strip roses, whose age and vigor allow them to bloom even in mid December. At Fremont, jog left and rejoin Commercial as it continues south.

6 Turn left on N Ivy, an alleylike street. At 311 stands Liberty Hall, a collectively run community center and event hall. Ivy runs into N Vancouver Avenue, where it is interrupted by the Wonder Bread Bakery and Retail Outlet. Wonder Bread was named by its founder in 1921 after he went to a hot air balloon festival and was filled with wonder at the sight of all those balloons aloft— hence the logo. Today the company is owned by Kansas City–based Interstate Bakeries Corporation, the largest baker and distributor of fresh baked goods in the United States. Stop by and browse the selection at the retail outlet. How long has it been since your mom packed a Twinkie in your lunch box?

Turn right on Vancouver and left on N Cook Street. Once you cross N Williams, you're in Northeast Portland. The homes at 19, 23, 27, and 33 NE Cook are like four sisters, all sharing the same bone structure but each with unique accessories and style. Turn right onto NE Rodney Avenue, a street of beautiful old homes. At the home on the corner of NE Monroe and Rodney stand two old cedars, flanking the front sidewalk in just the same fashion as the cedars in the vacant lot on N Knott Street.

At NE Morris Street, look one block to your right and you'll see the old brick Immaculata Academy, a Catholic girls school built in 1928. Today it houses Friends of the Children. Founded in 1993, this organization's goal is to provide vulnerable and challenged kids with a mentor, a "friend," who will stick with them for years, providing guidance, constancy, and support. Each friend is a full-time employee of the organization, mentoring eight children.

Continue south on Rodney. At the intersection of NE Stanton Street is a Methodist church from 1909 whose cornerstone is written in the German spoken by its parishioners, proudly announcing this as the "Deutsche Bisch. Meth. Kirche." Turn left on Stanton, and one block further, turn right on MLK.

7 Across MLK is the former Standard Dairy, which was turned into a retail and residential complex in 2000. All that remains of the old dairy is the curving brick façade. Behind the facade is Billy Reed's Restaurant and Bar. At the corner of NE Knott Street is Bridges Café and Catering, located inside a quirky pair of Queen Anne townhomes, conjoined by retail space on their first floors.

Pass the tiny, graceful Gladys McCoy Park, named for a former Multnomah County chairperson, and turn right onto one of my favorite tucked-away Portland streets: NE Knott, between MLK and Williams.

First you'll come to the former State of Oregon and Multnomah County Medical Examiner's Office at 301 NE Knott. This 1924 building, a strange hybrid of a bungalow and a Colonial, was the Pearson Funeral Home. In 1966, when Pearson moved, Multnomah County purchased the building as the county coroner's office, where it served much of Oregon and Multnomah County for almost forty years, until 2004. The building bridged the gap between the eras when the county coroner was an elected official, often not a medical doctor, to the current era of DNA testing and sophisticated forensic analysis by highly trained medical examiners. With antiquated facilities and only five coolers at the Knott Street facility, the move to the state-of-the-art, sixty-bed morgue and state crime laboratory in Clackamas County was much appreciated by all the living. The upstairs space in the Knott Street office was occupied by a revolving coterie of medical students, who lived at the morgue rent-free in exchange for pulling night shifts, opening the morgue to the incoming deceased, and doing general maintenance.

Across the street at 216 is the former Albina Library. Designed in 1912 in the Spanish Renaissance style, it originally housed books in most of the European languages to accommodate the needs of the neighborhood's diverse immigrant population. It was funded by the Carnegie Library Building Fund and is decorated with fabulous polychrome glazed terra-cotta pilasters and window boxes. In 1919 this building was designated by the American Institutes of Architects as one of the ten best buildings in Portland. In 1988 it was converted into Title Wave Used Books, where the county library system sells books it no longer needs. In its first fifteen years, the Title Wave sold more than 700,000 titles, generating $1.5 million in revenues. An afternoon spent browsing the ever-changing shelves of reasonably priced books in this lovely, light-filled building is one of Portland's signature charms. Ellis Lawrence designed the building.

In the next block on the right is the Matt Dishman Community Center, a Portland Parks facility with an indoor pool surrounded by windows, and other recreation facilities. This was once the site of the Eliot Grade School (now integrated into the Boise-Eliot Elementary School, seen earlier in the walk). In 1950 Portland Parks remodeled the building into a community center, later renaming it for Matt Dishman, the first African-American to be Multnomah County Sheriff and a Portland police officer.

In the 1950s the center was called the Knott Street Gym, home to the nationally famous Knott Street Boxers. From the 1950s to the early 1970s, Knott Street produced nine national Amateur Athletic Union champions. In 1964 two members made the U.S. Olympic boxing team. One retired boxer remembered those days, before it was the NBA that kids pinned their dreams on. "It was like

The award-winning building that was once the Albina Library is now the Title Wave, a library-run retail store selling cast-off books from throughout the Multnomah County library system.

we were the black Yankees," he said. "Portland was really put on the map, athletically, by Knott Street." Besides serving as a training ground for elite boxers, the gym was the neighborhood hangout, and weekly boxing shows drew crowds.

Across from Dishman is a 1906 substation originally owned by the Portland Railway, Light, and Power Company, the city's main streetcar line. Among other lines, it ran the train up to the top of Council Crest.

Turn left onto Williams and walk south one block to the beginning point of the walk.

WILLAMETTE COVE TO SAINT JOHNS BRIDGE LOOP

STARTING POINT N Ivanhoe Street and Richmond Avenue

DISTANCE 3.5 miles

ELEVATION 10 feet along the Willamette River; 150 feet along the river bluffs

GETTING THERE AND PARKING From Northwest Portland, drive west on Highway 30 (also called Saint Helens Road). From the intersection with NW Kittridge Avenue, drive 2.2 miles to a stoplight at NW Bridge Avenue (the last light before the road goes under the span of the Saint Johns Bridge). Signs direct you to turn left to get to the Saint Johns Bridge. Turn left, climb the hill, and turn right onto the bridge. At the first stoplight over the bridge, turn right onto N Ivanhoe Street (avoid making a hard right here onto Burlington Avenue). Drive four blocks and park on the street near the intersection of Ivanhoe and Richmond.

TriMet: From downtown, take bus 17 (NW 21st Avenue/Saint Helens Road) to the stop at N John Avenue and Ivanhoe Street. Walk two blocks east to the intersection of Ivanhoe and Richmond.

RESTROOMS AND DRINKING FOUNTAINS Restrooms and drinking fountains can be found at Cathedral Park and, for customers, at coffee shops or restaurants along N Lombard Street.

FOOD AND DRINK Saint Johns Theater and Pub at 8203 N Ivanhoe Street offers pub food, drinks, and movies, and is open for lunch and dinner every day; 503-

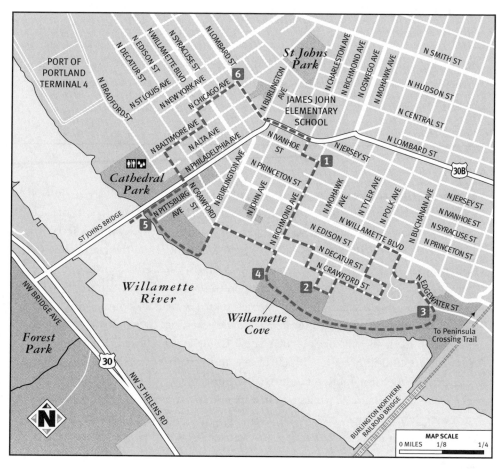

N

PORT OF
PORTLAND
TERMINAL 4

N BRADFORD ST

N DECATUR ST

N ST LOUIS AVE

N EDISON ST

N WILLAMETTE BLVD

N SYRACUSE ST

N LOMBARD ST

N NEW YORK AVE

N CHICAGO AVE

N BALTIMORE AVE

N ALTA AVE

N PHILADELPHIA AVE

6

St Johns
Park

N CHARLESTON AVE

N RICHMOND AVE

N OSWEGO AVE

N MOHAWK AVE

N SMITH ST

N HUDSON ST

N CENTRAL ST

N BURLINGTON AVE

JAMES JOHN
ELEMENTARY
SCHOOL

N IVANHOE
ST

N JERSEY ST

N LOMBARD ST

30B

*Cathedral
Park*

1

N PRINCETON ST

N JOHN AVE

N RICHMOND AVE

N MOHAWK
AVE

N TYLER AVE

N POLK AVE

N JERSEY ST

N IVANHOE ST

N SYRACUSE ST

N PRINCETON ST

N BURLINGTON AVE

N CRAWFORD
ST

N PITTSBURG
AVE

ST JOHNS BRIDGE

5

N EDISON ST

N WILLAMETTE BLVD

N BUCHANAN AVE

N EDGEWATER ST

4

N DECATUR ST

2

N CRAWFORD ST

3

*Willamette
River*

*Willamette
Cove*

To Peninsula
Crossing Trail

NW BRIDGE AVE

*Forest
Park*

30

NW ST HELENS RD

BURLINGTON NORTHERN
RAILROAD BRIDGE

MAP SCALE
0 MILES   1/8   1/4

WALK 20. *Willamette Cove to Saint Johns Bridge Loop*

MAP KEY

■ ■ ROUTE

▮▮▮▮▮ STAIRS

— — TRAILS

╞╪╪ RAILROAD TRACKS

PARKS/GREENSPACE

🚻 PUBLIC RESTROOMS

💧 WATER

🚏 BUS STOP

283-8520. John Street Café at 8338 N Lombard Street is open for breakfast and lunch Wednesday through Sunday, closed Monday and Tuesday; 503-247-1066. Additional restaurants and coffee shops can be found on N Lombard Street.

NOTE This hill walk cuts through Willamette Cove, an undeveloped riverside greenspace. The land is remote and lightly used. Walking alone, especially for women, is not a good idea.

SAINT JOHNS IS NAMED FOR JAMES (JIMMY) JOHNS, a reclusive man who in 1846 became the first white settler on the North Portland peninsula. He settled along the Willamette River, opening a store and operating a ferry. By 1850 there were twelve families in "old town" Saint Johns, on the land below the bluffs, and the area had taken the name of its first settler. His "sainthood" came, some people conjecture, from his support of schools and the community. (The neighborhood grade school is called James John Elementary.) Since 1867, Saint Johns has been a manufacturing mecca, starting with its first industry, a cooperage, which made barrels for Spreckles Sugar Company in Hawaii. It later became a major shipbuilding center. Much of the industry has moved on, but plenty remains, giving Saint Johns an industrial-historical feel that is different from anywhere else in Portland. With its rich history and its stunning views of downtown, the Saint Johns Bridge, and Forest Park, this hill walk is among my favorites, especially when it comes to getting off the usual Portland pedestrian paths.

1 Start at the corner of N Ivanhoe Street and Richmond Avenue, near the Saint Johns Theater and Pub. Today this historic building, like many other old and significant local structures, including a school, a Masonic lodge, and the county poor farm, has been renovated by the McMenamin brothers and now houses a restaurant and pub. The Saint Johns Theater and Pub building originated as the National Cash Register Building, built for the 1905 Lewis and Clark Exposition at Guilds Lake. During the exposition, multimedia lectures on various topics were held inside this building, using early motion picture technology. Its dome was topped with a cupola and a statue of a woman. After the exposition ended in October 1905, the First Congregational Church of Saint Johns barged the building downriver and converted it to a church. Over the years the building has undergone various incarnations and architectural assaults, including the removal of the cupola. Today, moving pictures are again shown under the dome. (See Walk 1 for more information about the Lewis and Clark Exposition.)

Walk south on Richmond toward the river. Cross N Willamette Boulevard and turn left two blocks further, onto N Decatur Street, a barely paved road. At this unprepossessing intersection is one of the city's loveliest views: the whole of the Saint Johns Bridge against a backdrop of forested mountains. The southern end of the bridge seems to disappear into the wilderness.

Turn right onto N Mohawk Avenue, then left onto N Crawford Street. Before turning right onto N Van Buren Avenue, note the large old home at 7821 Crawford. Built in 1886 in the Classic Revival style, it is the oldest standing house in Saint Johns. The home was built for Amos Miner, one of the first settlers in the area, and sits on his original land claim.

2 Walk down Van Buren one block and turn left on N Bradford Street, a tiny cliff-side street with nothing below it but bluff and river. The Willamette River is the tenth largest river, by volume, in the United States, and the largest north-flowing river in the continental United States. At this point on the hill walk you are about midway between the Saint Johns Bridge, at river mile 5.8, and the Burlington Northern Railroad Bridge, at river mile 7. River miles refer to the distance to the river's confluence, in this case with the Columbia River.

Bradford is a dead end and a bit off the beaten path but is well worth a meander for the lovely views across the river to Forest Park. Directly across the riverbank in the industrial area is an enormous gray and green complex of buildings along Front Avenue. They belong to Siltronic (formerly Wacker Siltronic), maker of high-purity silicon wafers for the semiconductor industry.

A staircase at the end of Bradford leads up to a locked gate on the grounds of Open Meadow High School, so at the end of Bradford turn left onto N Tyler Avenue. Walk one block and turn right on Crawford.

An 1887 Rural Vernacular farmhouse at 7706 sits far back from the road like a reticent relic from a more gracious era. This home, built by Amos Miner, was originally surrounded by gardens. Luzanna E. Graves once lived here, one of only two women doctors in Portland in the early twentieth century.

In 1910 Amos Benson, son of philanthropist Simon Benson, built the large home at 7654, which sits on the cliffs above Willamette Cove. (The Simon Benson House is on Walk 5.) Benson lived here until he divorced, selling the home in 1920 to the Chaneys, an extremely large family who lived here for decades. All the children attended Roosevelt High School, and for years the Chaney lawn was the site of annual end-of-year school celebrations. One of the Chaney daughters lives next to her former family home, at the dead end of N

Looking upriver to downtown Portland through the limbs of an ancient Oregon white oak on the grounds of the Benson-Chaney house, now Open Meadow High School.

Bradford Street. Dr. Graves, whose house you just passed, delivered at least one of the Chaney kids in an upstairs bedroom of the mansion.

In 1992 the Benson-Chaney house was reborn as Open Meadow High School, a private, nonprofit alternative for kids whose academic, behavioral, or emotional difficulties have kept them from succeeding in traditional school settings. The property boasts wide, estatelike lawns, heritage Oregon white oaks that predate the house by a hundred years or more, and a large English walnut. The school allows pedestrians to stroll across the lawn, and it is definitely worthwhile to meander over to the edge of the cliff. From there you'll have a sublime view of the river, downtown, and Willamette Cove, the next destination on the walk.

Follow Crawford to its end at N Pierce Avenue. Here the walk heads back up the hill a bit to avoid a steep, fenced-off ravine. Turn left on Pierce, then left on Decatur. The home behind the fence at 7530 was in 1912 part of a large estate owned by Augustus Stearns. Now the lovely home that once enjoyed river and mountain views is surrounded by a parking lot and modern, angular condominiums.

Turn right on N Polk Avenue. Walk two blocks to Willamette Boulevard, turn right, and in one block you'll to come to N Edgewater Street, where the tiny Portway Tavern has been offering beer and tavern food since the 1930s. This building started out around 1905 as a corner grocery store. Although it's a bit smoky, inside it is friendly, cozy, and full of personality. If the smoke bugs you, check out the beer garden out back under the trees. There are too few outdoor venues in Portland where you can eat and drink unmolested by the noise and smells of traffic; the Portway is one of them.

Turn right onto Edgewater, a long road that drops into a canyon darkened by maples. The canyon was probably carved into the face of the bluff by springs, much like Reed Canyon.

3 Soon after passing the driveway into the Edgewater Terraces condominiums, you're on public land acquired by Metro in 1996. The gates on Edgewater are meant to keep cars, partiers, and debris dumpers out, so unless you qualify in one of those categories, walk past them. This road down through the ravine leads eventually into the McCormick and Baxter Creosoting Company Superfund cleanup site. The company operated from 1944 to 1991, treating wood with preservatives that contained toxins such as creosote, pentachorophenol, and heavy metals. In the tradition of most commercial ventures of the era, untreated wastewater was dumped into the nearest river (the Willamette), and other industrial waste was dumped on-site. The extreme pollution came to public attention in 1988 when children wading in the river at the site suffered chemical burns. It has been a Superfund site since 1994. Through the Superfund program, administered by the Environmental Protection Agency, sites containing significant environmental pollutants are identified. Superfund status has been conferred on more than twelve hundred sites across the country since the program was established by Congress in 1980. In 2000 the McCormick and Baxter site was joined by others along a 6-mile stretch of the Portland Harbor, from Swan Island to the southern tip of Sauvie Island, that were all given Superfund status because of the harbor's industrial past.

After its designation, the creosoting plant was demolished, 33,000 tons of contaminated soil and 1950 gallons of contaminated groundwater were removed from the site, and a subsurface barrier wall was installed to keep remaining contaminants from migrating to the river. In 2003, however, funding dried up for further remediation, including a soil cap that would prevent rain from carrying contaminants into the groundwater. The plan is for the area to become a park once contaminants have been contained.

At the bottom of the road, cross the railroad tracks and head across an abandoned parking lot toward the river and the Burlington Northern Railroad Bridge. When it was built in 1908 this bridge was a swing span, its center rotating to allow river traffic to pass. Over the years the clearance became inadequate

Riverside at Willamette Cove, looking out toward the Burlington Northern Railroad Bridge and the West Hills.

due to the increasing size of ships, and so in 1989 the two towers were installed and the bridge was transformed into a lift span. When raised, the lifted bed provides 200 feet of clearance at low water, making it the fourth highest lift span in the world. The new 516-foot-long lift section and towers don't match the old sections of the bridge. The new section is made of steel, designed to weather to a brown color; the old sections are painted an aluminum color. These tracks provide Oregon's main rail link into Washington.

The Willamette Cove greenspace stretches from the northern side of the railroad embankment about half a mile along the Willamette River. It consists of 27 acres and was purchased by Metro to be preserved as a natural area. Despite its grimy past, this forested bottomland below the bluffs is a treasure of old specimen trees and out-of-the-ordinary river and mountain views. Willamette Cove's industrial uses date back to the early 1900s. A barrel manufacturer, lumber mill, plywood mill, and dry dock operated on this ground at various times until the late 1960s, when industrial activities ceased. The site has been vacant since then.

Metro has done some cleanup at Willamette Cove, removing obvious physical hazards and clearing blackberry, but the land remains undeveloped and hence warrants a higher level of care from pedestrians. Soil and groundwater contamination has been confirmed on-site. Near the southern end of the greenspace, a rotting, listing barge hull on the small cove beach adds romance—a romance cooled somewhat by the fact that toxic sediments make wading or beach play unsafe. However, despite the legacy of environmental devastation, there is plenty of beauty here. Just don't let your children make mud pies.

Follow the river downstream among several paths, one next to the railroad tracks and one near the river's edge. The people in charge of landscaping the grounds of the various companies that once existed here had good taste, because their horticultural picks provide year-round texture and color: mature and thriving figs, Lombardy poplars, cedars of Lebanon, and oaks. The madrona, with its distinctive bark, is a native of the coastal strip from California to British Columbia, and in Portland it seems to thrive best in areas along the Willamette bluffs. Archibald Menzies, a Scottish botanist, first described the Pacific madrona in 1792: "Its peculiar smooth bark of a reddish brown color will at all times attract the notice of the most superficial observer." Menzies was right: the bark is smooth, *except* when it's peeling, and reddish brown, *except* when it's green. Northwest Coast tribes chewed the leaves of the madrona and swallowed the juice for sore throats, and many tribes ate the berries, either raw, parched, roasted, or dried.

As you walk downstream you can see another environmental disaster across the river: the site of the former Gasco oil gasification plant, one part of which Siltronic occupies today. The stone Arts and Crafts–style Gasco headquarters building, with its clock tower and mossy roof, is a decaying landmark along the Saint Helens Road. Gasco was owned by one of the Linnton area's biggest employers, Portland Gas and Coke (predecessor to today's Northwest Natural). From 1913 to the late 1950s, gas was manufactured from oil at the site. Until 1925, tar and petroleum waste from the process were dumped directly into the Willamette. After 1925, tars were separated from the wastewater in settling ponds. When natural gas began being piped from New Mexico to Portland in the 1950s, the gas manufacturing plant closed. By 1956 an estimated 30,000 cubic yards of tar had settled in the ponds, which in the 1970s were buried under 10 feet of fill. Other pollutants are petroleum and cyanide. Cleanup of the contaminated soils and groundwater here, as in the rest of the Portland Harbor, will take years to resolve.

Above Gasco, the lush, steep hills of Forest Park rise as a green balm to the bio-mess below.

4 Leave Willamette Cove at the railroad crossing at Richmond Avenue. Walk one block on Richmond before turning left on Crawford. Follow this street, which is lined with scrap metal and barbed wire, to N Burlington Avenue; turn left and cross the railroad tracks. Stay straight and walk to the sidewalk that leads to the river's edge. Though nothing remains of it, you're at the site of the 1850s homestead of James John. After initially settling in Linnton in 1844, John took out a donation land claim in 1846 on the peninsula. Here he built a house, a barn, and a store (which he operated), all now buried beneath the riprapped and filled riverbank. This area was filled with homes in the late 1800s, most of which were torn down as industry moved in and people moved further up the hill.

The hopper dredge *Essayons* is often moored across the river. It is operated by the U.S. Army Corps of Engineers to keep the Willamette and Columbia river channels at 40 feet. Material dredged up by the *Essayons* gets stored on board the ship until it is dumped elsewhere in the river.

Turn right at the sidewalk's end, and walk on the path along the river. Ahead is the Water Pollution Control Laboratory. This lab, an environmentally green building that has won numerous architectural awards, is operated by the City of Portland Bureau of Environmental Services. Technicians in six different laboratories sample and analyze water from various sources, such as sewage treatment plant effluent, industrial waste discharges, stormwater, rivers, streams, and soil excavated during construction projects. The lab's 6.5 acres, from here to the edge of Cathedral Park, are a wonder of native landscaping reclaimed from industry. While the land reveals its grimy past through the rotting piers and broken concrete along the river, ashore you would never know the ground has been anything other than a well-tended park.

Planted in 1997, the grounds grow in beauty each year as native grasses, shrubs, and trees mature. The building and grounds demonstrate many ways to save energy and prevent untreated stormwater from running into streams. Water is directed into bioswales by simple but elegant designs: the parking lot is graded toward the center so that all runoff is directed into a bioswale; the roof has scuppers that direct rain, with Zen-like grace, off the edge and into a bioswale; and a flume directs other water into a quiet pond. Red osier dogwoods are planted abundantly on the grounds, and their reddish orange bark glows so vibrantly that they seem to create an orange light on otherwise gray winter days. The Flathead Indians of western Montana and Idaho would mix these dogwood berries with serviceberries and sugar to make a sweet and sour dish.

On the river path, walk past the laboratory. Just past a sculpture called "Water Please," by Doug Marks, is a path to the lab's crown jewel: a man-made pond surrounded by mass plantings of Oregon grape, reeds, roses, and grasses. The effect of the golds, greens, bronzes, and oranges, especially under low winter clouds, is stunning. A stone wall, starting high, curves into the pond, disappearing below the surface. After passing over so many abandoned sites on this hill walk, this wall brings to mind the impermanence of human endeavors.

After the pond, continue along the riverside path to its end at N Pittsburg Avenue. This was the Saint Johns ferry landing, which operated from 1852 until the Saint Johns Bridge was completed in 1931. Why was a ferry needed between what were then two sparsely settled areas? James Johns sited his ferry strategically, along the route of the Vancouver-to-Hillsboro road that had been used by fur trappers bringing their pelts to the Hudson Bay trading post in Vancouver. In the hills across the river, the portion of this road is likely the old Springville Road. Though now just a forest path, Springville was then one of the prime roads for farmers from northern Tualatin Valley bringing their produce to port. (See Walk 3 for more information.) In the early 1900s cattle ferried across the river were driven up the hill and through the streets of Saint Johns to their final destination at the Kenton stockyards. Rotting pilings in the river and broken concrete on the banks are the landing's last remains.

In 1910 the area underneath what would later become the Saint Johns Bridge was developed by the then-independent city of Saint Johns as a municipal dock, named Terminal 3. It was demolished to make way for the bridge.

5 Keep walking a short way until you come to a floating sidewalk that lets you walk out onto the river and up to the base of one of the massive concrete columns supporting the bridge. This is a wonderful vantage point from which to watch river traffic. Across the river, just downstream of the bridge, is the Whitwood Court subdivision. Surrounded on three sides by Forest Park and with only one road leading into it, Whitwood Court is a strong candidate for the city's most isolated neighborhood. At the foot of the hill below it was the ferry landing on the western side of the river.

The Saint Johns Bridge, opened in 1931, is the work of master bridge engineer David B. Steinman of New York. The Gothic arch motif in its fifteen progressively taller piers gave rise to the name of Cathedral Park at the eastern end of the bridge. Pier 10 is 183 feet high, the tallest reinforced concrete pier in the world at the time it was built. Its 1207-foot-long main span is flanked by two 430-foot-long side spans, and it soars 200 feet above the Willamette.

At the time the bridge was built, it had the world's largest and longest (at 2645 feet) prestressed twisted rope strand cables. The bridge's 408-foot-tall towers were designed to stand without traditional diagonal bracing; instead, they are supported by anchorages at either end. Peregrine falcons nest on the bridge's undercarriage; they have found that the city's taller bridges make fine substitutions for their native cliff-side habitat.

Renovations to the bridge took place from 2003 to 2005. Among other things, it was repainted and made more pedestrian-friendly. Unless you suffer from gephyrophobia (fear of crossing a bridge), consider a detour up to the top. The view from the sidewalk, 205 feet above the river at low water, is spectacular. Access the bridge sidewalks via N Syracuse Street.

After you leave the floating walkway, you're in Cathedral Park. This ground was the site of a year-round American Indian village, where the bounty of freshwater clams, wapato (a wetland plant whose tubers were a major source of carbohydrates), salmon, and berries provided sustenance. Just downstream of Cathedral Park, in the 9500 block of Bradford Street and now entombed by an immense parking lot, are the first graveyard and school in Saint Johns, dating from 1852.

Cathedral Park wasn't created when the bridge was complete, as might be expected. Forty years passed, and the site under the arches had become an unofficial dump. In the early 1970s, Saint Johns resident Howard Galbraith decided improvements were needed. He organized a drive to raise funds to turn the place into a park. Today, Cathedral Park's 23 acres include a boat ramp, picnic tables, greenspace, and stage, and feature superb river and forest views.

Walk uphill through the park and cross the railroad tracks. In the early 1900s a woman named Mother Gillespie took in travelers, fresh off the ferry, at her boarding house here, about where the tracks cross Burlington. The enormous concrete vault under the bridge is the east side anchorage for the bridge's suspension cables. On the western side of the bridge, the cables are anchored in 85-foot-deep tunnels drilled into the hillside's basalt.

Just past the vaults, turn left at Crawford, the first street you'll encounter. Walk two blocks. The warehouse building ahead of you at the intersection of Crawford and N Baltimore Avenue used to house Columbia Sportswear Company, one of Oregon's signature businesses. The company moved to Beaverton in late 2001, to the chagrin of the City of Portland. Before Columbia Sportswear, the building housed Portland Woolen Mills. A photo from 1920 shows the same building from Baltimore Avenue. Despite changes to the façade, the decorative raised brick visible under the roof peak identifies this building as the one in the photo.

Local chocolate maker Moonstruck Chocolate Company is located in the block on the left. Locally owned since its founding in 1993, the company wholesales its product nationally. Inside during regular business hours you can buy boxes of freshly made chocolate and treat your nose to some free whiffs of chocolate-scented air. The filtration system must be quite good here, because the aroma is not detectable outdoors.

Looking downhill toward the Portland Woolen Mills from N Baltimore Avenue, circa 1920. The building with the letters atop still stands. Beyond the mills are enormous wooden frames, berths for shipbuilding in World War I, and in the hills across the river is Linnton's Whitwood Court subdivision. The Saint Johns Bridge had not yet been built. Photo courtesy of Don Nelson.

Turn right on Baltimore, walk uphill three blocks to N Willamette Boulevard, and turn left. Willamette is a street of cute bungalows overshadowed by the looming, twelve-story Schrunk Riverview Tower, an apartment tower owned by the Housing Authority of Portland. Walk one block on Willamette and turn right onto N Chicago Avenue.

At 7011 Chicago is the 1908 home of Dr. Joseph McChesney, who lived just steps from his office, a commercial building you'll walk by on N Lombard Street. At 7207 is the 1900 home of Hiram Brice, the mayor of Saint Johns until its annexation to Portland in 1915. An ancient cherry tree in the backyard likely provided fruit for His Honor's pies. Walk two bocks further on Chicago, carefully cross Ivanhoe, a busy street, and come to Lombard, the commercial heart of Saint Johns.

6 While Lombard hasn't yet fully metamorphosed into the modern-day retail incarnation it will undoubtedly become—à la SE Hawthorne Boulevard or Multnomah Village—it has plenty of diversions to occupy a curious wanderer. The few blocks covered on this route contain a thriving camera store, bike shop,

Mexican grocer, old-fashioned bakery, discount grocer, theater, coffee shops, restaurants, thrift stores, and, my favorite, a 1930s filling station resplendent in its retro glory.

Just to the left of the intersection of Lombard and Chicago, including 8933–8953 N Lombard, is the McChesney Block. It and most of the other commercial buildings you'll pass were built between 1900 and the mid 1920s. Like many Streetcar-Era buildings, the McChesney Block had apartments above, and shops and offices with transom windows on the first floor. Here, unfortunately, the transoms have been replaced by overly large and stylistically anachronistic plate glass squares. But the renovation is less disruptive to the building's style than others on the street.

At 8704 is the lovely Saint Johns Theatre, built around 1925 in the California Mission style, with stuccoed walls, arched windows, and tile accents. It was called the Venetian then, and one of its managers was Walt Morey, the author of many beloved children's novels (his most famous, *Gentle Ben*, was turned into a Disney movie). Today the Saint Johns Theatre is a great place to go for second-run movies; you can even park your car at the curb instead of having to negotiate a mega parking lot.

At 8638 is another Streetcar-Era Commercial building, constructed in 1925 and unrecognizably transformed. This is also true of the 1908 Multnomah Theater, across the street at 8647–8641. This was one of the first moving picture theaters in the city, and to meet the demand for the new art form, it originally housed 850 people. As it turned out, demand wasn't *quite* that high, so in the 1920s the theater moved to the smaller Venetian. In 1935 this building was converted to a bowling alley.

Weir's Cyclery, still in the Weir family after eighty years, sits at 8621 in the 1904 Bickner Department Store, the oldest retail building in Saint Johns.

Here, near the end of the hill walk, is the intimate and highly rated John Street Café. Don't miss the Tulip Pastry Shop, a family-run shop that has been at this location since the 1950s, making all its delectables from scratch.

The icing on this little architectural tour is the 1938 Signal Tower Gas Station at 8302 Lombard, on the corner of N Charleston Avenue. Designed in a Streamline Modern style with neon accents, it has been lovingly restored, complete with pumps.

Turn right on Charleston and walk one block to the intersection of Ivanhoe. Turn left and walk one block to the starting point.

ACKNOWLEDGMENTS

Without the help of so many Portlanders, I could not have written the book that I wanted to write. Thank you to Vocational Village teacher Jerry Eaton and his students for sharing with me the GIS (Geographic Information System) map they created of Rocky Butte, and to Elizabeth Jensen and her high school students at Open Meadow Social Service CRUE (Corps Restoring the Urban Environment) for sharing their knowledge about North Portland history and the Benson-Chaney house.

Thank you to the city employees who stopped what they were doing in order to answer my questions, including Briggy Thomas at the Portland Water Bureau, who made sure I got the story of Portland's water supply right; Diana Banning, Brian Johnson, and Leanne Arndt at the City of Portland Archives, who ensured I didn't leave until I had the photographs I needed; Courtney Duke, pedestrian coordinator, who checked her maps so that I didn't walk on private property; Mark Hughes, city ecologist, who helped me unravel the mysteries of trails on Rocky Butte; Craig Jensen in city maintenance, who told me everything I wanted to know about elm trees and street trees; Pat Kolodich and Andrew Aebi, who gave me a primer on street maintenance, paving issues, and Local Improvement Districts; Sue Thomas at Portland Parks, who gave me access to her history files; Blair Fitzgibbon, who shared information on the history of Portland schools; and Amie Massier at the Hillside Community Center, who mailed me fascinating oral histories.

Thank you to the many Portland activists who see needs and then address them, especially David Lewis of the Rocky Butte Preservation Society, Paul Leistner of the Mount Tabor Neighborhood Association, and Tom Miller of the Homestead Neighborhood Association, all of whom generously shared much information with me. Thanks, too, to Don Baack, the catalyst behind the fabulous *SW Walking Map*; to my mother-in-law, Isabella Chappell, for inspiring me with her knowledge of and great interest in Portland history; to Glen and Marti Gordon, who put both their money and their enthusiasm into Linnton; to Pat Wagner, who shared her Linnton knowledge with me; to Don Nelson, for opening up his Portland photo archive for me; and to William Warren of Central Northeast Neighbors.

Thank you to Congressman Earl Blumenauer, for his career-long advocacy for transportation alternatives that keep us out of our cars. I am honored by both his and his staff's support for this book.

Thank you to Karen Alexander and Mark Kemball at OHSU; Townsend Angell and Gay Walker at Reed College; Janet Beale and George Domijan, who opened my eyes to the history and business of the Port of Portland's marine terminals; Susan Safford at the Port of Portland, who provided information about the Portland Harbor; Jim Morgan of Metro, who educated me on the history of Willamette Cove; Nan Finch of Leach Garden Friends, who shared a Saturday morning with me; Eugene Gray, forensic administrator, who answered my questions about the morgue when I wandered in off the street one day; Claire Kellogg at Lake Oswego Public Library, who solved my Dunthorpe photo quandary; John Lemma, who shared his stories about making wine in Linnton; Patricia Solomon at the State of Oregon Archives, who sent me information on the Stadium Freeway; Andrea Raven at Leach Botanical Garden, who shared her wealth of knowledge; and Lee Stewart, who let me borrow her fascinating memorabilia on Westover Heights.

I am indebted to fellow Timber Press authors William J. Hawkins III and Ellen Morris Bishop, who took time from their busy schedules to read the manuscript.

Thank you to Zeb Andrews and the extremely helpful folks at Blue Moon Camera and Machine in Saint Johns.

Thanks to the three women who made sure my baby was having as much fun as I was while I wrote this book: Andrea Carlstrom, Jolene Williams, and Brenda Rose-O'Donnell, and to my writing partner, Michelle McCann.

Thank you to the Regional Arts and Culture Council for helping fund my research for this book through its grants for artists. Thanks too to Rosie Williams, project manager in the office of Vera Katz, for her encouragement.

Thank you to Mindy Fitch, Rebecca Ragain, and the other consummate professionals at Timber Press. Finally, a huge thanks to Eve Goodman at Timber, for making my original idea much better and for her enthusiastic encouragement, which made writing this book a joy.

BIBLIOGRAPHY

Aalberg, Bryan. 2003. Oaks Amusement Park. *Oregon Historical Quarterly* 104 (2).

Abbott, Carl. 1981. *The Great Extravaganza: Portland and the Lewis and Clark Exposition*. Portland: Oregon Historical Society.

American Experience. 2004. Gutzon Borglum. http://www.pbs.org/wgbh/amex/rushmore/peopleevents.htm. Accessed March 17, 2004.

Bartels, Eric. A Castle Worth the Hassle. *Portland Tribune*, February 10, 2004.

Beeson, M. H., et al. 1989. *Geologic Map of the Lake Oswego Quadrangle, Clackamas, Multnomah and Washington Counties, Oregon*. Portland: Oregon Department of Geology and Mineral Industries.

———. 1991. *Geologic Map of the Portland Quadrangle, Multnomah and Washington Counties, Oregon, and Clark County, Washington*. Portland: Oregon Department of Geology and Mineral Industries.

Bishop, Ellen Morris. 2003. *In Search of Ancient Oregon: A Geological and Natural History*. Portland: Timber Press.

Bishop, Ellen Morris, and John Eliot Allen. 1996. *Hiking Oregon's Geology*. Seattle: Mountaineers.

Blandon, Peter. 2004. *Cryptomeria japonica*. http://www.blandon.co.uk/forestry/species/sugi.htm. Accessed February 4, 2004.

Blankenship, Judy. 2003. *Intersections: TriMet Interstate MAX Light Rail Community History Project*. Portland: TriMet.

Brenneman, Kristina. 2004. Graham's Tram. *Portland Tribune*, January 2, 2004.

Briggs, Kara. 2003. Maywood Park Mayor Brews Tea in the Town He Calls "Mayberry." *Oregonian*, July 10, 2003.

———. 2003. PSU Center for Native Americans a Landmark. *Oregonian*, October 24, 2003.

Brock, Kathy. 2003. Floods Recede but Tides of Change Keep Rolling through SW Miles Place. *Oregonian*, September 28, 2003.

———. 2003. Southwest Miles Place: A Street Flooded with Memories. *Oregonian*, September 28, 2003.

Business Journal of Portland. 1999. Bowles House: A Taste of Italy. http://www.bizjournals.com/portland. Written May 3, 1999. Accessed March 17, 2004.

Chauncey, Joy. 1998. *Oral History Interview*. Unpublished typescript. Portland: Catlin Gabel School.

Cleary, Beverly. 1988. *A Girl from Yamhill: A Memoir*. New York: Morrow.

Collette, Carlotta. 1985. The Bishop's Close. *Horticulture* (March).

Cone, Paul. 2003. *A History of Rocky Butte*. Unpublished typescript. Portland State University.

Corning, Howard McKinley. 1947. *Willamette Landings: Ghost Towns of the River*. Portland: Binfords & Mort for the Oregon Historical Society.

Cotton, Alice. 2001. *When Buildings Speak: Stories Told by Oregon's Historical Architecture*. Portland: Artemis.

Davis, Marguerite, Norris Tulley, and Cecil Tulley. 1976. *The Building of a Community*. Portland: Cecil Tulley.

Department of Veterans Affairs. 2004. National Cemetery Administration. http://www.cem.va.gov. Accessed March 17, 2004.

Dirr, Michael A. 1983. *Manual of Woody Landscape Plants*. Champaign, Illinois: Stipes.

Edwards, Margaret Watt, ed. 1973. *Land of the Multnomahs: Sketches and Stories of Early Oregon*. Portland: Binfords & Mort.

Encyclopedia Britannica. 2003. Horsetail. http://www.britannica.com/eb/article?eu=42029. Accessed July 7, 2003.

———. Abigail Jane Scott Duniway. 2003. http://www.britannica.com/eb/article?eu=137778. Accessed September 15, 2003.

———. John Loudon McAdam. 2003. http://www.britannica.com/eb/article?eu=50793. Accessed October 2, 2003.

——. Mount Tabor. 2003. http://www.britannica.com/eb/article?eu=72688. Accessed October 30, 2003.

——. Aesculapius. 2003. http://www.britannica.com/eb/article?eu=9912. Accessed November 14, 2003.

——. Caduceus. 2003. http://www.britannica.com/eb/article?eu=18792. Accessed November 14, 2003.

Fish, Peter. 2002. Names for the New World. *Sunset*. http://www.sunset.com/sunset/premium/travel/1998/westwander98/wwdoughlas.html. Accessed November 11, 2002.

Friends of Forest Park. 2003. *Hiking and Running Guide to Forest Park: Ten-Map Set*. Portland: Friends of Forest Park.

Fulton, Ann. 2002. *Iron, Wood and Water: An Illustrated History of Lake Oswego*. San Antonio, Texas: Lammert Publications.

Godfrey, Louise. 2002. A Woman, a Garden, an Organization: The Berry Botanic Garden at Twenty-Five. *Pacific Horticulture* (April/May/June).

Gronowski, Nancy H. 2003. *Ross Island: Past and Present Park Proposals*. Unpublished typescript. Portland State University.

Grotto Staff. 1994. *The Grotto: Seventy Years of Service*. Typescript. Portland: The Grotto.

Gurrad, Mathew, Ben Holmes, Casey Martin, and Austin Wiesner. 2003. *Mount Tabor Park*. Unpublished typescript. Portland Parks and Recreation.

Haught, Nancy. 2003. Relationships/Faith in Action Major Commitment. *Oregonian*, August 24, 2003.

Hawkins III, William J., and William F. Winningham. 1999. *Classic Houses of Portland, Oregon: 1850–1950*. Portland: Timber Press.

Heinz, Spencer. 2003. City of (Imported) Roses. *Oregonian*, March 3, 2003.

Hill, Richard, and Noelle Crombie. 2001. New Discovery Confirms Active Fault in Portland. *Oregonian*, May 30, 2001.

Hill, Sue. 2002. *The Parks of South Portland*. Unpublished typescript. Portland State University.

Historical Gazette. 1997. One Hundred Fifty Years on the Willamette, Saint Johns, Oregon. *Historical Gazette* 3 (7).

Hofmann, Jane. 1978. *Neighborhood in the Park: A History of Arlington Heights.* Unpublished typescript. Portland.

Houck, Michael C., and M. J. Cody, eds. 2000. *Wild in the City: A Guide to Portland's Natural Areas.* Portland: Oregon Historical Society.

Houle, Marcy Cottrell. 1996. *One City's Wilderness: Portland's Forest Park.* Portland: Oregon Historical Society.

Hunt, John Clark. 1964. Willamette Heights Comfortable, Friendly as Old Shoe. *Oregon Journal* (February 4).

———. 1964. Willamette Heights Had Ringside Seat. *Oregon Journal* (February 6).

Jacklet, Ben. 2003. Radon Risk High in Seven Areas of City. *Portland Tribune,* December 16, 2003.

Jensen, Edward, and Charles Ross. 1994. *Trees to Know in Oregon.* Corvallis: Oregon State University Extension Service and Oregon Department of Forestry.

Kershaw, Sarah. 2003. Time Capsule Mystery Stumps, Portland, Ore. *The New York Times,* May 18, 2003.

King, Bart. 2001. *An Architectural Guidebook to Portland.* Layton, Utah: Gibbs Smith.

Kirkpatrick, Golda, Charlene Holzwarth, and Linda Mullens. 1994. *The Botanist and Her Muleskinner: Lilla Irvin Leach and John Roy Leach, Pioneer Botanists in the Siskiyou Mountains.* Portland: Leach Garden Friends.

Klooster, Karl. 1986. Portland Prestige: Dunthorpe & Assoc. *This Week Magazine* (April 23).

———. 1987. *Round the Roses: Portland Past Perspectives.* Portland: K. T. Klooster.

———. 1992. *Round the Roses II: More Portland Past Perspectives.* Portland: K. T. Klooster.

Langer, Elinor. 2003. *A Hundred Little Hitlers: The Death of a Black Man, the Trial of a White Racist, and the Rise of the Neo-Nazi Movement in America.* New York: Metropolitan Books.

Linnton Community Center. 2002. *Linnton: A Town Too Tough to Die.* Typescript. Portland.

Linnton Neighborhood Association. 2000. *Linnton Neighborhood Plan.* Typescript. Portland.

Mapes, Jeff. 2000. Maurine Neuberger: United States Senator. *Oregonian*, February 23, 2000.

Marlitt, Richard. 1989. *Matters of Proportion: The Portland Residential Architecture of Whidden and Lewis*. Portland: Oregon Historical Society.

McArthur, Lewis A. 2003. *Oregon Geographic Names*. Portland: Oregon Historical Society.

McCammon, Michael. 1996. Oaks Park: Local Treasure Spans Generations. *Sellwood Bee*.

Metropolitan Service District. 2001. *Disappearing Streams*. Map. Portland.

Moerman, Daniel E. 1998. *Native American Ethnobotany*. Portland: Timber Press.

Montalbano, Andrea. 2000. Share-It Square. *New Village Journal* 2 (Spring).

Mount Tabor Neighborhood Association. 2001. *Mount Tabor Neighborhood Plan*. Draft. Portland.

Mullen, Ruth. 2003. Past Imperfect. *Oregonian*, May 22, 2003.

Munger, Thornton T. 1960. *History of Portland's Forest Park*. 50th anniversary ed. Portland: Friends of Forest Park. 1998.

Murphy, Todd. 2004. Requiem for a Dream: For Too Many Knott Street Boxers, Despair Displaces Glory. *Portland Tribune*, January 27, 2004.

Nafsinger, Janie. 1985. Bishop's Close: A Piece of the Past Preserved for the Ages. *Lake Oswego Review* (February 27–28).

Nelson, Grant. 1977. *The Early Years (1845–1895) at Mount Tabor: From Forest to Farms to Families*. Typescript. Portland: Pacific Northwest History.

Norman Jr., James B. 1991. *Portland's Architectural Heritage: National Register Properties of the Portland Metropolitan Area*. Portland: Oregon Historical Society.

Northwest Examiner. 2003. Tree Proves No Obstacle. *Northwest Examiner* 17 (12).

O'Donnell, Terence, and Thomas Vaughan. 1976. *Portland: A Historical Sketch and Guide*. Portland: Oregon Historical Society.

———. 1984. *Portland: An Informal History and Guide*. Portland: Oregon Historical Society.

Oregon Blue Book. 2004. Notable Oregonians: Oswald West—Governor. *Oregon Blue Book.* http://www.sos.state.or.us/bbook/notable/notwest.htm. Accessed March 17, 2004.

Oregon Department of Environmental Quality. 2004. Portland Harbor Superfund Site. http://www.deq.state.or.us/nwr/portlandharbor/ph.htm. Accessed February 2, 2004.

Oregon Health and Science University. 2003. *OHSU at a Glance.* Portland.

Oregon Journal. 1957. Scotch Nubbin Proved Tough but Finally Succumbed. *Oregon Journal* (November 10).

Oregonian. 1912. Carving Level Terraces. Advertisement. *Oregonian*, January 21, 1912.

———. 1912. Irresistible: The Verdict of 38. Advertisement. *Oregonian*, February 11, 1912.

———. 1912. Level Sites on the Heights. Advertisement. *Oregonian*, February 18, 1912.

———. 1912. Why Retaining Walls? Advertisement. *Oregonian*, February 25, 1912.

———. 2003. Port Agrees to Begin Early Cleanup at Part of Harbor's Superfund Site. *Oregonian*, October 7, 2003.

———. 2004. Ten NW Men Land on Forbes' Wealthiest List. *Oregonian*, February 27, 2004.

Patapoff, Elizabeth Dotson. 1999. Cougars on Mount Tabor. *Southeast Examiner*, February 1999.

Paulson, Rod. 1976. *Portland Neighborhood Histories.* Typescript, vols. 1 and 2. Portland.

Pennelly, Amanda. 2003. Native Wish Becomes Concrete Reality. *Portland Tribune*, October 21, 2003.

Pietsch, Margaret. 1980. *Riverwood Yesterday and Today.* Lake Grove, Oregon: Lake Grove Printing.

Pittock Mansion Society. 1999. *Simply Splendid: Portland's Pittock Mansion.* Portland.

Pokorny, Kym. 2002. Happy Birthday Dear Berry. *Oregonian*, May 2, 2002.

Portland, City of. 1903. *Report of the Park Board with the Report of Messrs. Olmsted Bros., Landscape Architects, Outlining a System of Parkways, Boulevards and Parks for the City of Portland.*

——. 1984. *Historic Resource Inventory: Selected Properties.*

——. 2003. *Portland Historical Timeline.* http://www.portlandonline.com. Accessed June 27, 2003.

Portland Bureau of Planning. 1978. *King's Hill: A Report to the Portland Historical Landmarks Commission.* Portland Bureau of Planning.

——. 1988. *Scenic Views, Sites, and Drives Inventory.* Portland Bureau of Planning.

Portland Historical Landmarks Commission. 1979. *Inventory of Historic Landmarks and Districts.* Portland Historical Landmarks Commission.

Portland Office of Transportation. 2004. *Local Improvement Districts.* http://www.portlandtransportation.org. Accessed March 3, 2004.

——. 2004. Russell Street Improvement Planning Project. http://www.trans.ci.portland. Accessed January 28, 2004.

Portland Office of Transportation and SW Trails. 2002. *SW Walking Map.*

Portland Parks and Recreation. 2003. *Historic Timeline.* http://www.parks.ci.portland.or.us/History/. Accessed October 1, 2003.

Portland Water Bureau. 2003. *Bull Run Watershed.* http://www.portlandonline.com/water. Accessed November 10, 2003.

Price, Larry, ed. 1987. *Portland's Changing Landscape.* Portland State University, Department of Geology; Association of American Geographers.

Reed College. 2003. Reed College Canyon plants. http://web.reed.edu/canyon/natu/plants. Accessed July 16, 2003.

Reynolds, Phyllis C., and Elizabeth Dimon. 1993. *Trees of Greater Portland.* Portland: Timber Press.

Richard, Terry. 1995. Rocky Butte Great Climb From Top Down. *Oregonian,* August 24, 1995.

Ritz, Richard E. 1991. *An Architect Looks at Downtown Portland.* Portland: Greenhills Press.

Rojas-Burke. 2003. Port Agrees to Begin Early Cleanup at Part of Harbor's Superfund Site. *Oregonian,* October 7, 2003.

Roos, Roy, and Jim Heuer. 2001. *A Preliminary Historical Review of Early Russell and Blythe Houses Designed by Emil Schacht.* Unpublished type-script. Portland: Oregon Historical Society archives.

Rose, Joseph. 2003. The Heights of Safety: Residents Say It Takes a Village. *Oregonian,* March 26, 2003.

Saint Johns Heritage Association. 2003. *Oral History of Bro. Holmes, O.M.S.* http://www.ccrh.org/comm/slough/or/holmes.htm. Accessed July 21, 2003.

Sloane, David Charles. 1991. *The Last Great Necessity: Cemeteries in American History.* Baltimore: Johns Hopkins University Press.

Smith, Bridget. 1997. One Hundred Fifty Years on the Willamette River: Legacy of James John. *Saint Johns, Ore. Historical Gazette* 3 (7).

Snyder, Eugene. 1970. *Early Portland: Stumptown Triumphant.* Portland: Binfords & Mort.

———. 1979. *Portland Names and Neighborhoods: Their Historic Origins.* Portland: Binfords & Mort.

———. 1991. *Portland Potpourri: Art, Fountains, and Old Friends.* Portland: Binfords & Mort.

Sullivan, Jane. 1991. Rocky Butte Still a Jewel, Still a Beaut. *Oregonian,* June 3, 1991.

Swanson, Lowell. 2001. *Multnomah School 1913–1979.* Portland: Multnomah Historical Association.

Swing, William. 1961. Heights Nearly Fell to Wildcatter's Idea. *Oregonian,* October 16, 1961.

Terry, John. 2003. Reeds' Desires, Riches Yield Premier Legacy of Learning. *Oregonian,* July 6, 2003.

Trimble, Donald. 2004. Geology of Portland and Adjacent Areas. *United States Geologic Service.* http://vulcan.wr.usgs.gov/volcanoes. Accessed March 17, 2004.

U.S. Centennial of Flight Commission. 2003. Evolution of Airway Lights and Electronic Navigation Aids. http://centennialofflight.gov/essay/government_rol/navigation/POL13.htm. Accessed July 31, 2003.

Vaughn, Thomas, and George McMath. 1967. *A Century of Portland Architecture.* Portland: Oregon Historical Society.

Willamette Heights Historical Archive Committee. 1991. *Willamette Heights Chronicles*. Portland.

Willamette National Cemetery. 2003. *Eligibility and Information*. Portland.

Wortman, Sharon Wood. 2001. *The Portland Bridge Book*. Portland: Oregon Historical Society.

Young, Stefana. 1996. *Portland's Little Red Book of Stairs*. Portland: Coobus Press.

INDEX